# COMMON CORE STANDARDS

*for* | Elementary
Grades 3–5 Math
& English Language Arts

SUSTAINABLE
FORESTRY
INITIATIVE

Certified Sourcing

www.sfiprogram.org
SFI-00774

*Edited by John Kendall*

# COMMON CORE STANDARDS

*for* | Elementary
Grades 3–5 Math
& English Language Arts

Amber Evenson

Monette McIver

Susan Ryan

Amitra Schwols

Alexandria, Virginia USA

Mid-continent Research for Education and Learning
Denver, Colorado USA

1703 N. Beauregard St. • Alexandria, VA 22311-1714 USA
Phone: 800-933-2723 or 703-578-9600 • Fax: 703-575-5400
Website: www.ascd.org • E-mail: member@ascd.org
Author guidelines: www.ascd.org/write

## MⱯREL®

Mid-continent Research for Education and Learning
4601 DTC Boulevard, Suite 500
Denver, CO 80237 USA
Phone: 303-337-0990 • Fax: 303-337-3005
Website: www.mcrel.org • E-mail: info@mcrel.org

PAPERBACK ISBN: 978-1-4166-1466-1          ASCD product #113015          n3/13
Also available as an e-book (see Books in Print for the ISBNs).

Quantity discounts: 10–49 copies, 10%; 50+ copies, 15%; for 1,000 or more copies, call 800-933-2723, ext. 5634, or 703-575-5634. For desk copies: www.ascd.org/deskcopy.

**Library of Congress Cataloging-in-Publication Data**

Evenson, Amber.
  Common core standards for elementary grades 3–5 math & English language arts a quick-start guide / Amber Evenson, Monette McIver, Susan Ryan, Amitra Schwols ; edited by John Kendall.
    pages cm
  Includes bibliographical references.
  ISBN 978-1-4166-1466-1 (pbk. : alk. paper) 1. Mathematics—Study and teaching (Elementary)—United States. 2. Mathematics—Study and teaching (Elementary)—Standards—United States. 3. Langauge arts (Elementary)—Curricula—United States—States. 4. Language arts (Elementary)—Standards—United States—States. I. Title.
  QA135.6.E85 2013
  372.6'043—dc23
                    2013001878

22 21 20 19 18 17 16 15 14          2 3 4 5 6 7 8 9 10 11 12

# COMMON CORE STANDARDS

*for* | Elementary
Grades 3–5 Math
& English Language Arts

# Editor's Preface

This book is part of a series on the Common Core State Standards designed to help educators quickly acquire a deeper understanding of what the standards mean, how they are related within and across grades, and how they help to ensure that, at the end of their schooling, students are prepared to succeed in postsecondary education or the working world.

To help facilitate that understanding, the authors of this guide provide a narrative "unpacking" of the standards. An *unpacking* is a close analysis of the language and structure of standards designed to make the content of the standards clear. The narrative approach to unpacking you will find here allows the authors to convey the many connections that can be found in the standards, and it seems a wiser approach than the kind of unpacking that breaks standards statements into disconnected pieces of knowledge and skill. To maintain coherence, the authors follow the structure of the standards closely; however, even a cursory comparison of the Common Core standards for English language arts and literacy (ELA/literacy) and the Common Core standards for mathematics makes obvious the striking structural differences between the two. That's why you will notice a very different approach to the discussion in the two subject-area sections of this guide.

Within the introduction to each subject area, the authors provide an overview of the standards structure they will use to organize the discussion to come. In the ELA/literacy standards, every standard serves to advance what is called an anchor standard, which describes an overall goal and area of focus that is supported in some way by each grade-level standard. Such a design invites a close grade-by-grade comparison of standards at adjacent grades to clarify how each standard builds from grade to grade and within each grade. It's a logical approach given that ELA/literacy processes, such as reading and writing, grow more complex over the years—in part because of the increasing complexity of the reading material on which many of the standards depend.

The Common Core's approach to mathematics does not include anchor standards, and the mathematics standards have a more complex structure. Whereas the ELA/literacy standards feature the same topics at nearly every grade, the math standards do not. It's probable that this organization reflects a deliberate intent to avoid a common pitfall observed in prior state standards for mathematics, which is the tendency to revisit the same content over again each year. Mathematics concepts and skills are more discrete than the kinds of processes students use in ELA classes and, once mastered, these concepts and skill reappear principally as either subskills or fundamental concepts required in service of more complex skills and tasks. As a result, new topics appear or disappear with each grade, requiring the authors of this guide to provide, in their Part II treatment of mathematics standards, a more expansive cross-standard description of the connections that apply.

Part III of the guide addresses lesson planning and lessons. It includes three sample lessons for each subject area, built to reflect the best of what we know about designing instruction. As the starting point for these lessons, the authors selected standards that, in light of previous state standards, teachers are likely to find instructionally challenging. The sample lessons also serve to show how the new standards, while they may present a greater challenge to students, are also articulated through the grades to ensure that students will come to each grade knowing what they need to in order to master the new and rigorous content.

*John Kendall*

# Acknowledgments

We would like to acknowledge Kirsten Miller and John Kendall for their crucial role in making our thoughts much more readable; Greg Gallagher and the North Dakota Curriculum Initiative committee, who provided us with valuable insights into the challenges facing teachers as they begin to work with the Common Core standards; Ceri Dean for her step-by-step guide to lesson planning; Megan Henry, Darcy Ballentine, Barbara Browning, and Kathleen Dempsey for their collaboration and content expertise in developing the lessons; our McREL colleagues, who provided an analytical ear as we discussed the work; and our families, for supporting us as we worked on this project.

# Introduction

In July 2009, nearly all state school superintendents and the nation's governors joined in an effort to identify a common set of standards in mathematics and English language arts and literacy (ELA/literacy), with the goal of providing a clear, shared set of expectations that would prepare students for success in both college and career. The Common Core State Standards Initiative (CCSSI) brought together researchers, academics, teachers, and others who routed multiple drafts of the standards to representatives including curriculum directors, content specialists, and technical advisors from all participating state departments of education. By spring 2010, drafts were submitted for comment to the national subject-area organizations and posted for public comment. In June 2010, the final versions were posted to a dedicated website: www.corestandards.org. (A minor update of the standards was posted in October 2010.)

At press time, 45 states, as well as Washington, D.C., and two territories, have adopted the Common Core State Standards (CCSS) for mathematics. (Minnesota has adopted the ELA/literacy standards but not the mathematics standards. Texas, Alaska, Virginia, and Nebraska have indicated that they do not plan to adopt either set, although both Virginia and Nebraska have aligned the Common Core standards with their existing standards.)

Adoption of the standards is, of course, voluntary for states and does not include a commitment to any other programs or policies. However, states that have adopted these standards will be eligible to join one of two federally funded assessment consortia that are currently tasked with developing assessments for the Common Core—the Smarter Balanced Assessment Consortium (SBAC) or the Partnership for Assessment of Readiness for College and Careers (PARCC). Sharing assessments across states promises financial relief from notoriously expensive state assessments. In addition, federal programs such as Race to the Top have required that applicants demonstrate that they have joined with other states in adopting a common set of standards and an assessment program. Although states may form new consortia, many either have opted to join or are considering joining SBAC or PARCC.

Sharing a set of standards across states offers other advantages. For example, teachers' well-designed lesson plans targeting Common Core standards will be immediately useful to a large number of colleagues. The shared language of standards should also provide teachers with more opportunities to participate in very specific discussions about content, a process that has been hampered somewhat by the variety of ways states have described virtually the same content.

For a lengthier discussion of the Common Core standards, including their link to previous standards-based education efforts and the benefits and challenges the Common Core presents, see *Understanding Common Core State Standards* (Kendall, 2011), the first booklet in this series. We also encourage readers to explore numerous resources available at corestandards.org, especially the standards documents themselves (CCSSI, 2010c, 2010g) and the guidelines for adapting standards instruction for English language learners (CCSSI, 2010a) and students with disabilities (CCSSI, 2010b).

## About This Guide

This guide is part of a series intended to further the discussion and understanding of Common Core standards on a subject-specific and grade-level basis and to provide immediate guidance to teachers who must either adapt existing lessons and activities to incorporate the Common Core or develop new lessons to teach concepts not addressed in their previous state standards.

In the pages ahead, we will look at the general structure of the Common Core standards for both ELA/literacy and mathematics in the upper elementary grades (3–5), examining how the standards build upon and extend the skills students have acquired in earlier grades. We then examine the standards more closely. In Part I, we focus on ELA/literacy, exploring the links among the standards' four strands and looking closely at the three domains within Reading. In Part II, we examine the content in and connections among the mathematics domains, highlighting the mathematical practice standards with the strongest connections to each mathematics domain. In Part III, we turn to practical lesson planning with the Common Core, presenting a process for creating standards-based lessons that make the best use of the effective instructional strategies explored in *Classroom Instruction That Works, 2nd edition* (Dean, Hubbell, Pitler, & Stone, 2012). The guide concludes with an illustration of this process's outcome: six sample lessons that address Common Core standards identified as representing notable changes to upper elementary school teachers' current practice.

# PART I

# English Language Arts and Literacy

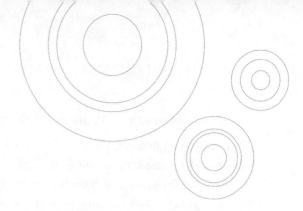

# CHAPTER 1

# About the Common Core ELA/Literacy Standards for Grades 3–5

This chapter focuses on key areas of the Common Core State Standards for English Language Arts and Literacy that represent the most significant changes to commonly used curricula and presents an overview of how the standards are organized, fit together, and reinforce one another. Reviewing the essential student knowledge and skills in the Common Core will allow teachers to quickly understand how they might adjust the materials and strategies used in their classroom to best meet these new expectations.

## Focus Areas and Instructional Implications

Although the Common Core ELA/literacy standards are comprehensive and address a broad range of communication skills, they place particular emphasis on four key areas: building knowledge through reading informational text, reading complex text, close reading and citing text evidence, and writing and speaking about texts. Let's take a closer look at each area and consider its implications for teachers.

## Building knowledge through reading informational text

During the last decade, the amount of nonfiction included in reading text-books and on national reading tests such as the National Assessment of Educational Progress has been increasing (National Assessment Governing Board, 2010a). The Common Core adds momentum to this trend, calling for a balance between literature and informational texts in the curriculum. Considering that as little as 7 percent of current elementary school instructional reading is expository (CCSSI, 2010d), adoption of the Common Core means elementary teachers will need to increase the number of informational texts they ask their students to read. Rather than compete with literary reading for "ELA class time," this reading should support learning across the curriculum, helping to build literacy and content-area knowledge in science, social studies, the arts, and other subjects. Additionally, it's essential that students' reading abilities not limit their acquisition of knowledge in areas like history and science; instruction should be designed to allow students to listen to complex informational texts that they may not be able to read on their own yet. This focus on using literacy skills to support subject-area learning is found throughout the Common Core standards, which also emphasize subject-specific vocabulary and writing about informational texts.

## Reading complex texts

The Common Core defines a three-part model for selecting appropriately complex texts that will lead to college and career readiness by the end of high school. Within this model, text readability—specifically, its quantitative measure for relative difficulty—is set higher than the mark set by prior readability systems and reading comprehension assessments for each grade span. Elementary school students are now expected to independently read and understand texts with Lexile scores between 420 and 820L by the time they finish 3rd grade. The high end of this range is notably higher than the high end of the prior levels (450–725L) set by the Lexile system. By the end of 5th grade, students are expected to comprehend texts with Lexile scores between 740 and 1010L, which is another increase from the former expectation (645–845L) (Nelson, Perfetti, Liben, & Liben, 2012). This move toward more challenging reading material will have a strong impact on which texts and, in particular, which *informational texts* teachers select for upper elementary school students. The qualitative measures and reader task considerations—the other two legs in the model for text selection in the Common Core—provide teachers with a set of criteria to use when evaluating titles for particular students and situations. For a complete description of the Common Core's text complexity model, please see Chapter 2.

## Close reading and citing text evidence

The Common Core has numerous reading standards that ask students to closely analyze the information, ideas, and rhetorical choices that appear in texts. Students are expected to provide text evidence to support their assertions about the content and attributes of the texts that they read.

The Common Core's publisher's criteria for ELA/literacy (Coleman & Pimentel, 2012) notes that teachers can foster close reading and the use of text evidence in their classrooms simply by increasing the number of text-based questions that they ask. Currently, many questions in the curriculum are designed to develop student background knowledge or to help students make connections between the text and their prior experience. These types of questions will remain important during prereading exercises and as support strategies, but the bulk of questions teachers use during instruction should be text-based and answerable only by examining the text. Additionally, the writers of the Common Core advise teachers to favor graphic organizers and activities that ask students to provide direct quotations from the text as evidence. Teachers may want to immediately begin to inventory and review their current curriculum to identify and modify the types of questions and organizers used to help ensure that students are required to review and cite the specific texts they read.

## Writing about texts

Many of the Common Core ELA/literacy standards emphasize writing in response to print and multimedia texts, including the use of research skills.

Students write pieces in which they support an opinion about the texts that they read and hear, and they write explanations of information they find in texts. In both cases, students' writing presents evidence that they draw directly from texts. These writing skills are key to the research process, which requires students to use texts to find answers to questions and to investigate topics. The Common Core emphasizes research skills across the ELA/literacy standards, specifying that teachers ask students to conduct both brief and sustained research and that teachers weave research requirements into many different classroom contexts. The Common Core's reading standards also support writing about texts and conducting research by asking students to compare and integrate information from diverse sources. Teachers who implement the Common Core standards will likely need to increase the number of writing activities based on reading and listening activities and decrease their use of writing activities in which students respond to a prompt by drawing only on prior knowledge or experiences.

## How the Standards Are Organized

The Common Core English language arts and literacy standards present content within a highly organized structure. Content is organized first by strands and then grouped under more specific headings. The standards themselves provide the most detailed level of content description: statements of student knowledge and skills for particular grades. In elementary school, there are standards for each grade, from kindergarten through 5th grade. Each grade-level set of content standards can be traced back to the Common Core's foundation: the set of College and Career Readiness Anchor (CCRA) standards that broadly describe what students should know and be able to do by the time they graduate high school.

To further clarify the structure of the Common Core standards, we will look at each organizational component in turn.

### Strands

The ELA/literacy standards are sorted into four strands: Reading, Writing, Speaking and Listening, and Language. The first three of these categories will be familiar, as they have been used to organize content in numerous state ELA standards documents. The category of Language, however, is found less frequently in state standards. The Common Core Language strand describes knowledge and skills that cross all the strands. Grammar, for example, is applicable to both writing and speaking activities, and vocabulary is an important element of reading, writing, speaking, and listening. The strands in the Common Core are also distinguished from some state standards in that research skills and media literacy are not separate categories; research is addressed in the Common Core Writing strand, and media is embedded throughout the ELA/literacy strands, although it is most emphasized in the Speaking and Listening strand.

The Reading strand is further divided into three subsections, known as domains: Reading Literature, Reading Informational Text, and Reading Foundational Skills. The standards in the first two domains are parallel, addressing the same basic reading skills but describing them in ways specific to reading fiction versus reading nonfiction. The Foundational Skills domain addresses content related to early reading, including decoding and fluency.

Each strand has an associated abbreviation code to identify its particular numbered standards, with each of the three domains of the Reading strand receiving its own shorthand:

- Reading Literature (RL)
- Reading Informational Text (RI)
- Reading Foundational Skills (RF)
- Writing (W)
- Speaking and Listening (SL)
- Language (L)

These strand abbreviations are used as part of the CCSSI's official identification system, which provides a unique identifier for each standard in the Common Core and can be very useful to school staffs developing crosswalks, planning lessons, and sharing lesson plans. For example, the third standard in the Writing strand can be referred to as "Writing Standard 3" or, using the full, formal "dot notation," as "CCSS.ELA-Literacy.W.3." To speak specifically of a standard for a particular grade level, the grade designation is inserted between the strand letter and standard number: "CCSS. ELA-Literacy.W.4.3," for example, is Writing Standard 3 for grade 4. In this guide, we use an abbreviated form of the CCSSI identification system, dropping the common prefix and using strand and standard number only (e.g., W.3) in our general discussion. We have included the grade-level indicators in figures that present or refer to standards at various grade levels and in the sample lessons.

## Headings

Within each strand, a set of two or more topic headings provide further organization. The same headings span all grade levels. In the Language strand, for example, the standards are organized under three headings: Conventions of Standard English, Knowledge of Language, and Vocabulary Acquisition and Use. The headings provide users with an overview of the topics that the particular strands address, group standards that share a similar focus, and provide context for understanding individual standards. For example, the Craft and Structure heading within the Reading strand signals that the standards beneath it will focus on the various choices that authors make when developing (crafting) and organizing (structuring) their writing.

## College and Career Readiness Anchor standards

As noted, the College and Career Readiness Anchor standards define the knowledge and skills students should acquire in each content strand over the course of their K–12 education. The more specific, grade-level content standard statements spell out the aspects of CCRA knowledge and skills appropriate for students within that grade. In other words, there is a version of every anchor standard for each grade level, and every grade level has the same anchor standards. For illustration, see Figure 1.1, which displays the 3rd grade, 4th grade, and 5th grade versions of the same anchor standard within the Reading strand's Reading Literature domain.

The use of anchor standards provides overarching goals for student learning. When a single standard includes many details and various aspects,

Figure 1.1 | **Upper Elementary Grade-Specific Versions of a CCRA Standard**

| CCRA | Grade 3 | Grade 4 | Grade 5 |
|---|---|---|---|
| **RL.3** Analyze how and why individuals, events, and ideas develop and interact over the course of a text. | **RL.3.3** Describe characters in a story (e.g., their traits, motivations, or feelings) and explain how their actions contribute to the sequence of events. | **RL.4.3** Describe in depth a character, setting, or event in a story or drama, drawing on specific details in the text (e.g., a character's thoughts, words, or actions). | **RL.5.3** Compare and contrast two or more characters, settings, or events in a story or drama, drawing on specific details in the text (e.g., how characters interact). |

teachers can identify that standard's primary focus by reviewing its associated anchor standard. The progression of grade-level standards provides a structure that indicates how students' skills are expected to advance over time. As teachers assess their students, the continuum of grade-level standards in the Common Core may enhance their understanding of how specific skills develop. Additional resources have also been developed to help teachers understand the precursor and postcursor skills for the Common Core standards at specific grade levels. The National Center for the Improvement of Educational Assessment has identified research-based learning progressions for use with the Common Core (Hess, 2011), and the Center on Instruction at RMC Research Corporation has identified learning progressions for the standards within the Reading Foundational Skills domain (Kosanovich & Verhagen, 2012). In contrast to the rest of the Common Core standards for ELA/literacy, those within the Foundational Skills domain are not directly associated with anchor standards.

## Connections Across Content Areas

It is important to note that although standards for literacy in history/social studies, science, and technical subjects are described separately in the

Common Core standards for grades 6–12, they are fully integrated into the standards for grades K–5. The standards for reading, writing, speaking and listening, and language should be applied across the curriculum in elementary classrooms. For example, students will be expected to use skills articulated in reading standards when reading history texts and skills addressed in writing and speaking and listening standards when reporting the results of science experiments. In this way, the Common Core ELA/literacy standards work in conjunction with other subject-area standards and provide a foundation for a broad spectrum of student learning.

## Appendices to the ELA/Literacy Standards

In addition to the standards themselves, the Common Core standards document for ELA/literacy includes a set of three appendices that provide further clarification and support.

Appendix A (CCSSI, 2010d) explains the research base and rationale for many of the key aspects of the standards. It describes how to use the Common Core text complexity model, which includes three factors for determining the appropriate complexity of texts for each grade range. Appendix A also describes the three major text types required by the standards in the Writing strand: argument, exposition, and narration. The role of oral language in literacy is also described in this appendix, as are various aspects of the Language strand, including vocabulary.

Appendix B (CCSSI, 2010e) supports teachers' efforts to determine appropriate levels of text complexity by excerpting portions of particular texts that illustrate the level of complexity required of students within each grade band. The Common Core standards for elementary school include two text complexity bands: grades 2–3 and grades 4–5. Short performance tasks accompany the exemplar texts and indicate the types of activities and student performances that support specific reading standards.

The standards document's Appendix C (CCSSI, 2010f) provides annotated samples of student writing for each grade level that meet or exceed the minimum level of proficiency the standards demand. Examples are provided across all three of the text types: argument, informational/expository, and narrative writing. In most cases, the samples are accompanied by a description of the context for writing (prompt, requirements, audience, and purpose). Annotations clarify how the sample meets the requirements of the grade-level standards.

✳✳✳

Our intention in Part I of this guide is to provide a sense of the meaning of each ELA/literacy standard for grades 3–5 and explain how the standards are related to each other across both grade levels and strands. Readers should be aware that what we present are examples of such connections; we do not mean to suggest that no other connections can or should be made. Teachers should build on the information here to strengthen their own practice and enhance their implementation of the Common Core standards.

Now that we've looked at the overall structure of the Common Core ELA/literacy standards, we will examine each strand in turn.

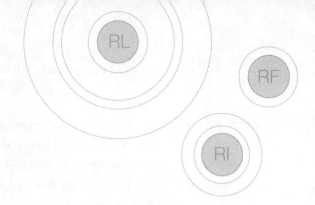

# CHAPTER 2

# Reading

The Common Core standards expect students to read both widely and deeply. Students read across a variety of genres to develop an appreciation for literature and to build content-area knowledge. At the same time, they engage in close reading, thinking critically and in depth about the author's ideas, techniques, and choices. As discussed later in this chapter, a key aspect of the reading standards is that they provide an opportunity for all students to encounter and learn from complex texts that will prepare them for the level of reading required in middle school and, ultimately, in college and careers. Finally, children in 3rd, 4th, and 5th grades continue to develop decoding skills and reading fluency, which were a major focus in grades K–2.

Both of the consortia currently designing assessments for the Common Core standards—the Smarter Balanced Assessment Consortium (SBAC) and the Partnership for Assessment of Readiness for College and Careers (PARCC)—have announced that they plan to assess mastery of the reading standards using selected-response items, such as multiple choice; performance-based items, such as research tasks; and constructed-response items that require short or long written responses. SBAC will use computer adaptive testing for both an optional interim assessment (designed to generate formative data) and a required, accountability-focused summative assessment; its aim is to provide educators and parents with specific information about each student's reading ability. Similarly, PARCC is developing a reading diagnostic assessment as an optional tool to help educators identify students' independent reading levels.

At the elementary school levels, the Reading strand is divided into three domains: Reading Standards for Literature ("Reading Literature" or "RL"), Reading Standards for Informational Text ("Reading Informational Text" or "RI"), and Reading Standards: Foundational Skills ("Foundational Skills" or "RF"). The first two domains have an identical structure; the standards in each are similar, although they highlight key differences between reading literature and informational texts. Both the Reading Literature and Reading Informational Text domains share the same 10 College and Career Readiness Anchor standards. As explained in Chapter 1, the anchor standards describe what students should know and be able to do by the time they graduate from high school. Each standard within these domains has a corresponding CCRA standard, which describes the standard's overall goal in preparing students for the demands of college or career. In other words, each standard in Reading Literature has a parallel standard in Reading Informational Text, and both of those standards are tied to the same CCRA standard. The Reading Literature and Reading Informational Text domains also organize standards under the same four headings: Key Ideas and Details, Craft and Structure, Integration of Knowledge and Ideas, and Range of Reading and Level of Text Complexity.

The Reading Foundational Skills domain, by contrast, contains the only ELA/literacy standards in the Common Core that are not directly associated with anchor standards and do not extend past 5th grade. As their name implies, the Foundational Skills standards specify discreet skills for early reading, including concepts associated with print conventions, phonemic awareness, mastery of phonics, and decoding strategies. The bulk of these standards are found in grades K–2, but decoding and fluency remain a focus for 3rd, 4th, and 5th grade.

Figure 2.1 provides an overview of the entire Reading strand at the upper elementary level.

**Figure 2.1  |  The Reading Strand: Grades 3–5 Overview**

**Domains: Reading Literature and Reading Informational Text**

| Heading | CCRA Standard | Grade 3 Standards | Grade 4 Standards | Grade 5 Standards |
|---|---|---|---|---|
| Key Ideas and Details | R.1 | RL.3.1 | RL.4.1 | RL.5.1 |
| | | RI.3.1 | RI.4.1 | RI.5.1 |
| | R.2 | RL.3.2 | RL.4.2 | RL.5.2 |
| | | RI.3.2 | RI.4.2 | RI.5.2 |
| | R.3 | RL.3.3 | RL.4.3 | RL.5.3 |
| | | RI.3.3 | RI.4.3 | RI.5.3 |
| Craft and Structure | R.4 | RL.3.4 | RL.4.4 | RL.5.4 |
| | | RI.3.4 | RI.4.4 | RI.5.4 |
| | R.5 | RL.3.5 | RL.4.5 | RL.5.5 |
| | | RI.3.5 | RI.4.5 | RI.5.5 |
| | R.6 | RL.3.6 | RL.4.6 | RL.5.6 |
| | | RI.3.6 | RI.4.6 | RI.5.6 |
| Integration of Knowledge and Ideas | R.7 | RL.3.7 | RL.4.7 | RL.5.7 |
| | | RI.3.7 | RI.4.7 | RI.5.7 |
| | R.8 | RI.3.8 | RI.4.8 | RI.5.8 |
| | R.9 | RL.3.9 | RL.4.9 | RL.5.9 |
| | | RI.3.9 | RI.4.9 | RI.5.9 |
| Range of Reading and Level of Text Complexity | R.10 | RL.3.10 | RL.4.10 | RL.5.10 |
| | | RI.3.10 | RI.4.10 | RI.5.10 |

**Domain: Reading Foundational Skills**

| Heading | CCRA Standard | Grade 3 Standards | Grade 4 Standards | Grade 5 Standards |
|---|---|---|---|---|
| Print Concepts | — | — | — | — |
| Phonological Awareness | — | — | — | — |
| Phonics and Word Recognition | — | RF.3.3 | RF.4.3 | RF.5.3 |
| Fluency | — | RF.3.4 | RF.4.4 | RF.5.4 |

*Note:* There are no CCRA standards for the Reading Foundational Skills domain, and standards under the Print Concepts and Phonological Awareness headings conclude in Grade 2.

# Reading Literature and Reading Informational Text

To effectively address the different formats of the three Reading domains, we will begin by looking at the similarly structured Reading Standards for Literature and Reading Standards for Informational Text, alternating our focus between them as we move from one heading to the next, using excerpts from the Common Core to frame the discussion.

# Key Ideas and Details

The Common Core authors note that the standards ask students to "read like a detective" (Coleman & Pimentel, 2012, p. 16). Detective readers carefully review the content, structure, and rhetorical techniques in a text for clues to its meaning. This type of investigation is at the heart of the reading standards, beginning with those under the Key Ideas and Details heading. Figure 2.2 shows the sequence of standards in the Reading Literature domain. Differences in each standard's phrasing from the prior grade level are shown in contrasting text to highlight how the standard's content changes from grade to grade.

The majority of standards in the Reading strand ask students to analyze texts. Reading Standard 1 (abbreviated as RL.1 and RI.1, respectively) asks students to support their analyses with text evidence. In this way, it works in tandem with many of the other reading standards that follow. Reading Standard 1 is identical in the literature and informational text domains, and it provides a foundation for the Common Core's emphasis on students' close, analytic reading by requiring that students' responses to literature be grounded in information and details from the text.

Reading Standard 1 also describes a continuum of advancing skill related to students' ability to support their ideas about books. In 3rd grade, students refer to details in the story when they answer questions. By 4th grade, students also find examples in the text to support the inferences they make, and by 5th grade, they are expected to quote specific

For an example of a 3rd grade lesson addressing Reading Informational Text Standard 1 (RI.3.1), please see **Sample Lesson 1.**

RL.1–3

| Figure 2.2 \| **Reading Literature Standards 1–3: Key Ideas and Details** | | |
| --- | --- | --- |
| Grade 3 | Grade 4 | Grade 5 |
| **RL.3.1** Ask and answer questions to demonstrate understanding of a text, **referring explicitly to the text as the basis for the answers.** | **RL.4.1 Refer to details and examples in a text when explaining what the text says explicitly and when drawing inferences from the text.** | **RL.5.1 Quote accurately from a text** when explaining what the text says explicitly and when drawing inferences from the text. |
| **RL.3.2** Recount stories, including fables, folktales, **and myths** from diverse cultures; determine the central message, lesson, or moral and **explain how it is conveyed through key details in the text.** | **RL.4.2 Determine a theme of a story, drama, or poem from details in the text; summarize the text.** | **RL.5.2** Determine a theme of a story, drama, or poem from details in the text, **including how characters in a story or drama respond to challenges or how the speaker in a poem reflects upon a topic;** summarize the text. |
| **RL.3.3** Describe characters in a story **(e.g., their traits, motivations, or feelings) and explain how their actions contribute to the sequence of events.** | **RL.4.3** Describe **in depth** a character, **setting, or event in a story or drama, drawing on specific details in the text (e.g., a character's thoughts, words, or actions).** | **RL.5.3 Compare and contrast two or more** characters, settings, or events in a story or drama, drawing on specific details in the text **(e.g., how characters interact).** |

*Note:* Boldface text identifies content that differs from the prior grade level.

evidence for their explanations of the text. Across grades, this standard asks students to support their observations about what they read with text evidence. To help students master this standard, the questions teachers ask students during instruction and classroom activities and on assessments should be "text-based," in that students need to refer to a text as the basis for their answers.

The second standard under the Key Ideas and Details heading, Reading Literature Standard 2 (RL.2), asks students to determine the central idea or themes in a text and summarize them, using text details rather than their own opinions as support. As they do with all skills addressed in the ELA/ literacy standards, students build facility with text analysis over the course of their K–12 education. They build the ability to discern major themes in literary texts, as required by Reading Literature Standard 2, by retelling stories and determining a central message during grades K–2. Beginning in 3rd grade, they connect the central message or lesson in the story to the specific details that convey its importance. In 4th and 5th grades, students' retelling or recounting of stories becomes more formalized summaries. Note that the 5th grade version of Reading Literature Standard 2 specifies that students understand how a text's themes are drawn out in details such as characters' actions or poetic descriptions.

For an example of a 5th grade lesson addressing Reading Literature Standard 2 (RL.5.2), please see **Sample Lesson 3.**

Reading Literature Standard 3 (RL.3) at the 3rd grade level focuses on character development and how character actions build plot. In 4th grade, it focuses on the *development* of a particular character, setting, or event, and in 5th grade, it addresses *comparing* characters, settings, or events in a story or drama. At all grade levels, RL.3 asks students to identify details from the text to support their ideas about the targeted story elements. Teachers accustomed to using graphic organizers and note-taking techniques that require students to quote descriptions, events, and dialogue from the text will find that these tools remain useful for addressing this standard. As students enter middle school and more fully explore the effects of and relationships among story elements, their ability to analyze story elements will continue to grow.

Figure 2.3 shows the full sequence of standards under the Key Ideas and Details heading of the Reading Standards for Informational Text. As described later in this chapter (see the discussion of Standard 10 for Reading Informational Text), the Common Core standards emphasize students' reading of informational texts in science, social studies, and other subjects. Within the Reading Informational Text domain, the Key Ideas and Details

Figure 2.3  |  **Reading Informational Text Standards 1–3: Key Ideas and Details**

| Grade 3 | Grade 4 | Grade 5 |
|---|---|---|
| **RI.3.1** Ask and answer questions to demonstrate understanding of a text, **referring explicitly to the text as the basis for the answers.** | **RI.4.1 Refer to details and examples in a text when explaining what the text says explicitly and when drawing inferences from the text.** | **RI.5.1 Quote accurately from a text** when explaining what the text says explicitly and when drawing inferences from the text. |
| **RI.3.2 Determine** the main idea of a text; **recount the key details and explain how they support the main idea.** | **RI.4.2** Determine the main idea of a text **and explain how it is supported by key details; summarize the text.** | **RI.5.2** Determine **two or more main ideas** of a text and explain how they are supported by key details; summarize the text. |
| **RI.3.3** Describe the **relationship** between a series of historical events, scientific ideas or concepts, or steps in technical procedures in a text, **using language that pertains to time, sequence, and cause/effect.** | **RI.4.3 Explain events, procedures, ideas, or concepts in a historical, scientific, or technical text, including what happened and why, based on specific information in the text.** | **RI.5.3** Explain **the relationships or interactions between two or more individuals, events, ideas, or concepts** in a historical, scientific, or technical text based on specific information in the text. |

*Note:* Boldface text identifies content that differs from the prior grade level.

heading covers standards that describe students' ability to comprehend the factual information and ideas in texts that they read while they are building content knowledge across the curriculum.

As previously noted, Reading Informational Text Standard 1 (RI.1) is identical to the first standard in the Reading Literature domain (RL.1), addressing the use of textual evidence as support for analysis of explicit and inferred information in texts. Teachers can promote mastery by asking students to respond to prompts and questions about the informational texts they read by referencing specific text details.

Reading Informational Text Standard 2 (RI.2) is very similar to its counterpart in Reading Literature. The primary differences are that students must identify main ideas rather than themes, and they must retell supporting facts rather than character or plot details. As with the Reading Literature standards, students progress from retelling to more formalized summaries, and they learn to connect details within a text to the text's main ideas. Learning how authors of informational texts support their ideas with factual details and other evidence not only will improve students' understanding of the subject matter but will also help them understand how to develop and support their own ideas when they write about information.

For an example of a 4th grade lesson addressing Reading Informational Text Standard 2 (RI.4.2), please see **Sample Lesson 2.**

Reading Informational Text Standard 3 (RI.3) focuses on how ideas and details in a text are related. The requirements of this standard vary for each grade, but the standard always focuses on students making connections among different types of detailed information. Across grades 3, 4, and 5, students focus on understanding the sequence of events, ideas, or steps and explaining cause-and-effect relationships. Students in earlier grades make similar connections, although the complexity of the ideas and information being studied steadily increases as the reading material and subject matter become more complex. In fact, across all reading standards, the increased difficulty from one grade to the next is directly related to the increasing complexity of the text being analyzed, an aspect that is described in detail within the discussion of Reading Standard 10 (see p. 32).

Notably, the reading standards do not specify the use of particular reading comprehension strategies (such as making predictions), as is common in many state standards documents. The Common Core publishers' criteria document states that, in ELA and literacy, "to be effective, instruction on specific reading techniques should occur when they illuminate specific aspects of a text. Students need to build an infrastructure of skills, habits, knowledge, dispositions, and experience that enables them to approach new challenging texts with confidence and stamina. As much as possible, this training should be embedded in the activity of reading the text rather than being taught as a separate body of material" (Coleman & Pimentel, 2012, p. 9).

In other words, classroom teachers should model and incorporate reading strategies into instruction as driven by curricula and student needs. However, teachers will note that many skills commonly referred to as reading comprehension strategies are clearly embedded within the standards. For example, the strategies of questioning and making inferences are clearly required in Reading Standard 1 (both RL.1 and RI.1). Strategies for determining the importance of information and ideas are clearly part of Reading Standard 2 (both RL.2 and RI.2). Making text-to-text connections is a key aspect of Reading Standard 3 (both RL.3 and RI.3). What the standards don't specify, however, is how students are to apply these strategies. Such instructional decisions (e.g., *Will students use a highlighter, an outline, a graphic organizer, or some other means to help them identify main ideas and related details in a text? Will they record their questions about a text on a sticky note or in an electronic comment feature?*) are left to the teacher, to be driven by the needs of individual students and the environment in which learning is taking place. Teachers should ask students to apply strategies and approaches in ways that are effective in the particular context of their classroom and their curriculum framework.

## Craft and Structure

The standards under the Craft and Structure heading require students to explain the techniques and strategies that authors employ in texts. Reviewing the author's craft not only supports students' close reading of texts but also provides them with models for their own writing. This heading covers three standards, which ask students to analyze the word choice, organization, and point of view or purpose present in a text. Figure 2.4 shows the sequence of these standards for the Reading Literature domain.

The first standard under this heading, Reading Literature Standard 4 (RL.4), emphasizes authors' word choices and asks students to determine the explicit and implied meaning of words in the texts that they read. In 3rd

Figure 2.4  |  **Reading Literature Standards 4–6: Craft and Structure**

RL.4–6

| Grade 3 | Grade 4 | Grade 5 |
|---|---|---|
| **RL.3.4 Determine the meaning of words and phrases as they are used in a text, distinguishing literal from nonliteral language.** | **RL.4.4** Determine the meaning of words and phrases as they are used in a text, **including those that allude to significant characters found in mythology (e.g., Herculean).** | **RL.5.4** Determine the meaning of words and phrases as they are used in a text, **including figurative language such as metaphors and similes.** |
| **RL.3.5 Refer to parts of stories, dramas, and poems when writing or speaking about a text, using terms such as chapter, scene, and stanza; describe how each successive part builds on earlier sections.** | **RL.4.5 Explain major differences** between poems, drama, and **prose, and refer to the structural elements of poems (e.g., verse, rhythm, meter) and drama (e.g., casts of characters, settings, descriptions, dialogue, stage directions)** when writing or speaking about a text. | **RL.5.5 Explain how a series of chapters, scenes, or stanzas fits together to provide the overall structure of a particular story, drama, or poem.** |
| **RL.3.6 Distinguish their own point of view from that of the narrator or those of the characters.** | **RL.4.6 Compare and contrast the point of view from which different stories are narrated, including the difference between first- and third-person narrations.** | **RL.5.6 Describe how a narrator's or speaker's point of view influences how events are described.** |

*Note:* Boldface text identifies content that differs from the prior grade level.

grade, the standard focuses on the difference between literal and nonliteral language; in 4th grade, the focus is on words that stem from literary allusions, a topic that is addressed again and in depth in RL.4 at the 8th grade level. The 5th grade focus is on figurative language, such as metaphors and similes.

The second standard under this heading, Reading Literature Standard 5 (RL.5), focuses on how stories, drama, and poetry are structured. In 3rd grade, students identify the structural elements of different genres and use literary terms for those elements when talking or writing about their reading. Prior to 3rd grade, RL.5 asks students to focus only on the basic characteristics of fiction and beginnings and endings; the specifics in the 3rd grade version of the standard (chapter, scene, and stanza) represent a significant expansion in the types of structural elements that students are expected to identify. In 4th grade, students learn to further differentiate among the structural elements of different genres, with a particular emphasis on elements of poetry and drama. In 8th grade, students study how structural elements in literary texts work together to guide the reader through a story or poetic experience.

Reading Literature Standard 6 (RL.6), the third and final standard under the Craft and Structure heading, is about point of view. In grades K–2, students compare the point of view of various characters and narrators. Beginning in grade 3, they consider how their own point of view might be different from the point of view conveyed in the text. In 4th grade, students compare stories with different points of view and learn the difference between narration in the first and third person. In 5th grade, they consider the effects of point of view on the story, including how a reader's understanding of events is influenced by who in the story is describing those events. As with all the reading standards, RL.6 requires students to support their assertions about point of view with specific evidence, referencing details, words, and phrases in the text.

Figure 2.5 shows the standards under the Craft and Structure heading of the Reading Standards for Informational Text. While the standards in this domain closely resemble their counterparts in Reading Literature, they include details specific to reading nonfiction.

Similar to the corresponding standard in Reading Literature, Reading Informational Text Standard 4 (RI.4) is focused on authors' word choices. Instead of considering the explicit and figurative meaning of words and phrases, as they do when reading literature, students reading informational

Figure 2.5 | **Reading Informational Text Standards 4–6: Craft and Structure**

| Grade 3 | Grade 4 | Grade 5 |
|---|---|---|
| **RI.3.4** Determine the meaning of **general academic and domain-specific** words and phrases in a text relevant to a ***grade 3*** *topic or subject area.* | **RI.4.4** Determine the meaning of general academic and domain-specific words or phrases in a text relevant to a ***grade 4*** *topic or subject area.* | **RI.5.4** Determine the meaning of general academic and domain-specific words and phrases in a text relevant to a ***grade 5*** *topic or subject area.* |
| **RI.3.5** Use text features and **search tools (e.g., key words, sidebars, hyperlinks)** to locate information relevant to a given topic efficiently. | **RI.4.5 Describe the overall structure (e.g., chronology, comparison, cause/effect, problem/ solution) of events, ideas, concepts, or information in a text or part of a text.** | **RI.5.5 Compare and contrast** the overall structure (e.g., chronology, comparison, cause/effect, problem/solution) of events, ideas, concepts, or information in **two or more texts.** |
| **RI.3.6 Distinguish their own point of view from that of the author of a text.** | **RI.4.6 Compare and contrast a firsthand and secondhand account of the same event or topic; describe the differences in focus and the information provided.** | **RI.5.6 Analyze multiple accounts** of the same event or topic, **noting important similarities and** differences in the point of view they represent. |

*Note:* Boldface text identifies content that differs from the prior grade level.

texts focus on the explicit meaning of general academic and domain-specific words. These word categories are described in detail on pages 32–35 of Appendix A to the ELA/literacy standards document (CCSSI, 2010d), and we address them in Chapter 5's discussion of the language standards under the Vocabulary Acquisition and Use heading (see p. 77). Essentially, general academic words are those often found in academic texts but rarely used in everyday speech. The meaning of these words is not always easily inferred from the context or learned through exposure to spoken language, and so explicit study of general academic words can bolster students' comprehension of complex academic texts. Domain-specific words and phrases are words that pertain to a specific subject or content area. Examples would be social studies and science terminology that is particular to those subjects.

For an example of a 4th grade lesson addressing Reading Informational Text Standard 5 (RI.4.5), please see **Sample Lesson 2.**

Reading Informational Text Standard 5 (RI.5) focuses on the structure and organization of nonfiction tests. In kindergarten through 2nd grade, students identify and use basic text features, such as headings, a table of contents, and a glossary. In 3rd grade, these skills are expanded to include using search tools to locate information in a digital text. In 4th grade, the focus of RI.5 changes to how specific information in the text is organized within paragraphs and sections. Many teachers are accustomed to using classroom activities that help students identify these nonfiction text structures—having students highlight topic sentences or create outlines as they read, for example. In 5th grade, students further their exploration of the ways that information can be organized by comparing the text structures of two or more pieces of writing.

As noted, RL.6 focuses on point of view and purpose. Its counterpart, Reading Informational Text Standard 6 (RI.6), introduces 3rd graders to the idea that their own point of view may differ from the point of view present in the text. Fourth graders compare how authors with different points of view treat the same subject, including what information is included and highlighted in each account. Fifth graders continue to develop these comparative skills, analyzing multiple perspectives on a subject and considering how the choices that authors make may be similar or different.

## Integration of Knowledge and Ideas

Standards under the Integration of Knowledge and Ideas heading ask students to compare and synthesize the ideas and information presented in different works, including multimedia and artistic mediums. Figure 2.6 shows the sequence of these standards for the Reading Literature domain.

| Figure 2.6 | **Reading Literature Standards 7 and 9:** **Integration of Knowledge and Ideas** | | |
|---|---|---|---|
| **Grade 3** | **Grade 4** | **Grade 5** | |
| **RL.3.7 Explain how specific aspects of a text's illustrations contribute to what is conveyed by the words in a story** (e.g., create mood, emphasize aspects of a character or setting). | **RL.4.7 Make connections between the text of a story or drama and a visual or oral presentation of the text, identifying where each version reflects specific descriptions and directions in the text.** | **RL.5.7 Analyze how visual and multimedia elements contribute to the meaning, tone, or beauty of a text (e.g., graphic novel, multimedia presentation of fiction, folktale, myth, poem).** | |

**RL.8** *Not applicable to literature*

| | | |
|---|---|---|
| RL.3.9 Compare and contrast the **themes, settings, and plots of stories written by the same author about the same or similar characters (e.g., in books from a series).** | RL.4.9 Compare and contrast the **treatment of similar themes and topics (e.g., opposition of good and evil) and patterns of events (e.g., the quest) in stories, myths, and traditional literature from different cultures.** | RL.5.9 Compare and contrast **stories in the same genre (e.g., mysteries and adventure stories) on their approaches to similar themes and topics.** |

*Note:* Boldface text identifies content that differs from the prior grade level.

The two standards under this heading both focus on comparing multiple texts. (Note that Reading Standard 8, which is about evaluating arguments, is found only in the Reading Informational Text domain). The first standard, Reading Literature Standard 7 (RL.7), asks students to analyze the effects of different media and formats. While students in grades K–2 learn to use illustrations to gain a better understanding of the explicit meaning of a text, students in 3rd grade are asked to consider how illustrations may extend a text's meaning and how pictures contribute to and enhance the words in the text. Students in 4th grade move beyond illustrations to compare written texts with live or recorded versions and study how written descriptions or stage directions are applied. Students in 5th grade extend these skills by considering the effects of visual and multimedia elements used in a text. At all grade levels, this standard requires students to infer how a text's visual or oral elements are related to its words.

For an example of a 5th grade lesson addressing Reading Literature Standard 9 (RL.5.9), please see **Sample Lesson 3.**

In Reading Literature Standard 9 (RL.9), students compare and contrast texts, focusing first on texts with similar characters (grade 3); then on texts from diverse cultural origins with similar themes, topics, or events (grade 4); and finally on texts within the same genre with similar themes, topics, or events (grade 5). Across grades, RL.9 underscores how critical it is for curricular units of study to give students opportunities to read and compare a variety of works. Students build knowledge and a deeper understanding of material by comparing a variety of texts and text types with similar themes. When addressing this standard, teachers should be sure to pair short and long texts and fiction and informational texts, allowing students to compare different treatments of the same theme or topic. Making connections among texts by identifying similarities and differences is a well-known strategy for aiding reading comprehension (Dean et al., 2012).

Figure 2.7 presents the standards under the Integration of Knowledge and Ideas heading in the Reading Informational Text domain. Similar to their counterparts in the Reading Literature domain, these three standards focus on comparing information from multiple texts but, with the addition of Reading Informational Text Standard 8 (RI.8), also cover evaluating logic and evidence in nonfiction.

For an example of a 4th grade lesson addressing Reading Informational Text Standard 7 (RI.4.7), please see **Sample Lesson 2.**

Reading Informational Text Standard 7 (RI.7) focuses on synthesizing information found in diverse formats. In 3rd grade, the standard emphasizes graphic illustrations, including maps and photographs. In 4th grade, it expands to include visual, oral, and numerical formats, such as graphs, timelines, and web pages. By 5th grade, students are expected to access information from a variety of sources and formats to address particular

Figure 2.7  |  **Reading Informational Text Standards 7–9:**
             **Integration of Knowledge and Ideas**

| Grade 3 | Grade 4 | Grade 5 |
|---|---|---|
| **RI.3.7 Use information gained from illustrations (e.g., maps, photographs) and the words in a text to demonstrate understanding of the text (e.g., where, when, why, and how key events occur).** | **RI.4.7 Interpret** information presented visually, orally, or quantitatively (e.g., in charts, graphs, diagrams, time lines, animations, or interactive elements on Web pages) and explain how the information contributes to an understanding of the text in which it appears. | **RI.5.7 Draw on information from multiple print or digital sources, demonstrating the ability to locate an answer to a question quickly or to solve a problem efficiently.** |
| **RI.3.8 Describe the logical connection between particular sentences and paragraphs in a text (e.g., comparison, cause/effect, first/second/third in a sequence).** | **RI.4.8 Explain how an author uses reasons and evidence to support particular points in a text.** | RI.5.8 Explain how an author uses reasons and evidence to support particular points in a text, **identifying which reasons and evidence support which point(s).** |
| RI.3.9 Compare and contrast the most important points **and key details** presented in two texts on the same topic. | **RI.4.9 Integrate information** from two texts on the same topic **in order to write or speak about the subject knowledgeably.** | RI.5.9 Integrate information from **several texts** on the same topic in order to write or speak about the subject knowledgeably. |

*Note:* Boldface text identifies content that differs from the prior grade level.

purposes, such as solving a problem or answering a question. Note that RI.7 addresses similar skills to those covered in Writing Standards 7–9, under the heading Research to Build and Present Knowledge (see p. 53).

The second standard here, Reading Informational Text Standard 8 (RI.8), appears only in the Reading Informational Text domain and focuses on evaluating the logic and reasoning an author uses. It is a key standard because it reflects the Common Core's emphasis on students' ability to examine arguments. Students in grades K–2 identify the reasons that authors give to support their points. Now, in 3rd grade, RI.8 asks students to explain how authors connect their points with supporting reasons within and across paragraphs. In 4th grade, students more generally evaluate how evidence is used by an author to support points, and in 5th grade, they must determine the specific evidence provided for each major point. When students reach middle school, they will extend their argumentation skills further, going on to evaluate the quality of the evidence supporting a claim.

For an example of a 3rd grade lesson addressing Reading Informational Text Standard 9 (RI.3.9), please see **Sample Lesson 1.**

The final standard under Integration of Knowledge and Ideas, Reading Informational Text Standard 9 (RI.9), is similar to its counterpart in the Reading Literature domain in that students compare and synthesize texts that share a topic or subject. Children in 1st and 2nd grades learn how to compare books; here in 3rd grade, RI.9 asks them to provide comparisons that are more detailed. By 4th grade, students are assumed to be capable of synthesizing information from at least two sources to build knowledge about a topic. By 5th grade, RI.9 asks them to integrate information from several texts. As with RI.8, teachers planning units and lessons may find it useful to address RI.9 in conjunction with the research standards in the Writing strand.

## Range of Reading and Level of Text Complexity

The final standard in the Reading strand, Reading Standard 10 (RL.10/RI.10), describes the range and complexity of student reading materials to which all other reading standards apply. It reflects the idea that students must apply their developing reading skills to texts that increase in complexity each year to ensure that they will graduate prepared to read entry-level college texts.

It's important to say a few words here about the Common Core text complexity model, which includes three factors: qualitative measures, quantitative measures, and reader and task considerations. These factors are described in detail within Appendix A to the ELA/literacy standards document (CCSSI, 2010d), and models for each grade are provided in Appendix B (CCSSI, 2010e). Teachers are encouraged to consider all three factors when deciding which texts will be sufficiently complex for their students, and in some cases, teachers may determine that one of the factors is more critical than the others in determining the appropriateness of a given text.

*Quantitative measures* are objective and may be evaluated using a readability measure, which calculates text difficulty by examining aspects such as word and sentence length. Six different measures for calculating readability were compared in a recent study (Nelson et al., 2012), and these measures now share a common scale that aligns to college and career readiness as described in the Common Core. These measures include ATOS®, Degrees of Reading Power®, Flesch Kincaid®, Lexile® Framework, Source Rater©, and Pearson Reading Maturity Metric©. Quantitative readability measures do not address drama and poetry, however, and are less accurate for literature than they are for informational texts.

The other factors in the text complexity model are more subjective. *Qualitative factors* include aspects of the text, such as levels of meaning, structure, language conventionality and clarity, and knowledge demands. Rubrics have been developed by the Kansas State Department of Education (2011) and the National Center for the Improvement of Educational Assessment (Hess & Hervey, 2011) to assess qualitative factors for literature and informational text.

These same groups have developed criteria to aid teachers addressing the third component of Common Core text complexity, *reader and task considerations*. This final aspect of the model takes into account students' individual motivation, knowledge, and experiences as well as the complexity of the assignment. As more educators work to implement the Common Core standards in the coming years, additional tools to aid teachers in evaluating text complexity and selecting appropriate texts for classroom use will likely be developed.

In both the Reading Literature and the Reading Informational Text domains, the standards describe text complexity in terms of grade bands. In elementary school, there are two grade bands: grades 2–3 and grades 4–5. Students at the lower end of these bands, in 2nd and 4th grades, may need supports, such as guided reading, to read texts with higher levels of complexity. Students at the higher end of the bands, in 3rd and 5th grades, are expected to be able to read complex texts in their respective bands independently by the end of the year—an indication that they are appropriately prepared for the next grade.

The publisher's criteria for the ELA/literacy Common Core standards indicate that when students need supports to access a complex text above their reading level, teachers should ask questions that guide students to find the answer in the text rather than answer the students' questions by explaining the text to them. Prereading supports that build students' background knowledge should concentrate on words and concepts that are important to understanding the text and that cannot be derived through the context of the text itself. The degree of support provided to students should correspond to their individual needs, and particular attention should be paid to designing supports for English language learners and other students who struggle with complex texts (Coleman & Pimentel, 2012).

With that explanation given, let's move on to look at the standards under the Range of Reading and Level of Text Complexity heading within the Reading Literature domain (see Figure 2.8).

**RL.10**

Figure 2.8  |  **Reading Literature Standard 10: Range of Reading and Level of Text Complexity**

| Grade 3 | Grade 4 | Grade 5 |
|---|---|---|
| **RL.3.10** By the end of the year, read and comprehend literature, including stories, **dramas,** and poetry, **at the high end of the** *grades 2–3 text complexity band* **independently and proficiently.** | **RL.4.10** By the end of the year, read and comprehend literature, including stories, dramas, and poetry, **in the** *grades 4–5 text complexity band* proficiently, **with scaffolding as needed at the high end of the range.** | **RL.5.10** By the end of the year, read and comprehend literature, including stories, dramas, and poetry, **at the high end of** the *grades 4–5 text complexity band* **independently and** proficiently. |

*Note:* Boldface text identifies content that differs from the prior grade level.

In addition to describing text complexity, RL.10 describes the range of student reading by identifying a variety of genres that students should read, including stories, dramas, and poetry. Stories appropriate to grades K–5 are further defined as children's adventure stories, folktales, legends, fables, fantasy, realistic fiction, and myth. Appropriate drama includes dialogue and brief dramatic scenes that depict settings familiar to students, and poetry includes nursery rhymes and the subgenres of the narrative poem, limerick, and free verse poetry (CCSSI, 2010c, p. 31).

Figure 2.9 shows the standards for Range of Reading and Level of Text Complexity within the Reading Informational Text domain.

The version of this standard within the Reading Informational Text domain (RI.10) mirrors RL.10, using identical phrasing to describe text complexity. In range of reading, RI.10 defines informational texts for grades K–5 as literary nonfiction and historical, scientific, and technical texts. These include biographies and autobiographies; books about history, social studies, science, and the arts; technical texts, such as directions, forms, and information displayed in graphs, charts, or maps; and digital sources on a range of topics. Although literary nonfiction includes genres that are

RI.10

Figure 2.9 | **Reading Informational Text Standard 10: Range of Reading and Level of Text Complexity**

| Grade 3 | Grade 4 | Grade 5 |
|---|---|---|
| **RI.3.10** By the end of the year, read and comprehend informational texts, including history/social studies, science, and technical texts, **at the high end of the** *grades 2–3 text complexity band* **independently** and proficiently. | **RI.4.10** By the end of the year, read and comprehend informational texts, including history/social studies, science, and technical texts, **in the** *grades 4–5 text complexity band* proficiently, **with scaffolding as needed at the high end of the range.** | **RI.5.10** By the end of the year, read and comprehend informational texts, including history/social studies, science, and technical texts, **at the high end of** the *grades 4–5 text complexity band* **independently** and proficiently. |

*Note:* Boldface text identifies content that differs from the prior grade level.

structured similarly to narratives (e.g., biographies), the standards emphasize nonfiction that is built on informational text structures, such as news or magazine articles.

Reading Standard 10 (both RL.10 and RI.10) has important implications for curriculum and instruction. It calls for teachers to select a variety of reading materials around topics or themes in order to systematically develop student knowledge. As the standards document states, "Within a grade level, there should be an adequate number of titles on a single topic that would allow children to study that topic for a sustained period" (CCSSI, 2010c, p. 33).

As acquiring knowledge through reading should be part of students' study of history/social studies, science, and the arts, teachers are encouraged to seek links to curriculum in those areas. The *PARCC Model Content Frameworks for ELA/Literacy, Grades 3–11* (Partnership for Assessment of Readiness for College and Careers, 2012) recommends that unit plans include a variety of short texts that complement longer texts. For example, short informational texts might build the background knowledge needed to analyze a historical novel. Short texts also may provide greater opportunity for students to reread, which in turn supports the type of close, analytic examination essential to many of the reading standards. Short complex texts, or short excerpts from longer texts, may be used to model reading strategies and analytic thinking. The mix of short and longer texts will also provide opportunities for students to engage with texts of varying levels of complexity.

Reading Standard 10 is clear that all students should build proficiency with grade-level complex texts and topics, but students also need opportunities to build fluency and vocabulary with texts matched to their individual reading levels—that is, with texts that they can comprehend independently. (Reading fluency is described further in the Foundational Skills domain, the discussion of which begins below.) Essentially, the Common Core calls for teachers to use the text complexity model to carefully select reading materials of various lengths, genres, and complexity, which will provide all students with the opportunity to increase their reading ability and prepare for the challenges they will face in middle school and beyond.

# Reading Foundational Skills

This domain within the Reading strand is found only in kindergarten through 5th grade. Its standards focus on basic decoding skills and knowledge of print conventions. The first two headings in the domain, Print Concepts and Phonological Awareness, have standards at grades K through 2 alone. These standards cover general concepts of print, such as how it is organized on a page, and phonological awareness, such as the ability to segment and blend phonemes (individual sounds). The foundational reading skills identified for students in 3rd through 5th grades are organized under two headings: Phonics and Word Recognition, and Fluency. We'll examine them in turn.

# Phonics and Word Recognition

Phonics teaches students about the relationship between phonemes and printed letters and enables them to apply this knowledge to reading and spelling. Explicit and systematic phonics instruction is correlated with improved reading skills (National Reading Panel, 2000). In support of phonics instruction, Appendix A to the ELA/literacy standards provides a variety of reference tables and lists of common orthography conventions, including consonant graphemes, types of syllable patterns, principles for syllabification, inflectional suffixes, and derivational suffixes (CCSSI, 2010d). These detailed resources support the single standard under the Phonics and Word Recognition heading, Foundational Skills Standard 3 (RF.3), shown in Figure 2.10.

In grades K–2, this standard focuses on building students' phonetic knowledge and their ability to decode words, including regularly spelled two-syllable words with long vowels and grade-appropriate irregularly spelled words. In 3rd grade, the focus turns to applying phonetic knowledge to decode multisyllabic words and words with common affixes. In 4th and 5th grade, students continue to practice reading, gaining familiarity with all letter-sound correspondences, syllable patterns, and common word parts.

Figure 2.10 | **Reading Foundational Skills Standard 3: Phonics and Word Recognition**

| Grade 3 | Grade 4 | Grade 5 |
|---|---|---|
| **RF.3.3** Know and apply grade-level phonics and word analysis skills in decoding words.<br>a. **Identify and know the meaning of the most common prefixes and derivational suffixes.**<br>b. **Decode words with common Latin suffixes.**<br>c. **Decode multi-syllable words.**<br>d. Read grade-appropriate irregularly spelled words. | **RF.4.3** Know and apply grade-level phonics and word analysis skills in decoding words.<br>a. **Use combined knowledge of all letter-sound correspondences, syllabication patterns, and morphology (e.g., roots and affixes) to read accurately unfamiliar multisyllabic words in context and out of context.** | **RF.5.3** Know and apply grade-level phonics and word analysis skills in decoding words.<br>a. Use combined knowledge of all letter-sound correspondences, syllabication patterns, and morphology (e.g., roots and affixes) to read accurately unfamiliar multisyllabic words in context and out of context. |

*Note:* Boldface text identifies content that differs from the prior grade level.

# Fluency

Foundational Skills Standard 4 (RF.4), the single standard for reading fluency (see Figure 2.11), is very similar across grade levels, but, as dictated by Reading Standard 10, the complexity level of the texts that students are expected to read increases each year. As students expand their reading vocabulary and become more confident decoding multisyllabic words, their fluency with grade-appropriate texts will grow. The kinds of reading assessments teachers are accustomed to using to evaluate a student's fluency level will be helpful when it comes to pairing individual students with appropriate texts for independent reading and for differentiating instruction for students who are not yet reading as fluently as their peers, including students who are learning English.

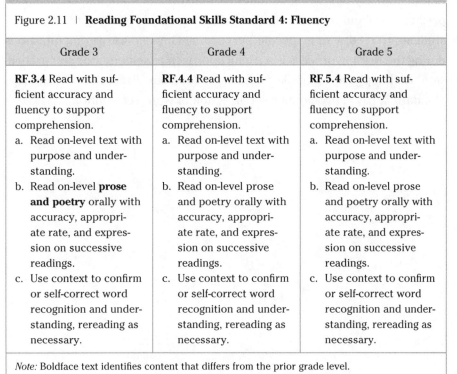

Figure 2.11 | **Reading Foundational Skills Standard 4: Fluency**

RF.4

| Grade 3 | Grade 4 | Grade 5 |
|---|---|---|
| **RF.3.4** Read with sufficient accuracy and fluency to support comprehension.<br>a. Read on-level text with purpose and understanding.<br>b. Read on-level **prose and poetry** orally with accuracy, appropriate rate, and expression on successive readings.<br>c. Use context to confirm or self-correct word recognition and understanding, rereading as necessary. | **RF.4.4** Read with sufficient accuracy and fluency to support comprehension.<br>a. Read on-level text with purpose and understanding.<br>b. Read on-level prose and poetry orally with accuracy, appropriate rate, and expression on successive readings.<br>c. Use context to confirm or self-correct word recognition and understanding, rereading as necessary. | **RF.5.4** Read with sufficient accuracy and fluency to support comprehension.<br>a. Read on-level text with purpose and understanding.<br>b. Read on-level prose and poetry orally with accuracy, appropriate rate, and expression on successive readings.<br>c. Use context to confirm or self-correct word recognition and understanding, rereading as necessary. |

*Note:* Boldface text identifies content that differs from the prior grade level.

The only difference in Foundational Skills Standard 4 from grade to grade is that beginning in 3rd grade, it specifies that students fluently read both prose and poetry. Reading poetry with appropriate expression and flow differs from reading prose, as punctuation and line and stanza conventions call for particular pauses and rhythms that are not found in texts with full sentences and paragraph organization.

In this standard, across grades, reading fluency of on-level texts is described in three ways: reading with purpose and understanding; reading accurately with appropriate rate and expression; and the ability to monitor one's own reading processes, using strategies to self-correct when needed. Teachers can evaluate all these skills by listening to students read aloud. It's worth stressing that the skills addressed in this standard are all closely tied to a variety of reading comprehension strategies. For example, making predictions about a book's content before reading is one way to encourage students to read with a specific purpose. Asking and answering questions during the reading process is a useful approach to self-monitor comprehension. And applying vocabulary strategies (see our discussion of Language Standard 4, p. 77) promotes self-correction of word recognition.

# CHAPTER 3

# Writing

The Common Core writing standards describe three types of writing: writing opinion pieces, writing about information, and writing stories. They also encompass skills related to writing processes, including using technology and conducting research. Taken together, the standards emphasize writing as a tool that develops students' critical thinking and learning across subject areas.

The standards of the Writing strand (W) are grouped under four headings: Text Types and Purposes, Production and Distribution of Writing, Research to Build and Present Knowledge, and Range of Writing. Figure 3.1 provides an overview of these standards for grades 3–5.

Our discussion of the Writing strand is organized by heading, but first we'll touch on how student writing is likely to be assessed.

Both consortia that are developing assessments for the Common Core will assess student writing. As currently described, SBAC will ask students to demonstrate their ability to write a variety of short pieces (one or more paragraphs) and longer pieces (planned and developed over multiple sessions) for different purposes and audiences. In addition, students will respond to at least one extended performance task that may draw on a variety of reading, writing, speaking, and research skills. PARCC plans to assess students' writing as part of its performance-based assessment, which will focus on writing effectively when analyzing text. Both consortia are likely to

Figure 3.1  |  **The Writing Strand: Grades 3–5 Overview**

| Heading | CCRA Standard | Grade 3 Standards | Grade 4 Standards | Grade 5 Standards |
|---|---|---|---|---|
| Text Types and Purposes | W.1 | W.3.1 | W.4.1 | W.5.1 |
| | W.2 | W.3.2 | W.4.2 | W.5.2 |
| | W.3 | W.3.3 | W.4.3 | W.5.3 |
| Production and Distribution of Writing | W.4 | W.3.4 | W.4.4 | W.5.4 |
| | W.5 | W.3.5 | W.4.5 | W.5.5 |
| | W.6 | W.3.6 | W.4.6 | W.5.6 |
| Research to Build and Present Knowledge | W.7 | W.3.7 | W.4.7 | W.5.7 |
| | W.8 | W.3.8 | W.4.8 | W.5.8 |
| | W.9 | — | W.4.9 | W.5.9 |
| Range of Writing | W.10 | W.3.10 | W.4.10 | W.5.10 |

*Note:* Writing Standard 9 begins in grade 4.

employ a mix of computer and human scoring to evaluate student writing. Technical aspects of student writing, such as correct use of English conventions, will be assessed not only through student performance tasks and constructed-response items but also through computer-based selected-response items, such as multiple choice. Skills related to using correct grammar and conventions are part of the Language strand of the Common Core standards because they pertain to both writing and speaking; see Chapter 5 for a full description of grammar and conventions for writing.

Now, let's take a closer look at the writing standards.

## Text Types and Purposes

Across all grades, the standards under the Text Types and Purposes heading address three primary types of writing: writing about opinions (argumentation), writing about information (exposition), and writing to tell a story (narration). For the first two writing types, students write organized, content-based paragraphs to support a claim or main idea. The reading standards' emphasis on reading informational texts that model both nonfiction structures and a formal tone will help students better understand how to write about information and ideas. For the third writing type, narration, students write a story, organized by a plot and featuring effective use of story elements. The Common Core standards call for the same balance of writing types found in the National Assessment of Educational Progress (NAEP). For 4th grade, this percentage is 30 percent persuasive (opinion pieces), 35 percent informative, and 35 percent narrative (National Assessment Governing Board, 2010b). Although the Common Core standards describe just three types of writing, they also indicate that students will employ a wide variety of forms or subgenres, such as speeches, scientific or historical reports, book reports, summaries, and research papers, to address specific purposes and audiences.

Notably, the standards do not dictate the length or particular format for writing within each text type, such as a five-paragraph essay for informative writing. They focus, rather, on the characteristics that each text type of student writing should exhibit in order to clearly develop the topic or story in a clear and coherent way. Not only should students be flexible in their ability to use different formats and subgenres, but Appendix A to the ELA/literacy standards document (CCSSI, 2010d) notes that effective student writing may blend text types to accomplish a given purpose, such as when an essay or speech includes a personal anecdote to illustrate a point. Effective writing assignments will provide students with opportunities to write in a variety of forms, and they will be flexible in how they allow students to apply characteristics from various writing types to best meet a given purpose and audience.

The three standards under the Text Types and Purposes heading are very specific, and each has numerous components that describe the attributes of the particular type of writing it addresses. Some of the attributes described in each standard's components are shared across more than one writing type and standard, while others are specific to that standard alone. For example, when students are writing about their opinions (the focus of

Writing Standard 1—W.1) and when they are writing about information (the focus of Writing Standard 2—W.2), they are expected to "provide a concluding statement or section" (W.1d, W.2d).

Note that the components of the Text Types and Purposes standards provide the type of descriptions and details about proficient student writing that may be useful in developing writing rubrics. In some instances, student writing that is either advanced or below proficient may demonstrate the skills articulated in the standard for the grade above or below, but in most cases distinguishing proficiency for a given writing standard is best accomplished by developing rubric descriptions about clarity, accuracy, degree of detail, and other descriptions of quality. SBAC has developed sample generic rubrics for writing that evaluate student writing in terms of content focus, organization, and elaboration, as well as use of conventions, language, and vocabulary (Measured Progress & ETS Collaborative, 2012). With the exception of conventions, which are described in the Language strand, these elements correspond roughly to the components of Writing Standards 1, 2, and 3.

Let's take a closer look at those standards and how they are structured to develop students' facility with the three targeted types of writing.

## Writing opinion pieces

In Writing Standard 1, students are expected to write about their opinions and provide supporting reasons. In the upper elementary grades, this standard lays the foundation students need to build more formal arguments, as they will begin to do in middle school. Appendix A to the ELA/literacy standards document cites a variety of research that identifies writing arguments as a key skill required for college readiness; the standards build this skill throughout the grades. Appendix A also draws a distinction between argument and persuasion. While argument is solely about making appeals to logic, persuasion also includes appeals to emotion and ethics. The Common Core standards emphasize the ability to make evidence-based arguments and to trace factual support for opinions in the informational texts that students read (see our discussion of RI.8, p. 31). Learning to recognize the difference between fact and unsupported opinion in their reading will support students' developing abilities to base their own opinions on facts and information that can be substantiated by appropriate sources.

Figure 3.2 shows Writing Standard 1 for grades 3, 4, and 5.

Figure 3.2 | **Writing Standard 1: Text Types and Purposes—Opinion Pieces**

| Grade 3 | Grade 4 | Grade 5 |
|---|---|---|
| **W.3.1** Write opinion pieces on familiar topics or texts, supporting a point of view with reasons.<br>a. Introduce the topic or text they are writing about, state an opinion, **and create an organizational structure that lists reasons.**<br>b. Provide reasons that support the opinion.<br>c. Use linking words **and phrases** (e.g., because, **therefore, since, for example**) to connect opinion and reasons.<br>d. Provide a concluding statement or section. | **W.4.1** Write opinion pieces on topics or texts, supporting a point of view with reasons **and information.**<br>a. Introduce a topic or text clearly, state an opinion, and create an organizational structure **in which related ideas are grouped to support the writer's purpose.**<br>b. Provide reasons that **are supported by facts and details.**<br>c. **Link opinion and reasons using** words and phrases **(e.g., for instance, in order to, in addition).**<br>d. Provide a concluding statement or section **related to the opinion presented.** | **W.5.1** Write opinion pieces on topics or texts, supporting a point of view with reasons and information.<br>a. Introduce a topic or text clearly, state an opinion, and create an organizational structure in which ideas are **logically grouped** to support the writer's purpose.<br>b. Provide **logically ordered** reasons that are supported by facts and details.<br>c. Link opinion and reasons using words, phrases, **and clauses (e.g., consequently, specifically).**<br>d. Provide a concluding statement or section related to the opinion presented. |

*Note:* Boldface text identifies content that differs from the prior grade level.

In grades K–2, students learn to write about their opinions on topics and books, supporting their opinions with reasons and connecting their ideas with linking words. When they reach 3rd grade, students must organize the reasons for their opinions within a structure and expand the types of linking words they use to build that structure beyond simple conjunctions. Improved organization of student writing and use of transitions continues as students move through elementary school. In 4th grade, they learn to group their ideas for a specific purpose and, in 5th grade, to improve the coherence or logic of those groups. Fourth graders are also expected to use transitional words and phrases to indicate a link between their opinion and their reasons, and 5th graders, to use clauses and sentence structures to make those links.

In both 4th and 5th grades, students are asked to support their ideas with facts and details. The requirement implies that students' writing will draw from what they have learned from reading or listening to informational texts. The skills necessary to support ideas with text-based facts and details are described in greater detail in writing standards under the Research to Build and Present Knowledge heading (see p. 53). As noted, when students enter middle school, they will be asked to develop more formal arguments, defining claims in relation to alternate or opposing ideas and supporting their claims with credible sources.

## Writing informative/explanatory texts

Writing Standard 2 focuses on explaining ideas or information in writing, a skill with applications in all content areas. Writing about information helps students build knowledge across a wide spectrum of topics and subjects, and this standard complements several Common Core reading standards in which students use multiple sources to build knowledge of subject-area topics (see RI.7 and RI.9). By writing explanatory texts, students exhibit their ability to think critically about the information they read and hear.

Appendix A to the ELA/literacy standards document describes a variety of purposes for students' explanatory writing, such as describing the types or component pieces of a subject; describing the size, function, or behavior of a subject; or explaining how things work or why things happen.

As students address such purposes, they may use a variety of subgenres that should be included in expository writing, such as academic reports, analyses, and summaries.

Just like Writing Standard 1, Writing Standard 2 asks students to draw detailed information from sources to support the ideas in their writing. They must select, organize, and analyze content on the subject in order to write clearly about it. Figure 3.3 shows the sequence of Writing Standard 2 in the upper elementary grades.

W.2

Figure 3.3 | **Writing Standard 2: Text Types and Purposes—Informative Writing**

| Grade 3 | Grade 4 | Grade 5 |
|---|---|---|
| **W.3.2** Write informative/ explanatory texts to **examine a topic and convey ideas and information clearly.**<br>a. Introduce a topic and **group related information together; include illustrations when useful to aiding comprehension.**<br>b. Develop the topic with facts, definitions, **and details.**<br>c. **Use linking words and phrases (e.g., also, another, and, more, but) to connect ideas within categories of information.**<br>d. Provide a concluding statement or section. | **W.4.2** Write informative/ explanatory texts to examine a topic and convey ideas and information clearly.<br>a. Introduce a topic **clearly** and group related information **in paragraphs and sections; include formatting (e.g., headings),** illustrations, and **multimedia** when useful to aiding comprehension.<br>b. Develop the topic with facts, definitions, **concrete details, quotations, or other information and examples related to the topic.**<br>c. Link ideas within categories of information using words and phrases (e.g., another, **for example,** also, **because).** | **W.5.2** Write informative/ explanatory texts to examine a topic and convey ideas and information clearly.<br>a. Introduce a topic clearly, **provide a general observation and focus,** and group related information **logically;** include formatting (e.g., headings), illustrations, and multimedia when useful to aiding comprehension.<br>b. Develop the topic with facts, definitions, concrete details, quotations, or other information and examples related to the topic.<br>c. Link ideas within **and across** categories of information using words, phrases, **and clauses (e.g., in contrast, especially).** |

*(continued)*

W.2

| Figure 3.3 | Writing Standard 2: Text Types and Purposes—Informative Writing *(continued)* | | |
| --- | --- | --- | --- |
| Grade 3 | Grade 4 | Grade 5 |
| | d. **Use precise language and domain-specific vocabulary to inform about or explain the topic.**<br><br>e. Provide a concluding statement or section **related to the information or explanation presented.** | d. Use precise language and domain-specific vocabulary to inform about or explain the topic.<br><br>e. Provide a concluding statement or section related to the information or explanation presented. |

*Note:* Boldface text identifies content that differs from the prior grade level.

For an example of a 5th grade lesson addressing a specific component of Writing Standard 2 (W.5.2b), please see **Sample Lesson 3.**

Like the other standards under the Text Types and Purposes heading, the components of Writing Standard 2 describe the characteristics of proficient writing of this type, including introductions, organization, supporting details, transitions, word choice, and conclusions. Note that both W.1 and W.2 focus on improving students' abilities to organize their writing and use transition words and phrases as they progress through the 3rd, 4th, and 5th grades. Note, too, that beginning in 4th grade, students are expected to pay close attention to their word choices, using precise language and words that are specific to a subject or content area. Making these kinds of choices is the first step toward establishing a formal tone and style.

## Writing narratives

The third standard under the Text Types and Purposes heading, Writing Standard 3 (W.3), focuses on narration, or storytelling. Students write about experiences, either real or imaginary. Figure 3.4 shows the sequence of this standard in the upper elementary grades. In contrast to the first two writing types, narration is structured by time and place. Narrative writing

Figure 3.4 | **Writing Standard 3: Text Types and Purposes—Narration**

W.3

| Grade 3 | Grade 4 | Grade 5 |
|---|---|---|
| **W.3.3** Write narratives to **develop real or imagined experiences or events using effective technique, descriptive details, and clear event sequences.**<br><br>a. **Establish a situation and introduce a narrator and/or characters; organize an event sequence that unfolds naturally.**<br>b. **Use dialogue and** descriptions of actions, thoughts, and feelings **to develop experiences and events or show the response of characters to situations.**<br>c. Use temporal words **and phrases** to signal event order.<br>d. Provide a sense of closure. | **W.4.3** Write narratives to develop real or imagined experiences or events using effective technique, descriptive details, and clear event sequences.<br><br>a. **Orient the reader by** establishing a situation and introducing a narrator and/or characters; organize an event sequence that unfolds naturally.<br>b. Use dialogue and description to develop experiences and events or show the responses of characters to situations.<br>c. **Use a variety of transitional words and phrases to manage the sequence of events.**<br>d. **Use concrete words and phrases and sensory details to convey experiences and events precisely.**<br>e. **Provide a conclusion that follows from the narrated experiences or events.** | **W.5.3** Write narratives to develop real or imagined experiences or events using effective technique, descriptive details, and clear event sequences.<br><br>a. Orient the reader by establishing a situation and introducing a narrator and/or characters; organize an event sequence that unfolds naturally.<br>b. **Use narrative techniques,** such as dialogue, description, **and pacing,** to develop experiences and events or show the responses of characters to situations.<br>c. Use a variety of transitional words, phrases, and **clauses** to manage the sequence of events.<br>d. Use concrete words and phrases and sensory details to convey experiences and events precisely.<br>e. Provide a conclusion that follows from the narrated experiences or events. |

*Note:* Boldface text identifies content that differs from the prior grade level.

may serve a variety of purposes and appear in a variety of formats, including narrative poems or short stories. Narrative writing increases students' appreciation of the story elements and narrative techniques they encounter when reading, which suggests that students may benefit from addressing some reading literature standards (specifically RL.4, RL.5, and RL.6 under the Craft and Structure heading; see p. 24) as they learn how and where to employ story elements in their own writing. Narrative writing also provides students with the opportunity to engage in their learning by expressing their personal ideas, culture, and experiences.

Overall, Writing Standard 3 expects students in elementary school to write a story that is structured by a series of events and that includes characters and descriptions engaging to the audience. As compared to students in the primary grades, 3rd graders are better able to introduce the situation and characters of their story clearly and organize the plot events. Students in 3rd grade are also able to write dialogue and describe their characters in greater depth than students in grades K–2. Students in 4th grade are asked to guide their reader through the story with transitional words and phrases and to include a conclusion that draws the details of the story to a satisfactory end. Similar to the standards for writing informative texts, beginning in 4th grade, students are expected to pay close attention to their word choices, using concrete words and phrases that create clear mental images and sensory details to engage the reader in the story. Students in 5th grade continue to practice their narrative writing skills. They are asked to pay attention to how they pace the plot of a story and how they use sentence structure (e.g., phrases and clauses) to transition the reader through the story.

## Production and Distribution of Writing

While the first set of standards in the Writing strand details the qualities and characteristics of different writing types, the rest focus on writing processes. The three standards under the Production and Distribution of Writing heading, shown in Figure 3.5, address adapting writing to task, purpose, and audience; using the writing process; and using technology.

Figure 3.5  |  **Writing Standards 4–6: Production and Distribution of Writing**

W.4–6

| Grade 3 | Grade 4 | Grade 5 |
|---|---|---|
| **W.3.4 With guidance and support from adults, produce writing in which the development and organization are appropriate to task and purpose. (Grade-specific expectations for writing types are defined in standards 1–3.)** | **W.4.4** Produce **clear and coherent** writing in which the development and organization are appropriate to task, purpose, and **audience.** (Grade-specific expectations for writing types are defined in standards 1–3.) | **W.5.4** Produce clear and coherent writing in which the development and organization are appropriate to task, purpose, and audience. (Grade-specific expectations for writing types are defined in standards 1–3.) |
| **W.3.5** With guidance and support from peers and adults, **develop and** strengthen writing as needed by **planning,** revising, and editing. **(Editing for conventions should demonstrate command of Language standards 1–3 up to and including *grade 3*.)** | **W.4.5** With guidance and support from peers and adults, develop and strengthen writing as needed by planning, revising, and editing. (Editing for conventions should demonstrate command of Language standards 1–3 up to and including *grade 4*.) | **W.5.5** With guidance and support from peers and adults, develop and strengthen writing as needed by planning, revising, editing, **rewriting, or trying a new approach.** (Editing for conventions should demonstrate command of Language standards 1–3 up to and including *grade 5*.) |
| **W.3.6** With guidance and support from adults, **use technology to** produce and publish writing **(using keyboarding skills) as well as to interact and** collaborate with others. | **W.4.6** With **some** guidance and support from adults, use technology, **including the Internet,** to produce and publish writing as well as to interact and collaborate with others; **demonstrate sufficient command of keyboarding skills to type a minimum of one page in a single sitting.** | **W.5.6** With some guidance and support from adults, use technology, including the Internet, to produce and publish writing as well as to interact and collaborate with others; demonstrate sufficient command of keyboarding skills to type a minimum of **two pages** in a single sitting. |

*Note:* Boldface text identifies content that differs from the prior grade level.

Writing Standard 4 (W.4) requires students to adapt their writing for specific tasks and purposes (grades 3–5) and for specific audiences (grades 4–5). It acknowledges that students need to be flexible writers who can adjust their selected details and text structure to meet the demands of a given task and situation. This standard appears for the first time in the Common Core at the 3rd grade level, and it remains largely the same in the succeeding grades, although middle and high school students are also expected to adjust their writing style to suit a given task and situation. Note, too, that the difficulty level of Writing Standard 4 increases commensurate with the complexity of the texts and topics that students address in their writing as they get older.

The second standard under the Production and Distribution of Writing heading, Writing Standard 5 (W.5), focuses on the writing process. While Writing Standard 10 (see p. 56) makes it clear that students need not apply the full writing process to everything they write, they do need practice planning, revising, and editing their written work. In elementary school, it's a given that students will receive guidance and support from peers and adults during the writing process. This level of support is scaled back when students reach middle school, and the focus shifts to developing their ability to produce polished writing while working independently. The types of guidance and supports teachers might use include writing process activities, such as peer review, and writing tools, such as editing checklists and graphic organizers that help students with prewriting.

In the primary grades, students are asked to use feedback from peers and adults to revise and edit their writing; 3rd grade marks the point at which students begin to use feedback to *develop* their writing. At this level, students are also expected to begin planning their writing through prewriting exercises and editing their work to conform to the convention and grammar rules specified in the language standards for each grade level (see Chapter 5). By the time students reach 5th grade, their ability to revise their writing is fairly sophisticated, with students rewriting or taking their writing in a different direction based on feedback from both peers and adults.

Finally, Writing Standard 6 (W.6) asks students to use technology to produce and publish individual and collaborative writing. In grades K–2, this standard specifies that students use a variety of digital tools for these purposes; as students progress through elementary school, the standard expands, asking students to use technology to interact with peers (3rd grade) and use the Internet (4th grade). In grades 3–5, a primary focus of Writing Standard 6 is keyboarding skills, which are not mentioned prior to 3rd grade. By 4th grade, students are asked to type a minimum of one page in a single sitting, and by 5th grade, they must type two pages. The requirement grows to three pages by 6th grade. As they progress through the elementary grades, students are also expected to use technology more independently. Although it's expected that they will still need adult guidance and support when using technology, from 4th grade on, this support is expected to be necessary only some of the time.

## Research to Build and Present Knowledge

In the Common Core standards, research is more than a single type of assignment; it is described as a set of skills that may be applied, as needed, to many different types of reading, speaking, and writing tasks. Although the standards under the Writing strand's Research heading articulate specific aspects of research processes, the basic skill of locating information in sources is embedded in many different standards across the ELA/literacy strands. In response to this emphasis on research skills, both consortia developing assessments for the Common Core have designed items to test students' research skills, including performance-based tasks that ask students to select appropriate sources and compare information.

The three standards under the Research to Build and Present Knowledge heading (see Figure 3.6) address the scope and purpose of research projects, the gathering and organizing of source information, and the use of analytical reading skills to draw on text evidence.

Writing Standard 7 (W.7) focuses on research projects. In grades K–2, students participate in shared research and writing projects. With this foundation, they are expected to be able to conduct short independent research projects that build knowledge about a topic (3rd grade), investigate different aspects of a topic (4th grade), and use several sources (5th grade). In the middle school grades, Writing Standard 7 will focus on developing these

W.7–9

Figure 3.6 | **Writing Standards 7–9: Research to Build and Present Knowledge**

| Grade 3 | Grade 4 | Grade 5 |
|---|---|---|
| **W.3.7 Conduct short research projects that build knowledge about a topic.** | W.4.7 Conduct short research projects that build knowledge **through investigation of different aspects** of a topic. | W.5.7 Conduct short research projects that **use several sources** to build knowledge through investigation of different aspects of a topic. |
| **W.3.8 Recall information from experiences or gather information from print and digital sources; take brief notes on sources and sort evidence into provided categories.** | **W.4.8 Recall relevant information from experiences or gather relevant information from print and digital sources; take notes and categorize information, and provide a list of sources.** | W.5.8 Recall relevant information from experiences or gather relevant information from print and digital sources; **summarize or paraphrase information in notes and finished work,** and provide a list of sources. |
| [W.9 is not applicable at Grade 3] | **W.4.9 Draw evidence from literary or informational texts to support analysis, reflection, and research.**<br>a. **Apply *grade 4* Reading standards to literature (e.g., "Describe in depth a character, setting, or event in a story or drama, drawing on specific details in the text [e.g., a character's thoughts, words, or actions].").**<br>b. **Apply *grade 4* Reading standards to informational texts (e.g., "Explain how an author uses reasons and evidence to support particular points in a text.").** | W.5.9 Draw evidence from literary or informational texts to support analysis, reflection, and research.<br>a. Apply *grade 5* Reading standards to literature (e.g., "Compare and contrast two or more characters, settings, or events in a story or a drama, drawing on specific details in the text [e.g., how characters interact].").<br>b. Apply *grade 5* Reading standards to informational texts (e.g., "Explain how an author uses reasons and evidence to support particular points in a text, **identifying which reasons and evidence support which point[s].").** |

*Note:* Boldface text identifies content that differs from the prior grade level.

skills further, with students learning to adjust the scope of their research and their research questions in response to the information they find.

The second standard under the Research heading, Writing Standard 8 (W.8), focuses on searching for and gathering information, and on comprehending and sorting that information once it's found. In the primary grades, students are asked to recall information from experiences and gather information necessary to answer specific questions by looking in sources that the teacher provides. By 3rd grade, they are expected to

For an example of a 5th grade lesson addressing Writing Standard 8 (W.5.8), please see **Sample Lesson 3.**

be able to access print and digital sources independently, take notes on the information they find, and then sort that information into categories that the teacher provides. In 4th grade, students are asked to be selective about the information that they gather, ensuring that it is relevant to the question or task. Fourth graders are also required to sort gathered information into categories that *they* determine and provide a simple list of their sources. In 5th grade, the focus of W.8 is developing students' ability to summarize or paraphrase the information gathered into notes and a finished written product or oral presentation. When students reach middle school, they will extend these skills, becoming more adept at conducting searches and evaluating the credibility of their sources.

The final research-focused writing standard, Writing Standard 9 (W.9), begins at the grade 4 level and addresses the use of analytical reading skills to draw evidence from texts, underscoring how research activities connect to both reading and writing. It explicitly requires students in grades 4 and 5 to apply the Common Core reading standards for their grade level during the research process as they look for specific information or ideas in written texts. The reference to reading in this writing standard reminds us that gathering information from texts is not only central to the research process but also a key aspect of reading. Because this skill will be constant in academic activities from this point on, Writing Standard 9 is phrased the same at every grade level, from 4th grade through high school, with only the references to the reading standards changing to reflect the particular standards for each grade level.

## Range of Writing

The writing standards conclude with a single standard focused on the variety of writing tasks in which students should engage. Writing Standard 10 (W.10), which is phrased exactly the same across grade bands, is shown in Figure 3.7.

To meet this standard, students need opportunities to write routinely. Writing assignments should be a regular part of classroom activities, and they should incorporate both *extended writing tasks* that involve reflection, revision, and multiple drafts and *focused writing tasks,* such as responding to text-dependent questions or reflecting on a particular aspect of a print or non-print text, which may take place within short timeframes. Both consortia developing assessments for the Common Core plan to include a mix of short and long writing tasks; thus, students need to be able to produce a high-quality first draft under a tight deadline and to review and improve their writing through revision processes. Because student writing should address a variety of tasks, purposes, and audiences, students will need multiple opportunities to practice various writing types and forms. Teachers should design writing activities and assignments with a wide range of authentic purposes and audiences in mind.

**W.10**

Figure 3.7  |  **Writing Standard 10: Range of Writing**

| Grade 3 | Grade 4 | Grade 5 |
|---|---|---|
| **W.3.10 Write routinely over extended time frames (time for research, reflection, and revision) and shorter time frames (a single sitting or a day or two) for a range of discipline-specific tasks, purposes, and audiences.** | **W.4.10** Write routinely over extended time frames (time for research, reflection, and revision) and shorter time frames (a single sitting or a day or two) for a range of discipline-specific tasks, purposes, and audiences. | **W.5.10** Write routinely over extended time frames (time for research, reflection, and revision) and shorter time frames (a single sitting or a day or two) for a range of discipline-specific tasks, purposes, and audiences. |

*Note:* Boldface text identifies content that differs from the prior grade level.

# CHAPTER 4

# Speaking and Listening

Analyzing spoken messages, communicating with a variety of audiences, and integrating oral, visual, and graphic information are the key skills in the Common Core's Speaking and Listening strand. Although these skills are frequently evaluated in classroom and local assessments, they have not traditionally been included in high-stakes tests. At the time of this writing, both consortia developing assessments for the Common Core plan to include speaking and listening components. As teachers are likely unaccustomed to formal speaking and listening assessments, and because the approaches taken by the consortia differ, the details are worth examining here.

The Partnership for Assessment of Readiness for College and Careers is developing performance-based items to assess oral communication skills, which will be associated with research tasks. PARCC's speaking assessment will be required and will be scored locally by teachers, but it will not be part of students' final summative score for the overall assessment (PARCC, 2010). In contrast, the Smarter Balanced Assessment Consortium, according to its draft content specifications for ELA/literacy assessments (Hess, 2011), plans to develop short summative speaking assessments that ask students to respond to a prompt. These responses will be recorded and scored externally. Other SBAC assessments will address oral presentation and collaborative discussion skills in connection with investigations or research tasks and will be scored locally by teachers. SBAC's current design calls for scores from these classroom assessments to be "certified" at the district level and reported to the state; recorded student performances will be audited to ensure consistent scoring. SBAC also plans to develop computer-based items to assess student listening skills regarding non-print texts.

The six standards in the Common Core's Speaking and Listening strand (SL) are grouped under two headings: Comprehension and Collaboration and Presentation of Knowledge and Ideas. Figure 4.1 provides an overview of these standards at the upper elementary level, and we'll review them in turn.

Figure 4.1  |  **The Speaking and Listening Strand: Grades 3–5 Overview**

| Heading | CCRA Standard | Grade 3 Standards | Grade 4 Standards | Grade 5 Standards |
|---|---|---|---|---|
| Comprehension and Collaboration | SL.1 | SL.3.1 | SL.4.1 | SL.5.1 |
| | SL.2 | SL.3.2 | SL.4.2 | SL.5.2 |
| | SL.3 | SL.3.3 | SL.4.3 | SL.5.3 |
| Presentation of Knowledge and Ideas | SL.4 | SL.3.4 | SL.4.4 | SL.5.4 |
| | SL.5 | SL.3.5 | SL.4.5 | SL.5.5 |
| | SL.6 | SL.3.6 | SL.4.6 | SL.5.6 |

Note that the Common Core State Standard Initiative's *Application to Students with Disabilities* (CCSSI, 2010b) clarifies that the speaking and listening standards may be applied to students' use of sign language.

## Comprehension and Collaboration

There are three standards under this heading: one focused on discussion and two focused on listening and viewing.

Speaking and Listening Standard 1 (SL.1) targets discussion skills and describes a variety of ways that students learn from each other during thoughtful academic conversations. This standard (see Figure 4.2)

Figure 4.2 | **Speaking and Listening Standard 1: Comprehension and Collaboration—Discussion**

SL.1

| Grade 3 | Grade 4 | Grade 5 |
|---|---|---|
| **SL.3.1 Engage effectively in a range of** collaborative discussions **(one-on-one, in groups, and teacher-led) with diverse partners** on *grade 3 topics and texts,* **building on others' ideas and expressing their own clearly.**<br>a. **Come to discussions prepared, having read or studied required material; explicitly draw on that preparation and other information known about the topic to explore ideas under discussion.**<br>b. Follow agreed-upon rules for discussions (e.g., gaining the floor in respectful ways, listening to others with care, speaking one at a time about the topics and texts under discussion).<br>c. Ask questions **to check understanding of information presented, stay on topic,** and link their comments to the remarks of others.<br>d. **Explain their own ideas and understanding in light of the discussion.** | SL.4.1 Engage effectively in a range of collaborative discussions (one-on-one, in groups, and teacher-led) with diverse partners on *grade 4 topics and texts,* building on others' ideas and expressing their own clearly.<br>a. Come to discussions prepared, having read or studied required material; explicitly draw on that preparation and other information known about the topic to explore ideas under discussion.<br>b. Follow agreed-upon rules for discussions **and carry out assigned roles.**<br>c. **Pose and respond to specific** questions to **clarify or follow up on** information, **and make comments that contribute to the discussion** and link to the remarks of others.<br>d. **Review the key ideas expressed** and explain their own ideas and understanding in light of the discussion. | SL.5.1 Engage effectively in a range of collaborative discussions (one-on-one, in groups, and teacher-led) with diverse partners on *grade 5 topics and texts,* building on others' ideas and expressing their own clearly.<br>a. Come to discussions prepared, having read or studied required material; explicitly draw on that preparation and other information known about the topic to explore ideas under discussion.<br>b. Follow agreed-upon rules for discussions and carry out assigned roles.<br>c. Pose and respond to specific questions by making comments that contribute to the discussion and **elaborate on** the remarks of others.<br>d. Review the key ideas expressed and **draw conclusions** in light of **information and knowledge gained from** the discussion. |

*Note:* Boldface text identifies content that differs from the prior grade level.

supports collaborative learning strategies and encourages teachers to create a variety of opportunities for students to discuss the material they are reading or otherwise learning about. The components within SL.1 describe specific skills that will support successful student collaboration, such as contributing information to discussions, working effectively with others, asking and answering questions, and summarizing a discussion.

When focusing on Speaking and Listening Standard 1, teachers should provide students with opportunities to engage in varied types of discussions, including "pair shares" and small- and large-group discussions. Although students in kindergarten, 1st grade, and 2nd grade are also expected to engage in a variety of conversations, 3rd grade marks the first time SL.1 asks students to read or prepare information for discussion in advance so that they can share what they've learned in order to contribute to the group's collective knowledge about a text or topic. Students in 4th grade are asked to practice interpersonal communication skills as they learn to connect their ideas to the remarks of others and fulfill an assigned role within a group. By the time students are in 5th grade, they are expected to be able to draw conclusions about the information and ideas shared in a discussion. As students enter middle school, they further their ability to monitor the progress of their group and ground their discussions in text evidence.

For an example of a 3rd grade lesson addressing Speaking and Listening Standards 1 and 2 (SL.3.1–2), please see **Sample Lesson 1.** For a 4th grade lesson addressing a specific component of Standard 1 (SL.4.1b), please see **Sample Lesson 2.**

The second and third standards under the Comprehension and Collaboration heading (see Figure 4.3) focus on listening skills—understanding and summarizing information obtained from various media and from a speaker.

Speaking and Listening Standard 2 focuses on understanding "seen" and "heard" content conveyed from three different types of media: *oral texts,* such as speeches or stories read aloud; *visual texts,* such as videos or presentation slides; and *graphic texts,* such as numerical charts and graphs. Third grade students are expected to identify the main ideas and details presented in these sources; 4th grade students, to

Figure 4.3 | **Speaking and Listening Standards 2–3: Comprehension and Collaboration—Listening**

| Grade 3 | Grade 4 | Grade 5 |
|---|---|---|
| **SL.3.2 Determine the main** ideas **and supporting** details of a text read aloud or information presented in **diverse media and formats, including visually, quantitatively,** and orally. | **SL.4.2 Paraphrase portions of a text** read aloud or information presented in diverse media and formats, including visually, quantitatively, and orally. | **SL.5.2 Summarize a written text** read aloud or information presented in diverse media and formats, including visually, quantitatively, and orally. |
| **SL.3.3** Ask and answer questions about information from a speaker, **offering appropriate elaboration and detail.** | **SL.4.3 Identify the reasons and evidence a speaker provides to support particular points.** | **SL.5.3 Summarize the points a speaker makes and explain how each claim is supported by reasons and evidence.** |

*Note:* Boldface text identifies content that differs from the prior grade level.

paraphrase the content; and 5th grade students, to summarize the content. Essentially, this standard asks students to build their note-taking abilities over time and apply increasingly complex viewing and listening strategies to texts that they see and hear.

The third standard, Speaking and Listening Standard 3 (SL.3), focuses on analyzing the information and ideas in spoken messages. Third graders learn to review the information that they hear by asking and answering questions. Fourth and 5th graders learn to analyze the supporting evidence presented by making connections between that evidence and the speaker's main ideas. The skills described in this standard, particularly at the 4th and 5th grade levels, parallel those described in Standard 8 of the Reading Informational Text domain (RI.8). In both this listening standard and that reading standard, students must identify the main points of spoken content and link these points to the evidence or reasons provided as support.

## Presentation of Knowledge and Ideas

As its name implies, the standards under this heading focus on oral presentation skills, asking students to present appropriate information clearly, use multimedia, and make appropriate language choices. Figure 4.4 shows the sequence of these standards across the upper elementary grade levels.

Speaking and Listening Standard 4 (SL.4) focuses on the content, organization, and delivery of student presentations. In grades K–2, students practice speaking through oral descriptions and storytelling, but the scope of this standard expands in later grades as students begin presenting on topics and texts they have studied (grade 4) and presenting their opinions (grade 5). In 4th grade, the organization of student presentations is expected to be more defined than in prior grades, with students required to ensure that the details they provide clearly support the main ideas they are communicating. Note that this emphasis on linking key ideas with their supporting details also begins at the grade 4 level of two related standards, SL.1 and RI.8. In 5th grade, students are expected to organize presentations in a logical sequence.

Another emphasis of Speaking and Listening Standard 4 at all the upper elementary grade levels is oral delivery—using a clear voice and maintaining an understandable pace throughout a presentation. Students will continue to develop their delivery skills in middle school, when SL.4 expands to address using eye contact, choosing and using appropriate voice volume, and using proper pronunciation.

Speaking and Listening Standard 5 (SL.5) focuses on the formats students use to present information or ideas. It places special emphasis on using multimedia, such as audio recordings and visual displays, to support presentations. In 3rd grade, students are expected to create audio recordings that demonstrate their reading fluency (see the discussion of RF.4 on p. 38 for additional descriptions of students' reading fluency). In 3rd and 4th grades, students learn to select visual displays, such as the pictures for a poster, to help develop the main ideas or themes that they want to emphasize. In 5th grade, the standard asks students to use

Figure 4.4 | **Speaking and Listening Standards 4–6: Presentation of Knowledge and Ideas**

| Grade 3 | Grade 4 | Grade 5 |
| --- | --- | --- |
| **SL.3.4 Report on a topic or text,** tell a story, or recount an experience with appropriate facts and relevant, descriptive details, speaking **clearly at an understandable pace.** | **SL.4.4** Report on a topic or text, tell a story, or recount an experience **in an organized manner,** using appropriate facts and relevant, descriptive details **to support main ideas or themes;** speak clearly at an understandable pace. | **SL.5.4** Report on a topic or text **or present an opinion, sequencing ideas logically and** using appropriate facts and relevant, descriptive details to support main ideas or themes; speak clearly at an understandable pace. |
| **SL.3.5** Create **engaging** audio recordings of stories or poems that **demonstrate fluid reading at an understandable pace;** add visual displays when appropriate **to emphasize or enhance certain facts or details.** | **SL.4.5 Add** audio recordings and visual displays to presentations when appropriate to **enhance the development of main ideas or themes.** | **SL.5.5 Include multimedia components (e.g., graphics, sound)** and visual displays in presentations when appropriate to enhance the development of main ideas or themes. |
| **SL.3.6** Speak in complete sentences when appropriate to task and situation in order to provide requested detail or clarification. (See **grade 3** Language standards 1 and 3 for specific expectations.) | **SL.4.6 Differentiate between contexts that call for formal English (e.g., presenting ideas) and situations where informal discourse is appropriate (e.g., small-group discussion); use formal English when appropriate to task and situation.** (See **grade 4** Language standards 1 and 3 for specific expectations.) | **SL.5.6 Adapt speech to a variety of contexts and tasks,** using formal English when appropriate to task and situation. (See **grade 5** Language standards 1 and 3 for specific expectations.) |

*Note:* Boldface text identifies content that differs from the prior grade level.

multiple modes of media, combining visual and audio components to support their message.

The final standard under the Presentation of Knowledge and Ideas heading, Speaking and Listening Standard 6 (SL.6), concerns the language that students use when speaking. The expectation that students be able to speak in complete sentences, when appropriate, first appears in the 2nd grade version of this standard and carries through 3rd grade. As students grow older, they develop the ability to understand when formal or informal language is required (grade 4) and to adapt their spoken language accordingly (grade 5). For example, students learn to recognize that some contexts, such as academic presentations, call for a formal tone and adherence to correct grammatical conventions, whereas other purposes and contexts, such as working in collaborative groups with peers, call for less formality.

For students to achieve Speaking and Language Standard 6, they need a variety of opportunities to address different types of audiences and engage in a range of collaborative tasks. Furthermore, they should practice their speaking and listening skills as they work with a variety of topics and subjects. For these reasons, we recommend SL.6 be addressed in conjunction with a wide variety of content, including science, social studies, and other subject-area material. SBAC has indicated that the stimuli for its listening and speaking tasks may come from any subject area or content discipline (Hess, 2012).

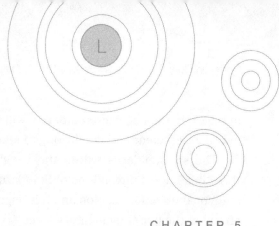

CHAPTER 5

# Language

The Language strand (L) focuses on skills related to standard English grammar and usage, vocabulary, sentence fluency, and word choice. Students study the language choices of authors and speakers, and they practice making effective language choices in their own writing and speaking. Because the skills in this strand support skills described in the Reading, Writing, and Speaking and Listening strands, they are easily addressed in conjunction with other Common Core standards in curricular units and daily lessons.

The consortia that are developing assessments for the Common Core will assess the language standards as part of constructed-response items and performance tasks that ask students to read, write, speak, and listen. For example, PARCC will assess students' ability to use correct English spelling and grammar as part of its performance-based assessment for English language arts and literacy. Both PARCC and SBAC are likely to evaluate students' knowledge of English conventions and vocabulary skills within computer-scored, selected-response questions, such as multiple-choice items.

Teachers of students who are learning English as a second language should note that "it is possible to achieve the standards for reading and literature, writing & research, language development and speaking & listening without manifesting native-like control of conventions and vocabulary" (CCSSI, 2010a, p. 1). Expectations for English language learners, particularly in regard to the language standards, will need to be adjusted based on individual assessment and monitoring of student progress.

The six standards within the Language strand are organized under three headings: Conventions of Standard English, Knowledge of Language, and Vocabulary Acquisition and Use. Figure 5.1 provides an overview of the strand at the upper elementary level.

Figure 5.1  |  **The Language Strand: Grades 3–5 Overview**

| Heading | CCRA Standard | Grade 3 Standards | Grade 4 Standards | Grade 5 Standards |
|---|---|---|---|---|
| Conventions of Standard English | L.1 | L.3.1 | L.4.1 | L.5.1 |
| | L.2 | L.3.2 | L.4.2 | L.5.2 |
| Knowledge of Language | L.3 | L.3.3 | L.4.3 | L.5.3 |
| Vocabulary Acquisition and Use | L.4 | L.3.4 | L.4.4 | L.5.4 |
| | L.5 | L.3.5 | L.4.5 | L.5.5 |
| | L.6 | L.3.6 | L.4.6 | L.5.6 |

# Conventions of Standard English

There are two standards under the Conventions of Standard English heading. The first, Language Standard 1 (L.1), details grammar and usage conventions for both writing and speaking. The second, Language Standard 2 (L.2), lists specific rules related to capitalization, punctuation, and spelling in students' written work. The detailed components listed within these standards differ significantly from grade level to grade level, identifying distinct and specific skills that build students' understanding of language and their ability to use it effectively as they progress through their schooling.

Figure 5.2 shows the sequence of Language Standard 1 for grades 3–5.

This standard describes a variety of specific grammatical constructions that students are expected to produce correctly. These skills develop

Figure 5.2 | **Language Standard 1: Conventions of Standard English**

L1

| Grade 3 | Grade 4 | Grade 5 |
|---------|---------|---------|
| **L.3.1** Demonstrate command of the conventions of standard English grammar and usage when writing or speaking.<br>a. **Explain the function of nouns, pronouns, verbs, adjectives, and adverbs in general and their functions in particular sentences.**<br>b. **Form and use regular and irregular plural nouns.**<br>c. **Use abstract nouns (e.g., childhood).**<br>d. **Form and use regular and irregular verbs.**<br>e. **Form and use the simple (e.g., I walked; I walk; I will walk) verb tenses.**<br>f. **Ensure subject-verb and pronoun-antecedent agreement.**<br>g. **Form and use comparative and super-**lative adjectives and adverbs, **and choose between them depending on what is to be modified.**<br>h. **Use coordinating and subordinating conjunctions.** Produce simple, compound, and **complex** sentences. | **L.4.1** Demonstrate command of the conventions of standard English grammar and usage when writing or speaking.<br>a. **Use relative pronouns (who, whose, whom, which, that) and relative adverbs (where, when, why).**<br>b. **Form and use the progressive (e.g., I was walking; I am walking; I will be walking) verb tenses.**<br>c. **Use modal auxiliaries (e.g., can, may, must) to convey various conditions.**<br>d. **Order adjectives within sentences according to conventional patterns (e.g., "a small red bag" rather than "a red small bag").**<br>e. **Form and use prepositional phrases.**<br>f. **Produce complete sentences, recognizing and correcting inappropriate fragments and run-ons.**<br>g. **Correctly use frequently confused words (e.g., to, too, two; there, their).** | **L.5.1** Demonstrate command of the conventions of standard English grammar and usage when writing or speaking.<br>a. **Explain the function of conjunctions, prepositions, and interjections in general and their function in particular sentences.**<br>b. **Form and use the perfect (e.g., I had walked; I have walked; I will have walked) verb tenses.**<br>c. **Use verb tense to convey various times, sequences, states, and conditions.**<br>d. **Recognize and correct inappropriate shifts in verb tense.**<br>e. **Use correlative conjunctions (e.g., either/or, neither/nor).** |

*Note:* Boldface text identifies content that differs from the prior grade level.

explicitly from grade to grade. For example, 2nd grade students are expected to use *frequently occurring* irregular plural nouns, a precursor skill to using *all* regular and irregular plural nouns, which they are expected to be able to do in 3rd grade. In this way, the specific skills described in Standard 1 work together to build the complexity of students' grammar as they progress through school. Because the standards for grammar and conventions are so specific, teachers will need to review and adjust their curriculum resources across grades to ensure that they emphasize the skills that are a focus for their particular grade level. In Figure 5.3, you'll find an overview of the specific grammar and usage skills addressed in the various components of Language Standard 1 in grades 3–5.

Figure 5.3  |  **Language Standard 1: Grammar and Usage—Component Definitions and Examples for Grades 3–5**

**L.1.** Demonstrate command of the conventions of standard English grammar and usage when writing or speaking.

| Standard Component | Component Terminology | Definition and Examples |
|---|---|---|
| **L.3.1a** | Explain the function of **nouns, pronouns, verbs, adjectives, and adverbs** in general and their functions in particular sentences. | **Nouns** are words for a person, place, thing, or idea. Nouns function as subjects and objects within sentences.<br>**Pronouns** take the place of a noun (e.g., *he, she, they, it*). Pronouns function as subjects and objects in sentences.<br>**Verbs** express an action, occurrence, or state of being. They function as the predicate of a sentence.<br>**Adjectives** describe nouns. Within sentences they modify nouns and pronouns.<br>**Adverbs** describe verbs. Within sentences they modify verbs, adjectives, and other adverbs. |
| **L.3.1b** | Form and use **regular and irregular plural nouns.** | **Regular plural nouns** are formed by adding an *–s* or *–es* (e.g., *dog/dogs; bus/buses*).<br>**Irregular plural nouns** do not follow a pattern (e.g., *children, mice, geese, women*). |

Figure 5.3 | **Language Standard 1: Grammar and Usage—Component Definitions and Examples for Grades 3–5 (*continued*)**

**L.1.** Demonstrate command of the conventions of standard English grammar and usage when writing or speaking.

| Standard Component | Component Terminology | Definition and Examples |
|---|---|---|
| L.3.1c | Use **abstract nouns** (e.g., *childhood*). | **Abstract nouns** are the names of ideas, events, qualities, and concepts (e.g., *trust, liberty, goodness, wisdom, comfort, courage*). |
| L.3.1d | Form and use **regular and irregular verbs.** | **Regular verbs** change very little when suffixes are added to change the tense (e.g., *talk/talks/talked/talking*). **Irregular verbs** have unique spelling for different tenses (e.g., *sing, sang, sung, singing*). |
| L.3.1e | Form and use the simple (e.g., I walked; I walk; I will walk) **verb tenses.** | **Verb tenses** include present, past, and future (e.g., *kick/kicked/will kick*). **Simple verb tenses** do not include forms or combinations of the progressive (e.g., *is kicking*) and perfect (e.g., *has kicked*). |
| L.3.1f | Ensure subject-verb and pronoun-**antecedent** agreement. | **Antecedents** are the nouns that pronouns replace. Pronouns and their antecedents and subjects and their verbs must **agree in number.** They should both be singular or plural. |
| L.3.1g | Form and use **comparative and superlative adjectives and adverbs,** and choose between them depending on what is to be modified. | **Comparative adjectives and adverbs** compare different objects and are formed with the suffix *–er* (e.g., *faster, colder*). **Superlative** forms show which object is "the most" and are formed with the suffix *–est* (e.g., *fastest, coldest*). |
| L.3.1h | Use **coordinating and subordinating conjunctions.** | **Coordinating conjunctions** connect words, phrases, and clauses (i.e., *and, but, for, nor, or, so, yet*). **Subordinating conjunctions** connect dependent clauses to independent clauses (e.g., *until, when, before, since, while*). |

(*continued*)

Figure 5.3  |  **Language Standard 1: Grammar and Usage—Component Definitions and Examples for Grades 3–5 (*continued*)**

**L.1.** Demonstrate command of the conventions of standard English grammar and usage when writing or speaking.

| Standard Component | Component Terminology | Definition and Examples |
|---|---|---|
| **L.3.1i** | Produce **simple, compound, and complex sentences.** | **Simple sentences,** also called independent clauses, have a subject and predicate (verb) and express a complete thought (e.g., *Joe walked the dog*).<br>**Compound sentences** are two or more independent clauses connected with a comma and coordinating conjunction or semicolon (e.g., *Joe walked the dog, and Maria fed the cat*).<br>**Complex sentences** have an independent clause connected to one or more dependent clauses with a subordinating conjunction (e.g., *Joe walked the dog until he got too tired*). |
| **L.4.1a** | Use **relative pronouns** (who, whose, whom, which, that) and **relative adverbs** (where, when, why). | **Relative pronouns** introduce dependent clauses that modify a word, phrase, or idea in the main clause (e.g., *Marta is the girl <u>who</u> won the spelling bee*).<br>**Relative adverbs** introduce dependent clauses that modify words or phrases in the main clause by describing a place (where), time (when), or reason (why) (e.g., *I like to play basketball <u>when</u> I get home from school*). |
| **L.4.1b** | Form and use the **progressive** (e.g., I was walking; I am walking; I will be walking) **verb tenses.** | **Progressive verb tenses** describe ongoing actions in the present, past, or future. |

| Figure 5.3 | **Language Standard 1: Grammar and Usage—Component Definitions and Examples for Grades 3–5 (*continued*)** |
| --- | --- |

**L.1.** Demonstrate command of the conventions of standard English grammar and usage when writing or speaking.

| Standard Component | Component Terminology | Definition and Examples |
| --- | --- | --- |
| **L.4.1c** | Use **modal auxiliaries** (e.g., can, may, must) to convey various conditions. | **Modal auxiliaries** (i.e., *shall/should, will/would, may/might, can/could, must*) are verbs that precede a main verb to form the predicate in a sentence. They are a subset of auxiliaries (also called "helping verbs") that are not inflected, or changed, for tense, person, or number. |
| **L.4.1d** | **Order adjectives** within sentences according to conventional patterns (e.g., "a small red bag" rather than "a red small bag"). | **The order of adjectives** in standard English follows this pattern: quantity, quality, size, age, shape, color, origin, material, and purpose (e.g., . . . *three comfortable, large, old, square, blue, American cotton sleeping blankets*). |
| **L.4.1e** | Form and use **prepositional phrases.** | **Prepositional phrases** begin with a preposition and end with a noun, which acts as the "object" of the preposition (e.g., *in the garden, along the bike path*). |
| **L.4.1f** | Produce **complete sentences**, recognizing and correcting inappropriate **fragments** and **run-ons.** | **Complete sentences**, also called independent clauses, contain a subject and predicate (verb phrase) and express a complete thought (e.g., *Juan eats apples*).<br>**Fragments** are incomplete sentences. They are missing a subject or predicate, or they express an incomplete thought (e.g., *Juan eats*).<br>**Run-on sentences** contain two or more independent clause, which are not connected by the required semicolon or comma and conjunction (e.g., *Juan eats red apples and Larry eats green apples*). |

(*continued*)

**Figure 5.3  |  Language Standard 1: Grammar and Usage—Component Definitions and Examples for Grades 3–5 (*continued*)**

**L.1.** Demonstrate command of the conventions of standard English grammar and usage when writing or speaking.

| Standard Component | Component Terminology | Definition and Examples |
|---|---|---|
| **L.4.1g** | Correctly use **frequently confused words** (e.g., to, too, two; there, their). | **Frequently confused words** include homophones (words that sound the same but have different spellings and meanings) and words that are prone to a particular mistake (*a lot* is two words, *already* vs. *all ready, among* vs. *between, farther* vs. *further*). |
| **L.5.1a** | Explain the function of **conjunctions, prepositions,** and **interjections** in general and their function in particular sentences. | **Conjunctions** are words that connect words, phrases, and clauses within a sentence. **Prepositions** are words that express temporal (e.g., *after, during*), spatial (e.g., *above, in, around*), or logical (e.g., *for, except*) relationships of a noun to the rest of the sentence. **Interjections** are words that express an emotion (e.g., *wow, ouch, yikes*) or response (e.g., *no, yes, thanks, well*) by a writer or speaker. They are found at the beginning or middle of a sentence, set off by commas, or sometimes stand alone, followed by an exclamation point. |
| **L.5.1b** | Form and use the **perfect** (e.g., I had walked; I have walked; I will have walked) **verb tenses.** | **Perfect verb tenses** describe actions already completed. |
| **L.5.1c** | Use **verb tense** to convey various times, sequences, states, and conditions. | Basic **verb tenses** include present and past. When auxiliaries ("helping verbs") are added, a wide variety of tenses that indicate time, sequence, state, and condition may be created to express an exact meaning. |

Figure 5.3 | **Language Standard 1: Grammar and Usage—Component Definitions and Examples for Grades 3–5 (*continued*)**

**L.1.** Demonstrate command of the conventions of standard English grammar and usage when writing or speaking.

| Standard Component | Component Terminology | Definition and Examples |
|---|---|---|
| **L.5.1d** | Recognize and correct inappropriate **shifts in verb tense.** | **Shifts in verb tense** within and among sentences should occur only when appropriate to meaning. Verb tenses should generally be consistent, without shifts, in academic writing and speaking. |
| **L.5.1e** | Use **correlative conjunctions** (e.g., *either/or, neither/nor*). | **Correlative conjunctions** (i.e., *either/or, not only/ but also, neither/nor, both/and, whether/or, just as/ so*) work in pairs to connect words, phrases, and clauses (e.g., *Not only do I like syrup on pancakes, but I also like jelly*). |

In many cases, students who are reading and listening to academic language will exhibit the grammatical constructions described in Figure 5.3 without having received explicit instruction; in other cases, explicit instruction may be needed. For example, Language Standard 1 requires 3rd and 5th graders to explain the function of particular parts of speech. They should be able to identify and explain the five basic parts of speech—nouns, pronouns, verbs, adjectives, and adverbs—in 3rd grade. The remaining parts of speech—conjunctions, prepositions, and interjections—are introduced in 5th grade. Although the ability to categorize words within the basic parts of speech was common in prior sets of elementary school English language arts standards, identifying the function of parts of speech within a sentence was a skill that was often not addressed until middle school. Teachers may find additional attention to this area necessary as students transition to the greater degree of rigor that the Common Core demands.

As noted, Language Standard 2, the second standard under the Conventions of Standard English heading, focuses on print conventions. Figure 5.4

shows the sequence of this standard for grades 3, 4, and 5, illustrating how it is designed to build an overall knowledge of sentence structure and print conventions by targeting various rules of capitalization, punctuation, and spelling.

Similar to the grammar-focused standard that precedes it, Language Standard 2 has many detailed components describing the specific skills that are the focus for each grade level. The very precise rules for both capitalization and spelling conventions that appear in the 3rd grade standards become more generally stated in later grades, as students apply these rules to 4th and 5th grade writing. Progressive punctuation skills are also detailed in each grade, reflecting students' growing ability to produce complex sentence structures.

The level of grade-by-grade specificity in both L.1 and L.2 can be a great help to teachers, alerting them not only to instructional targets for the current grade level but also to prerequisite skills they may find necessary to revisit. The chart showing Language Progressive Skills included in both the body of the Common Core standards document and its Appendix A can provide teachers with further support. This chart identifies skills first introduced in lower grades that are likely to require continued attention in higher grades as students are challenged to apply the conventions of English to increasingly sophisticated forms of writing and speaking. Note that fully a third of the skills listed in the Language Progressive Skills chart are introduced in the upper elementary grades.

Because grammar and conventions are encountered in all literacy contexts, instruction and assessment focused on these skills have long been integrated into a wide variety of classroom activities. They are often addressed, for example, when students edit their own written assignments (editing is part of the writing process as defined in Writing Standard 5; see p. 52). The SBAC content specifications draft (Hess, 2012) indicates conventions may be assessed within a variety of reading, writing, and speaking tasks, as well as within focused editing tasks and items.

The Common Core standards do not dictate a change to the traditional approach of addressing conventions within the writing process; however,

L.2

Figure 5.4 | **Language Standard 2: Conventions of Standard English—Print**

| Grade 3 | Grade 4 | Grade 5 |
|---|---|---|
| **L.3.2** Demonstrate command of the conventions of standard English capitalization, punctuation, and spelling when writing. | **L.4.2** Demonstrate command of the conventions of standard English capitalization, punctuation, and spelling when writing. | **L.5.2** Demonstrate command of the conventions of standard English capitalization, punctuation, and spelling when writing. |
| a. **Capitalize important words in titles.** | a. Use correct capitalization. | a. **Use punctuation to separate items in a series.** |
| b. **Use commas in addresses.** | b. Use commas and quotation marks to mark direct speech **and quotations from a text.** | b. **Use a comma to separate an introductory element from the rest of the sentence.** |
| c. **Use commas and quotation marks in dialogue.** | c. **Use a comma before a coordinating conjunction in a compound sentence.** | c. **Use a comma to set off the words yes and no (e.g., Yes, thank you), to set off a tag question from the rest of the sentence (e.g., It's true, isn't it?), and to indicate direct address (e.g., Is that you, Steve?).** |
| d. **Form and use possessives.** | d. **Spell grade-appropriate words correctly,** consulting references as needed. | |
| e. **Use conventional spelling for high-frequency and other studied words and for adding suffixes to base words (e.g., sitting, smiled, cries, happiness).** | | d. **Use underlining, quotation marks, or italics to indicate titles of works.** |
| f. Use spelling patterns and generalizations **(e.g., word families, position-based spellings, syllable patterns, ending rules, meaningful word parts)** in writing words. | | e. Spell grade-appropriate words correctly, consulting references as needed |
| g. Consult reference materials, including beginning dictionaries, as needed to check and correct spellings. | | |

*Note:* Boldface text identifies content that differs from the prior grade level.

because very detailed skills are assigned to specific grades, teachers may need to provide direct instruction on skills targeted for their grade level. The PARCC frameworks document for ELA/literacy (PARCC, 2012) notes that while grammar is meant to be a normal, everyday part of what students do, they also need explicit lessons in grammar as they read, write, and speak.

## Knowledge of Language

There is just one standard under the Knowledge of Language heading: Language Standard 3 (L.3), shown in Figure 5.5.

Overall, this standard focuses on developing students' understanding of how words, phrases, and sentence structures may be adjusted for different purposes and contexts. In 3rd grade, students select words and phrases

L.3

Figure 5.5 | **Language Standard 3: Knowledge of Language**

| Grade 3 | Grade 4 | Grade 5 |
|---|---|---|
| **L.3.3** Use knowledge of language and its conventions when writing, speaking, reading, or listening.<br>a. **Choose words and phrases for effect.**<br>b. **Recognize and observe differences between the conventions of spoken and written standard English.** | **L.4.3** Use knowledge of language and its conventions when writing, speaking, reading, or listening.<br>a. Choose words and phrases **to convey ideas precisely.**<br>b. **Choose punctuation for effect.**<br>c. **Differentiate between contexts that call for formal English (e.g., presenting ideas) and situations where informal discourse is appropriate (e.g., small-group discussion).** | **L.5.3** Use knowledge of language and its conventions when writing, speaking, reading, or listening.<br>a. **Expand, combine, and reduce sentences for meaning, reader/ listener interest, and style.**<br>b. **Compare and contrast the varieties of English (e.g., dialects, registers) used in stories, dramas, or poems.** |

*Note:* Boldface text identifies content that differs from the prior grade level.

for a specific effect, recognizing that different conventions may apply to spoken and written English. In 4th grade, they learn to select precise words, choose punctuation that creates a particular effect, and recognize how language is shaped by its context. In 5th grade, students go on to adjust sentence structures for different purposes and then to compare different types of English. In middle school, students will extend these skills by learning to vary words, phrases, and sentence structures for more subtle effects, such as creating a specific mood.

## Vocabulary Acquisition and Use

As noted in Appendix A to the ELA/literacy standards document, even though research supports vocabulary acquisition as a key element in student academic success, traditionally, students' vocabulary acquisition tends to taper off by grade 4 or 5 (CCSSI, 2010d). The three standards under the Vocabulary Acquisition and Use heading are designed to keep vocabulary development moving forward. They describe strategies for comprehending words and phrases encountered in texts, analysis of figurative meanings and word relationships, and the expansion of students' working vocabulary.

Much of these standards' content is essentially the same across grades—not only across the upper elementary grades but in the middle and high school grades as well. That is not to say that student vocabulary skills are expected to stagnate—far from it. As the complexity of the texts that students encounter increases, so do the demands these standards place on students' working vocabulary. For example, students may apply the same essential strategies for vocabulary acquisition across grades, but the words themselves reflect more sophisticated topics and texts from one grade level to the next. When designing lessons that address vocabulary, teachers should note that the content of Language Standard 4 (L.4) and Language Standard 5 (L.5) is similar to that of Reading Standard 4 (RL.4/RI.4), which addresses the comprehension of words and phrases in a text.

Figure 5.6 shows the sequence of standards for grades 3–5 under the Vocabulary Acquisition and Use heading.

**L.4–6**

Figure 5.6 | **Language Standards 4–6: Vocabulary Acquisition and Use**

| Grade 3 | Grade 4 | Grade 5 |
|---|---|---|
| **L.3.4** Determine or clarify the meaning of unknown and multiple-meaning words and phrases based on *grade 3* reading and content, choosing flexibly from a range of strategies.<br>a. Use sentence-level context as a clue to the meaning of a word or phrase.<br>b. Determine the meaning of the new word formed when a known **affix** is added to a known word **(e.g., agreeable/disagreeable, comfortable/uncomfortable, care/careless, heat/preheat).**<br>c. Use a known root word as a clue to the meaning of an unknown word with the same root **(e.g., company, companion).**<br>d. Use glossaries **or** beginning dictionaries, both print and digital, to determine or clarify the **precise** meaning of **key** words and phrases. | **L.4.4** Determine or clarify the meaning of unknown and multiple-meaning words and phrases based on *grade 4* reading and content, choosing flexibly from a range of strategies.<br>a. Use context **(e.g., definitions, examples, or restatements in text)** as a clue to the meaning of a word or phrase.<br>b. **Use common, grade-appropriate Greek and Latin affixes and roots as clues to the meaning of a word (e.g., telegraph, photograph, autograph).**<br>c. Consult reference materials (e.g., dictionaries, glossaries, **thesauruses**), both print and digital, **to find the pronunciation** and determine or clarify the precise meaning of key words and phrases. | **L.5.4** Determine or clarify the meaning of unknown and multiple-meaning words and phrases based on *grade 5* reading and content, choosing flexibly from a range of strategies.<br>a. Use context **(e.g., cause/effect relationships and comparisons** in text) as a clue to the meaning of a word or phrase.<br>b. Use common, grade-appropriate Greek and Latin affixes and roots as clues to the meaning of a word (e.g., photograph, **photosynthesis**).<br>c. Consult reference materials (e.g., dictionaries, glossaries, thesauruses), both print and digital, to find the pronunciation and determine or clarify the precise meaning of key words and phrases. |

Figure 5.6 | **Language Standards 4–6: Vocabulary Acquisition and Use (*continued*)**

| Grade 3 | Grade 4 | Grade 5 |
|---|---|---|
| **L.3.5** Demonstrate understanding of word relationships and nuances in word meanings.<br>a. **Distinguish the literal and nonliteral meanings of words and phrases in context (e.g., take steps).**<br>b. Identify real-life connections between words and their use **(e.g., describe people who are friendly or helpful).**<br>c. Distinguish shades of meaning among **related words that describe states of mind or degrees of certainty (e.g., knew, believed, suspected, heard, wondered).** | **L.4.5** Demonstrate understanding of **figurative language,** word relationships, and nuances in word meanings.<br>a. **Explain the meaning of simple similes and metaphors (e.g., as pretty as a picture) in context.**<br>b. **Recognize and explain the meaning of common idioms, adages, and proverbs.**<br>c. **Demonstrate understanding of words by relating them to their opposites (antonyms) and to words with similar but not identical meanings (synonyms).** | **L.5.5** Demonstrate understanding of figurative language, word relationships, and nuances in word meanings.<br>a. **Interpret figurative language,** including similes and metaphors, in context.<br>b. Recognize and explain the meaning of common idioms, adages, and proverbs.<br>c. **Use the relationship between particular words (e.g., synonyms, antonyms, homographs) to better understand each of the words.** |
| **L.3.6 Acquire and use accurately grade-appropriate conversational, general academic, and domain-specific words and phrases, including those that signal spatial and temporal relationships (e.g., After dinner that night we went looking for them).** | **L.4.6** Acquire and use accurately grade-appropriate general academic and domain-specific words and phrases, including those that signal **precise actions, emotions, or states of being (e.g., quizzed, whined, stammered) and that are basic to a particular topic (e.g., wildlife, conservation, and endangered when discussing animal preservation).** | **L.5.6** Acquire and use accurately grade-appropriate general academic and domain-specific words and phrases, including those that signal **contrast, addition, and other logical relationships (e.g., however, although, nevertheless, similarly, moreover, in addition).** |

*Note:* Boldface text identifies content that differs from the prior grade level.

The first standard under this heading, Language Standard 4 (L.4), describes strategies for comprehending words and phrases found within oral and written texts. Students choose among vocabulary strategies, such as using context clues, word parts, and reference materials. The standard specifies that 3rd graders use sentence-level context to determine the meaning of an unknown word; 4th and 5th graders are expected to use sentence-level context but also to consider clues found in the text overall. At each grade level, students study how prefixes, suffixes, and root words form words and how to use reference materials to clarify the meaning of a word or phrase. Although the study of word parts is associated with an increased vocabulary for all students, this approach will be particularly beneficial to students who are learning English as a second language and whose first language shares cognates with English as they learn to apply their first-language vocabulary knowledge when reading English (CCSSI, 2010b).

The second standard focused on vocabulary acquisition and use, Language Standard 5 (L.5), targets the understanding of word relationships and subtle word meanings. The details and examples provided in the various statements of L.5 are specific to each grade level, helping to focus teachers' instruction and exposing students to a wide variety of figurative language and word relationships over the course of their schooling. In each grade, students build their understanding of nonliteral and figurative meanings, how words reflect and connect to people and culture, and how words relate to other words. Studying how words and phrases are used in the texts they read or hear will improve students' ability to select effective language in their own writing or speaking.

The final standard under this heading, Language Standard 6 (L.6), addresses students' working vocabulary. In grades K–2, L.6 emphasizes acquiring words through conversations and reading. When students reach 3rd grade, they are also expected to learn general academic vocabulary (words common across a variety of scholarly writings but rarely found in speech) and domain-specific words (words related to subject-area topics), as described in Appendix A of the standards document. After 3rd grade, the standard no longer focuses on words learned through conversation.

In grades 3–5, Language Standard 6 specifies the type of general academic vocabulary that is the focus for each grade. Students in 3rd grade focus on words that show spatial and temporal relationships; students in 4th grade focus on words that signal actions, emotions, or states of being; and students in 5th grade focus on words that signal contrast, addition, and other logical relationships.

Remember that students in upper elementary grades are also expected to learn domain-specific words, related to the topics they study in history, social studies, science, and other subjects. Although it is common for teachers to provide explicit instruction on domain-specific words prior to and while reading subject-specific materials, it is less common for teachers to provide direct instruction on general academic words. This kind of direct instruction is absolutely necessary, however; students are not likely to learn the meaning of general academic words from everyday conversation, and the meaning of these words can be difficult to discern from context clues. Direct instruction, in addition to planning reading and listening activities that allow students to encounter the same word in multiple authentic contexts, is a way for teachers to support all students' vocabulary acquisition—and the vocabulary acquisition of struggling learners in particular.

# PART II

# Mathematics

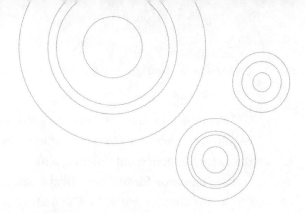

# CHAPTER 6

# About the Common Core Mathematics Standards for Grades 3–5

The Common Core mathematics standards are organized into two sets: the Standards for Mathematical Content, designed to cross traditional course boundaries and cover all the conceptual mathematical understanding necessary for students to develop from kindergarten through 12th grade, and the Standards for Mathematical Practice, which highlight the kinds of expertise that are essential for students to develop and use throughout this same grade span.

As we noted in Part I of this guide, the Common Core standards differ in many ways from most existing state standards documents, providing a greater level of detail about concepts, thought processes, and approaches. This level of detail often leads to much longer, more involved standards, some of which are up to a paragraph in length. Some of the mathematics standards detail conceptual methods of teaching and learning skills and concepts (e.g., combining data collection and representation with measurement, relating area to the operations of multiplication and addition and subtraction to length) that are not typically explicit in other standards documents.

Another example of this detailed focus on the mental processes required to understand mathematical concepts is found in the set of Standards for Mathematical Practice, which receives the same level of emphasis as the Standards for Mathematical Content.

In this chapter, we will walk you through the structure of the mathematics standards, provide an overview of how the standards work together, and offer some guidance on what to focus on as you begin your implementation efforts.

## The Standards for Mathematical Content

In the elementary levels, the Standards for Mathematical Content are organized first by grade. Each grade level is introduced with a one- or two-page introduction, which consists of two parts—a summary of the three to four critical areas (topics) for each grade and an in-depth narrative description of those critical areas. Figure 6.1 provides a brief, grade-by-grade summary for the upper elementary grades.

In order to delve as deeply into each of these critical areas as the standards' degree of rigor requires, grade-level teachers should commit to spending the majority of their mathematics instructional time on these topics. This emphasis necessitates a reduced focus on other content. It also means teachers will need to cut customary curriculum topics that have been moved to a different grade level—a step that some teachers may be wary of taking, as it requires a baseline level of trust in the Common Core's grade-level progression of content. It's our hope that the discussion in Part II of this guide will help teachers gain an understanding of these progressions, allowing them to let go of mathematics content that is no longer a critical area or an area of support for their grade.

In the chapters to come, we will review each domain of the grades 3–5 mathematics standards separately, providing an overview of its critical areas and illustrating how the content of each domain relates to the mathematical practices. We will then look at each cluster within the domain, identifying the connections among clusters and describing how the content

Figure 6.1 | **Critical Areas Within the Upper Elementary Domains by Grade Level**

| Domain Name | Grade 3 | Grade 4 | Grade 5 |
|---|---|---|---|
| Operations and Algebraic Thinking | • Meanings of multiplication and division<br>• Using properties of operations to calculate products of whole numbers<br>• Relationship between multiplication and division | • Methods to compute products and quotients involving multi-digit whole numbers | *No critical areas identified for this domain at this grade level* |
| Number and Operations in Base Ten | *No critical areas identified for this domain at this grade level* | • Place value to 1,000,000 | • Division procedures<br>• Addition and subtraction of decimals |
| Number and Operations— Fractions | • Understanding fractions (unit fractions, parts of a whole)<br>• Using fractions to represent numbers<br>• Solving problems that involve comparing fractions | • Fractional equivalence<br>• Operations with fractions with like denominators<br>• Composing and decomposing fractions from unit fractions<br>• Multiplying fractions by a whole number | • Addition and subtraction of fractions with unlike denominators<br>• Procedure for multiplying and dividing fractions (limited to division of unit fractions by whole numbers) and decimals<br>• Relationship between decimals and fractions |
| Measurement and Data | • Area of rectangles | *No critical areas identified for this domain at this grade level* | • Volume |
| Geometry | • Properties of two-dimensional shapes (quadrilaterals) | • Classification of two-dimensional shapes (using parallel or perpendicular lines; angles of a specified size)<br>• Symmetry | *No critical areas identified for this domain at this grade level* |

*Note:* Content in this table was adapted from the descriptions in the grade-level introductions within the mathematics standards document (CCSSI, 2010g).

differs and builds across grades. This close analysis will provide a clearer understanding of the meaning of each standard within the context of the entirety of the Common Core standards for mathematics. We believe it will better teachers' understanding of how students have been prepared throughout the grades for each concept—insight they can use to reassure themselves of the appropriateness of the content their grade-level standards address and then apply during lesson planning to deliver more effective instruction and improve students' learning.

After the grade-level introductions, the standards within each grade are organized hierarchically, as follows:

• *Domain:* Expressed in short phrases, a domain articulates big ideas that connect standards and topics. Elementary school standards for grades 3–5 are categorized into five domains: Operations and Algebraic Thinking (OA), Number and Operations in Base Ten (NBT), Number and Operations—Fractions (NF), Measurement and Data (MD), and Geometry (G).

• *Cluster:* A cluster captures several ideas that, taken with all the other clusters within that domain, summarize the important aspects of mathematics students will encounter. For example, there are nine clusters in the Operations and Algebraic Thinking domain in grades 3–5: four for grade 3, three for grade 4, and two for grade 5. The first of the two clusters at the 5th grade level ("Cluster A") is "Write and interpret numerical expressions." The second ("Cluster B") is "Analyze patterns and relationships." The content addressed in different domains and clusters may be closely related, reflecting the standards writers' emphasis on the interconnections throughout mathematics.

• *Standard:* A standard is a specific description of what students should understand and be able to do. It may be one sentence or several sentences long, and it sometimes includes lettered subsections, known as components. There are at least one and often several standards within every cluster. For example, the single standard in Cluster B of Operations and Algebraic Thinking at the 5th grade level, which is Standard 3 within the domain overall, is "Generate two numerical patterns using two given rules. Identify apparent relationships between corresponding terms. Form ordered pairs consisting of corresponding terms from the two patterns, and graph the ordered pairs on a coordinate plane."

This part of the guide contains one chapter focused on each of the five upper elementary school mathematics domains. At the beginning of these chapters, you will find a chart that provides an overview of that domain's clusters and standards by grade level. As in Part I's look at the ELA/literacy standards, here in Part II we will be referencing the content standards using a slightly abbreviated version of the CCSSI's official identification system. Again, we have dropped the first part of the code, the formal prefix ("CCSS. Math.Content"). The next piece of the code for standards in grades K–8 is the specific grade level, which is followed by the domain abbreviation, the letter identifying the particular cluster within the domain, and then the specific standard number. For example, "5.G.B.3" is shorthand for Grade 5, Geometry (the domain name), Cluster B (of the domain's two clusters, identified A–B), Standard 3. The shorthand way to refer to all standards within Cluster B of the 5th grade Geometry domain is "5.G.B."

Taken as a whole, the Common Core's mathematical content standards for grades 3–5 identify what students should know and be able to do in order to prepare for mathematics study in middle and high school and, ultimately, to graduate college- or career-ready. It is the nature of mathematics to build on concepts throughout the grades. The foundational multiplication concepts learned in 3rd grade, for example, will allow students to understand multiplication with fractions in 5th grade; that understanding will allow students to understand algebraic concepts in middle school and high school. Development of conceptual understandings and procedural fluencies in these lower grades is essential for students' success throughout their mathematics education.

## The Standards for Mathematical Practice

Emphasis on students' conceptual understanding of mathematics is an aspect of the Common Core standards that sets them apart from many state standards. The eight Standards for Mathematical Practice, listed in Figure 6.2 and consistent throughout grades K–12, play an important role in ensuring that students are engaged in the actual use of mathematics, not just in the acquisition of knowledge about the discipline. Indeed, the table of contents in the standards document gives equal weight to the Standards for Mathematical Practice and to the Standards for Mathematical Content. This dual focus, echoed throughout the document's introductory material, has been undertaken to ensure the standards "describe varieties of expertise that mathematics educators at all levels should seek to develop in their students" (CCSSI, 2010g, p. 6).

The writers of the Common Core describe these practice standards in an introduction, explaining that the standards are derived from the National Council of Teachers of Mathematics' process standards and the strands of mathematical proficiency found in the National Research Council report *Adding It Up* (2001). A brief description of the meaning of the practice standards is provided in the front of the mathematical standards document (CCSSI, 2010g, pp. 6–8).

In addition to stressing mathematics proficiencies that cross all domains, the mathematical practice standards ensure that students who are focused on skills and processes don't find themselves engaged in rote activities that provide them no deeper sense of how mathematics works

---

Figure 6.2  |  **The Standards for Mathematical Practice**

**MP1.** Make sense of problems and persevere in solving them.

**MP2.** Reason abstractly and quantitatively.

**MP3.** Construct viable arguments and critique the reasoning of others.

**MP4.** Model with mathematics.

**MP5.** Use appropriate tools strategically.

**MP6.** Attend to precision.

**MP7.** Look for and make use of structure.

**MP8.** Look for and express regularity in repeated reasoning.

as an integrated whole. For example, calculating areas can be seen as a simple process of solving a formula. In the past, many standards documents required nothing more than that the process be taught, which meant that often students were shown formulas, which they were expected to memorize and use, but were not exposed to the reasoning behind the algorithms. In contrast, the Common Core standards explicitly require that students be able to explain *why* the process captured in the formula for calculating area works. Third grade students are expected to grasp that area is an attribute of plane figures, and they begin measuring area by counting unit squares (3.MD.5–6). The formula for area is not taught until 4th grade (4.MD.3). By focusing in 3rd grade on just this small aspect of area, the standards provide a firm foundation for understanding area as a whole and promote students' ability to see the utility of the process over a wider range of problems.

Please note that, as with the content standards, the mathematical practice standards have official identifiers, which we have shortened in this guide's sample lessons. For example, we abbreviate Mathematical Practice Standard 1, officially "CCSS.Math.Practice.MP1," as "MP1."

## Implications for Teaching and Learning

A recent survey of more than 13,000 K–12 math teachers and 600 district curriculum directors across 40 states shows that teachers are highly supportive of the Common Core standards. That's the good news. On the other hand, the same survey shows that an overwhelming majority (80%) mistakenly believe that the standards are "pretty much the same" as their former state standards, and only about 25 percent of respondents are willing to stop teaching a topic that they currently teach, even if the Common Core State Standards do not support teaching that topic in their current grade (Schmidt, 2012).

These findings suggest some damaging possible consequences. For example, if teachers don't recognize the Common Core standards' new focus on depth of understanding, they may attempt to teach a broad curriculum that doesn't give students the time they need to develop that deeper understanding. Furthermore, teachers' unwillingness to stop teaching familiar or favorite content that the standards do not require reinforces the possibility that, while students may be exposed to a wide variety of mathematical concepts, they will not reach the required level of mastery set for concepts that have been identified as critical.

We want to highlight a document that can provide significant support for teachers' instructional efforts: the *Progressions for the Common Core State Standards in Mathematics* (Common Core Standards Writing Team, 2011). Still in draft form at the time of this writing but available online, it details some useful strategies for teaching the grades 3–5 mathematics standards, and we urge anyone interested in specific strategies and examples to read it.

# How to Begin Implementation

As noted, the writers of the Common Core have offered some ideas for how to get started planning instruction and teaching the mathematics standards, and here in this guide, we share our own best advice.

## Focus on the mathematical practice standards

The Standards for Mathematical Practice are one of the potentially challenging aspects of Common Core implementation. As described on page 90, the mathematical practice standards are found in two places in the standards document: in the overall introduction and in the introduction to each grade level. The guidance found in the document's introduction provides valuable insight into each mathematical practice standard, and we recommend that teachers become extremely familiar with these descriptions and spend some time planning how to incorporate the practices into their units. Throughout Part II of this guide, we offer our own ideas about how teachers might integrate the mathematical practice standards with each of the domains in the mathematical content standards.

## Focus on critical areas

By sharpening the focus of each grade on three to four critical areas identified by the Common Core writers, teachers can help students develop a deeper understanding of those concepts than previous sets of mathematics standards required or allowed. The outcome is stronger foundational knowledge.

## Focus on connections

Remember that the Common Core mathematics standards are designed to be coherent within and across grades. In our upcoming discussion of each domain, we will clarify how the concepts found in the elementary school mathematics standards are organized across grades, underscoring that each standard is best understood not as new knowledge but as an extension of ideas presented in previous school years. We believe that the better teachers understand these progressions, the easier it will be for them to let go of content that is no longer a critical area or an area of support for their grade.

The Standards for Mathematical Practice provide further connective tissue between the standards at the grade levels and within the various domains; we highlight these connections in the ensuing chapters. However, it is important to stress that what we present are only a few examples of such connections; we do not mean to suggest that no other connections can or should be made. We encourage teachers to build on the proposals here to strengthen their own practice and enhance their implementation of the Common Core standards.

✳✳✳

Now that we've looked at the overall structure of the Common Core standards for mathematics in upper elementary school, we will examine each domain, addressing the specific standards at grades 3, 4, and 5.

CHAPTER 7

# Operations and Algebraic Thinking

The Operations and Algebraic Thinking domain (OA) is found in the mathematics standards in grades K–5. Figure 7.1 provides an overview of the domain's clusters and standards in the upper elementary grades.

Taken as a whole, in grades 3–5, the Operations and Algebraic Thinking domain focuses on the flexible and fluent use of the four operations (with a strong emphasis on multiplication and division), analysis of patterns and relationships, and writing and interpreting numerical expressions. Many of the skills associated with this domain are also addressed in other domains, most particularly in Number and Operations in Base Ten (see Chapter 8).

In this chapter and the chapters that follow, we will first look at how the content of the domain relates to the Standards for Mathematical Practice and then provide an overview of how standards in each cluster relate to other mathematics content standards, both within and across grades. This close analysis is intended to clarify the meaning of every standard within the context of the entire set of Common Core mathematics standards and illustrate how students have been prepared for this content through the standards that appear in the early elementary grades.

Figure 7.1 | **The Operations and Algebraic Thinking Domain: Grades 3–5 Overview**

| Grade Level | Clusters | Standards |
|---|---|---|
| Grade 3 | **3.OA.A** Represent and solve problems involving multiplication and division. | 3.OA.A.1, 3.OA.A.2, 3.OA.A.3, 3.OA.A.4 |
| | **3.OA.B** Understand properties of multiplication and the relationship between multiplication and division. | 3.OA.B.5, 3.OA.B.6 |
| | **3.OA.C** Multiply and divide within 100. | 3.OA.C.7 |
| | **3.OA.D** Solve problems involving the four operations, and identify and explain patterns in arithmetic. | 3.OA.D.8, 3.OA.D.9 |
| Grade 4 | **4.OA.A** Use the four operations with whole numbers to solve problems. | 4.OA.A.1, 4.OA.A.2, 4.OA.A.3 |
| | **4.OA.B** Gain familiarity with factors and multiples. | 4.OA.B.4 |
| | **4.OA.C** Generate and analyze patterns. | 4.OA.C.5 |
| Grade 5 | **5.OA.A** Write and interpret numerical expressions. | 5.OA.A.1, 5.OA.A.2 |
| | **5.OA.B** Analyze patterns and relationships. | 5.OA.B.3 |

# Connections to the Standards for Mathematical Practice

Students will use several mathematical practice standards as they learn operations and algebraic thinking. As they gain familiarity with addition, subtraction, multiplication, and division, students will begin to use operations to solve problems within real-world contexts developed by either the teacher or themselves. As students' confidence and fluency with operations and problem solving develop, teachers can begin to assign complex word problems that include some ambiguity about what the "best approach" may be. An example might be a multi-step designing and planning task featuring a number of constraints (design a football stadium, given a limited area and a fixed budget) that students are free to handle any way they like so long as they meet the needs of the project. This kind of problem solving gives students an opportunity to practice skills described by Mathematical Practice Standard 1—"Make sense of problems and persevere in solving them."

The standards within this domain that ask students to solve problems involving multiplication and division also focus on students' interpretation of the meaning of the quantities and operations involved. As students in grades 3–5 learn how to interpret numbers in a given context, they are not only developing fluency with the mathematical operations but also developing the abilities described in Mathematical Practice Standard 2, "Reason abstractly and quantitatively." Furthermore, as students write multiplication and division equations to describe a real-world or word problem, they are modeling with mathematics (Mathematical Practice Standard 5).

Many of the standards in grades 3–5 that ask students to solve problems and identify patterns also call upon them to explain how they arrived at a given answer or why a pattern generates a given result. Explaining thinking in this way requires students to engage in conjecture and generate a logical progression of statements to back up that conjecture—both of which are skills related to Mathematical Practice Standard 3 ("Construct viable arguments and critique the reasoning of others"). In addition, any time a teacher calls on students to explain their mathematical reasoning is an opportunity to develop students' ability to use mathematical terms precisely and correctly and to express their answers carefully and fully. Precision in communication skills is a key aspect of "attending to precision" (Mathematical Practice Standard 6).

Students in grades 3–5 are beginning the see the structure and patterns found in multiplication and division problems. For example, as they interpret the meaning of multiplication and division, and see that five groups of seven objects is the same as seven groups of five objects, the commutative property of multiplication becomes apparent. Students' understanding of these properties employs Mathematical Practice Standard 7, "Look for and make use of structure."

## Conceptual Pathway Through the Grades

This overview provides a summary of the conceptual pathway for the Operations and Algebraic Thinking domain, which students begin studying in kindergarten. Teachers may also find it a useful tool for determining students' readiness for instruction on operations and algebraic thinking. Figure 7.2 traces the development of these ideas in grades K–2.

Now that we've taken a high-level look at the domain as a whole, we will explore the clusters found within each grade level and examine the standards they contain.

| Figure 7.2 | **Operations and Algebraic Thinking: Conceptual Pathway to Grades 3–5** | |
|---|---|
| **Grade Level** | **Concepts** |
| Kindergarten | • Understand addition as putting together and adding to<br>• Understand subtraction as taking apart and taking from |
| Grade 1 | • Representation of addition and subtraction problems within 20 with symbols for the unknown number<br>• Properties of operations (addition and subtraction)<br>• The relationship between addition and subtraction<br>• Add and subtract within 20<br>• Understand the meaning of the equal sign<br>• Understand the concept "equal shares" |
| Grade 2 | • Representation of addition and subtraction problems with symbols for the unknown number<br>• Add and subtract within 20<br>• Determining whether a group of objects are odd or even<br>• Write an equation to express an even number as a sum of two equal addends<br>• Express the sum of a rectangular array of objects as a sum of equal addends |

# Grade 3

The Common Core mathematics standards document (CCSSI, 2010g) identifies understanding the meaning of the multiplication and division operations as a critical area for 3rd grade. These concepts, the primary focus of the Operations and Algebraic Thinking domain, are also highlighted by both the *PARCC Model Content Frameworks*: *Mathematics Grades 3–8* (PARCC, 2011) and the Smarter Balanced Consortium's *Content Specifications for the Summative Assessment of the Common Core State Standards for Mathematics* (Schoenfeld, Burkhardt, Abedi, Hess, & Thurlow, 2012). As noted, critical areas provide educators with a place to focus their efforts, minimizing the chance that they will take on too much and struggle to implement the substantive changes the Common Core standards may require.

At the 3rd grade level, the Operations and Algebraic Thinking domain contains nine standards, grouped in four clusters.

## Represent and solve problems involving multiplication and division

In 3rd grade, students begin to learn about numbers and operations by representing and solving multiplication and division problems, as described in Cluster A (see Figure 7.3).

This cluster focuses on the critical area of multiplication and division. The first standard (3.OA.A.1) asks students to interpret products of whole numbers as equal groups; the second (3.OA.A.2), to divide numbers as equal shares; and the third (3.OA.A.3), to use multiplication and division to solve word problems and simple equations. Students' ability to understand each of these concepts is rooted in what they learned about addition in earlier grades—particularly the content presented in 2nd grade.

The Common Core standards' focus on developing a deep understanding of the concept and properties of addition begins in kindergarten (K.OA.A, 1.OA.A–D). By 2nd grade, students are asked to express the sum of a rectangular array of objects as the sum of equal addends (2.OA.4). This is a natural foundation for understanding the concept of multiplication, and

---

Figure 7.3 | **Represent and Solve Problems Involving Multiplication and Division**     3.OA.A

---

1. Interpret products of whole numbers, e.g., interpret 5 × 7 as the total number of objects in 5 groups of 7 objects each. For example, describe a context in which a total number of objects can be expressed as 5 × 7.

2. Interpret whole-number quotients of whole numbers, e.g., interpret 56 ÷ 8 as the number of objects in each share when 56 objects are partitioned equally into 8 shares, or as a number of shares when 56 objects are partitioned into equal shares of 8 objects each. For example, describe a context in which a number of shares or a number of groups can be expressed as 56 ÷ 8.

3. Use multiplication and division within 100 to solve word problems in situations involving equal groups, arrays, and measurement quantities, e.g., by using drawings and equations with a symbol for the unknown number to represent the problem.

4. Determine the unknown whole number in a multiplication or division equation relating three whole numbers. For example, determine the unknown number that makes the equation true in each of the equations 8 × ? = 48, 5 = □ ÷ 3, 6 × 6 = ?.

---

students who master 2.OA.C.4 will find it easier to understand multiplication as the repeated addition of equal groups. Interpreting multiplication in this way prepares students to grasp the concept of division as the number of objects in each share when a given number is partitioned equally into a given number of shares—equal shares being a concept addressed in 1st and 2nd grades (1.G.A.3, 2.G.A.3). A firm foundation in both multiplication and equal shares will benefit students when they are introduced to the idea of division.

From 1st grade on, students have been asked to represent addition and subtraction problems using equations featuring a symbol as the stand-in for the unknown number. Here in 3rd grade, students will extend that skill to multiplication and division problems. Being able to use symbols for unknown quantities will ultimately allow students to use variables in mathematical expressions (as well as in equations and inequalities). They will need these skills in later school years to valuate expressions and generate equivalent expressions, abilities that will promote success with algebra.

## Understand properties of multiplication and the relationship between multiplication and division

Cluster B of the 3rd grade Operations and Algebraic Thinking domain extends students' understanding of multiplication to include the properties of multiplication (see Figure 7.4).

Although the Common Core mathematics standards document does not explicitly state that one standard or cluster should be taught prior to another, the logical organization of ideas described here—specifically, that Cluster B is an extension of Cluster A—indicates that there is such a sequence; it should be of special interest to those developing curriculum guides.

As students learn about each operation throughout the elementary grades, they also spend ample time focusing on the operation's properties. Students in kindergarten learn the basic meaning of addition and subtraction and gain a conceptual understanding of what is meant by each operation. In 1st and 2nd grades, students apply the properties of operations as strategies to add and subtract whole numbers. Here in 3rd grade and later in 4th, students begin to apply what they know about the properties of operations to develop strategies for multiplying and dividing whole numbers and adding and subtracting fractions. In later grades, they will extend their understanding of the properties of operations to include operations

**3.OA.B**

Figure 7.4  |  **Understand Properties of Multiplication and the Relationship
Between Multiplication and Division**

5. Apply properties of operations as strategies to multiply and divide. *Examples: If 6 × 4 = 24 is known, then 4 × 6 = 24 is also known. (Commutative property of multiplication.) 3 × 5 × 2 can be found by 3 × 5 = 15, then 15 × 2 = 30, or by 5 × 2 = 10, then 3 × 10 = 30. (Associative property of multiplication.) Knowing that 8 × 5 = 40 and 8 × 2 = 16, one can find 8 × 7 as 8 × (5 + 2) = (8 × 5) + (8 × 2) = 40 + 16 = 56. (Distributive property.)* (Note: Students need not use formal terms for these properties.)

6. Understand division as an unknown-factor problem. *For example, find 32 ÷ 8 by finding the number that makes 32 when multiplied by 8.*

on rational numbers and, eventually, how these properties are used in solving algebraic expressions. Applying the properties of multiplication and division, as Standard 5 (3.OA.B.5) requires, increases students' fluency with those properties, which they will need in later grades to develop the proficiencies we have highlighted.

As is often the case in the Common Core standards, Standard 6 (3.OA.B.6) focuses on a conceptual understanding—here, an understanding of division as an unknown-factor problem—and addresses the skill involved (solving a given division problem) as a secondary goal.

## Multiply and divide within 100

Cluster C of the 3rd grade Operations and Algebraic Thinking domain contains a single standard and continues the focus on multiplication and division of whole numbers (see Figure 7.5).

The first part of Standard 7 (3.OA.C.7), "Fluently multiply and divide within 100," was a common standard statement in many state standards documents predating the Common Core. The second part of this standard adds key specifics that were often lacking in past documents: the requirement that students not only be able to quickly and easily multiply and divide within 100 and know from memory all products of two one-digit numbers but also be able to use strategies and their understanding of the properties of operations to solve multiplication and division problems. The ability to fluently multiply and divide has its immediate roots in the standards of the previous two clusters (3.OA.A, 3.OA.B), which focus on understanding multiplication and division at a conceptual level and

Figure 7.5 | **Multiply and Divide Within 100**

3.OA.C

7. Fluently multiply and divide within 100, using strategies such as the relationship between multiplication and division (e.g., knowing that 8 × 5 = 40, one knows 40 ÷ 5 = 8) or properties of operations. By the end of Grade 3, know from memory all products of two one-digit numbers.

applying properties of multiplication and division. Students with a deep understanding of these concepts and who are fluent with multiplication and division will be prepared for the skills required in later grades, such as finding factors and multiples.

## Solve problems involving the four operations, and identify and explain patterns in arithmetic

The final 3rd grade cluster in the Operations and Algebraic Thinking domain focuses on word problems and arithmetic patterns, expanding the focus on solving word problems involving multiplication and division found in 3.OA.A.3 to word problems that include all four of the operations (see Figure 7.6).

The first of the two standards in Cluster D, Standard 8 (3.OA.D.8), requires another expansion of established skills. Since 1st grade, students have been expected to solve simple word problems by using a symbol to represent the unknown (1.OA.A). Now, in 3rd grade, they are asked to use a letter to represent an unknown, which is a clear precursor to algebraic equations. This standard also communicates a new level of rigor for students, who are now expected to assess the reasonableness of answers and

**3.OA.D**

Figure 7.6  |  **Solve Problems Involving the Four Operations, and Identify and Explain Patterns in Arithmetic**

8. Solve two-step word problems using the four operations. Represent these problems using equations with a letter standing for the unknown quantity. Assess the reasonableness of answers using mental computation and estimation strategies including rounding. (*Note:* This standard is limited to problems posed with whole numbers and having whole number answers; students should know how to perform operations in the conventional order when there are no parentheses to specify a particular order [Order of Operations].)

9. Identify arithmetic patterns (including patterns in the addition table or multiplication table), and explain them using properties of operations. For example, observe that 4 times a number is always even, and explain why 4 times a number can be decomposed into two equal addends.

to use the order of operations (without parentheses). The idea of estimation using rounding is introduced in 3rd grade in the Number and Operations in Base Ten domain, and it builds on students' understanding of place value (see the discussion of 3.NBT.A.1, p. 114).

The second standard in this cluster, Standard 9 (3.OA.D.9), introduces the idea of identifying arithmetic patterns and explaining them in terms of the properties of operations that the patterns reflect. In traditional state standards, the concept of patterns was typically and explicitly addressed in the primary grades (K–2). Although the ability to find patterns is not directly called out in the Common Core standards until this standard's appearance in 3rd grade, the expectation that students find and use mathematical patterns is stated in the Standards for Mathematical Practice, which teachers are expected to integrate into all grade levels. The use of patterns to understand a mathematical concept is indirectly addressed in a number of content standards at different grade levels and in different domains. For example, a kindergarten Geometry standard asks students to describe similarities and differences between shapes as they analyze them (K.G.B.4). A 1st grade standard in the Number and Operations in Base Ten domain calls for students to mentally find 10 more or 10 less than a given number and explain their reasoning (1.NBT.C.5). When Standard 9 in this cluster asks 3rd graders to find and explain arithmetic patterns, the assumption is that they will be applying what they have learned about discerning patterns and the mathematics communication skills they have been practicing throughout the earlier grades to develop these skills.

# Grade 4

In 4th grade, students develop, discuss, and use methods of multiplication and division to compute products of multi-digit whole numbers. The Common Core standards identify multiplication and division content as a critical area in 4th grade, and PARCC (2011) highlights this content in its frameworks document. As noted, critical areas help teachers identify where they should be focusing their instructional efforts.

The Operations and Algebraic Thinking domain at the 4th grade level contains five standards, grouped in three clusters.

## Use the four operations with whole numbers to solve problems

Let's take a look at the first cluster (Cluster A) in the 4th grade Operations and Algebraic Thinking domain (see Figure 7.7).

In 3rd grade, students were introduced to the idea of multiplication as the total number of objects in a number of equal groups (3.OA.A.1). In 4th grade, they begin to build on this understanding of multiplication. As you see, Standard 1 (4.OA.A.1) and Standard 2 (4.OA.A.2) expand the conceptualization of multiplication to include multiplicative comparisons. These standards connect closely to a 4th grade standard in the Number and Operations in Base Ten domain (see Chapter 8), in which students begin to add, subtract, and multiply with multiple digits (4.NBT.B.3). The understanding of multiplicative comparisons developed here will help students to interpret word problems, which often are stated as multiplicative comparisons

4.OA.A

**Figure 7.7  |  Use the Four Operations with Whole Numbers to Solve Problems**

1. Interpret a multiplication equation as a comparison, e.g., interpret 35 = 5 × 7 as a statement that 35 is 5 times as many as 7 and 7 times as many as 5. Represent verbal statements of multiplicative comparisons as multiplication equations.

2. Multiply or divide to solve word problems involving multiplicative comparison, e.g., by using drawings and equations with a symbol for the unknown number to represent the problem, distinguishing multiplicative comparison from additive comparison.

3. Solve multistep word problems posed with whole numbers and having whole-number answers using the four operations, including problems in which remainders must be interpreted. Represent these problems using equations with a letter standing for the unknown quantity. Assess the reasonableness of answers using mental computation and estimation strategies including rounding.

(e.g., "Maria has four times as many donuts as Karl. Karl has four donuts. How many donuts does Maria have?").

The third and last standard in this cluster, Standard 3 (4.OA.A.3), asks students to apply their fluency with all four operations and their ability to solve word problems. Students have been working on both these skills since the introduction of simple addition and subtraction word problems in kindergarten (K.OA.A.2). In 1st and 2nd grades, they are asked to represent addition and subtraction word problems with equations that include symbols that stand for the unknown quantity (1.OA.A, 2.OA.A.1). And, as we have seen, in 3rd grade, students add multiplication and division to their tool kit and begin to solve two-step word problems involving all four operations (3.OA.D.8). It's also in 3rd grade that students begin to use letters for unknown quantities and assess the reasonableness of their answers using mental computation and rounding. Here in 4th grade, Standard 4 is very similar to its 3rd grade predecessor (3.OA.A.4), requiring students to represent problems with equations that include letters and to assess the reasonableness of the results. In addition, Standard 4 asks students to solve more complex problems that involve more than two steps and to include division problems in which the remainder must be interpreted.

## Gain familiarity with factors and multiples

Next, let's look at Cluster B in the 4th grade Operations and Algebraic Thinking domain (see Figure 7.8).

| Figure 7.8   I   **Gain Familiarity with Factors and Multiples** | 4.OA.B |
| --- | --- |

4. Find all factor pairs for a whole number in the range 1–100. Recognize that a whole number is a multiple of each of its factors. Determine whether a given whole number in the range 1–100 is a multiple of a given one-digit number. Determine whether a given whole number in the range 1–100 is prime or composite.

While finding factor pairs and multiples is not identified as a critical area in the 4th grade, the concept does provide a valuable bridge between critical concepts found in the 3rd grade Operations and Algebraic Thinking domain and the 4th grade Number and Operations—Fractions domain (see Chapter 9, p. 129). In 3rd grade, students were introduced to the meaning of multiplication, developing fluency in multiplying and dividing numbers within 100 using strategies based on the properties of the two operations. They develop this fluency further in 4th grade as they begin multiplying and dividing multi-digit numbers (4.NBT.B.5, 4.NBT.B.6) and, as articulated by the standards in this cluster, begin finding factors and multiples of numbers within 100. All these concepts are identified as critical in the introductory text to the 4th grade standards. Students who exhibit this kind of fluency with multiplication and division and who are able to find factors and multiples of numbers within 100 should find it easier to generate equivalent fractions by creating common denominators, skills addressed in the 4th grade level of the Number and Operations—Fractions domain (4.NF.A).

## Generate and analyze patterns

Cluster C of the 4th grade Operations and Algebraic Thinking domain is another single-standard one (see Figure 7.9).

Standard 5 (4.OA.C.5) further develops the idea of identifying patterns that was formally introduced to the mathematical content standards in 3rd grade. (As noted earlier, although the concept of finding patterns is not explicit in the content standards until 3rd grade, the expectation that students find and use mathematical patterns is found in the mathematical practice standards, which should be integrated into all grade levels.) In 3rd grade, students are asked to identify patterns and explain them, using the properties of operations. Now, in 4th grade, students must build on that introduction to patterns by generating a number or shape pattern and identifying features of the pattern that were not explicit in the rule. Practice generating patterns and explaining the features of patterns that are not explicit in the rules helps students develop number sense and a deeper understanding of operations.

Figure 7.9  |  **Generate and Analyze Patterns**

5. Generate a number or shape pattern that follows a given rule. Identify apparent features of the pattern that were not explicit in the rule itself. For example, given the rule "Add 3" and the starting number 1, generate terms in the resulting sequence and observe that the terms appear to alternate between odd and even numbers. Explain informally why the numbers will continue to alternate in this way.

# Grade 5

In 5th grade, students extend their understanding of how to evaluate numerical expressions and how to analyze patterns. While the Common Core standards do not identify expressions or patterns as critical areas in 5th grade, this content can support students as they learn about critical content, such as graphing expressions (see the discussion of Cluster B, p. 108), in later grades.

At the 5th grade level, the Operations and Algebraic Thinking domain contains three standards, grouped into two clusters.

## Write and interpret numerical expressions

The first cluster, Cluster A, asks students to write and interpret numerical expressions (see Figure 7.10).

In 3rd grade, students are introduced to the order of operations without parentheses as they begin to solve problems involving all four operations (3.OA.D.8). Fluency with the four operations, including the order of operations, will assist them as they work toward mastery of the first standard in this cluster (5.OA.A.1), which asks them to write and evaluate numerical expressions involving parentheses, brackets, and braces.

Standard 2 within this domain (5.OA.A.2) builds upon students' ability to solve word problems, which they have been developing throughout elementary school. In kindergarten, students are expected to solve simple word problems involving addition and subtraction by translating the words

5.OA.A

Figure 7.10  |  **Write and Interpret Numerical Expressions**

1. Use parentheses, brackets, or braces in numerical expressions, and evaluate expressions with these symbols.

2. Write simple expressions that record calculations with numbers, and interpret numerical expressions without evaluating them. For example, express the calculation "add 8 and 7, then multiply by 2" as 2 × (8 + 7). Recognize that 3 × (18932 + 921) is three times as large as 18932 + 921, without having to calculate the indicated sum or product.

into simple equations (K.OA.A.2). In 1st and 2nd grades, these translation skills extend to using symbols as stand-ins for the unknown qualities, and students take on increasingly complex problems (1.OA.A, 2.OA.A.1). In 3rd and 4th grades, as students add multiplication and division to their skill repertoire, they begin to translate word problems into equations for all four of the operations. Here in 5th grade, the two standards in Cluster A introduce students to the idea of expressions and to the idea that words can be translated into expressions without evaluation being necessary. Both understandings will assist students in middle school, as they further extend their conceptions of algebraic expressions.

## Analyze patterns and relationships

The single standard making up Cluster B of the 5th grade Operations and Algebraic Thinking domain (see Figure 7.11) extends the learning about patterns and relationships first introduced in 3rd grade.

Again, although the concept of finding patterns is not explicitly addressed in the content standards until 3rd grade (3.OA.D), the expectation that students find and use mathematical patterns is found in Mathematical Practice Standard 7, which should be integrated into instruction at all grade levels. The 3rd grade standards mentioned ask students to identify and explain patterns, using the properties of operations. In 4th grade, students must generate a number or shape pattern and identify features

Figure 7.11  |  **Analyze Patterns and Relationships**

5.OA.B

3. Generate two numerical patterns using two given rules. Identify apparent relationships between corresponding terms. Form ordered pairs consisting of corresponding terms from the two patterns, and graph the ordered pairs on a coordinate plane. For example, given the rule "Add 3" and the starting number 0, and given the rule "Add 6" and the starting number 0, generate terms in the resulting sequences, and observe that the terms in one sequence are twice the corresponding terms in the other sequence. Explain informally why this is so.

of the pattern that were not explicit in the rule (4.OA.C.5). Now, in 5th grade, they are asked to generate *two* numerical patterns using two given rules and to graph the results. While this standard focuses 5th graders on the analysis of patterns, they are also expected to form ordered pairs and graph them, which supports their work in the Geometry domain to graph points on the coordinate plane (5.G.A.1; see p. 162). This combination of concepts provides teachers with a way to develop students' graphing skills while teaching pattern analysis. In addition, the work students are doing to generate and graph numerical patterns is a good foundation for understanding the graphing of equations, which they will undertake in 6th grade (6.EE.C.9). In other words, this single standard about pattern analysis, while not considered critical content for 5th grade, not only addresses students' ability to use the coordinate plane but also introduces them to ideas that will support a fuller understanding of the graphing of equations later in their study of mathematics.

# CHAPTER 8

# Number and Operations in Base Ten

The Number and Operations in Base Ten domain (NBT) appears in the Common Core mathematics content standards for grades K–5. Here at the upper elementary level, it focuses on the development and use of place value understanding and the use of the properties of operations to perform multi-digit arithmetic (see Figure 8.1).

After a look at how the contents of the domain relate to the mathematical practice standards, we'll move on to examine the clusters at grades 3, 4, and 5, clarifying the meaning of each standard within the context of the entirety of the Common Core standards for mathematics and examining how the standards at earlier grade levels have prepared students by laying the foundation for mastery.

## Connections to the Standards for Mathematical Practice

Content within the Number and Operations in Base Ten domain provides a foundational understanding of the base ten number system. Students learn about place value and are asked to perform operations on numbers

| Figure 8.1 \| **The Number and Operations in Base Ten Domain: Grades 3–5 Overview** | | |
| --- | --- | --- |
| Grade Level | Clusters | Standards |
| Grade 3 | **3.NBT.A** Use place value understanding and properties of operations to perform multi-digit arithmetic. | 3.NBT.A.1, 3.NBT.A.2, 3.NBT.A.3 |
| Grade 4 | **4.NBT.A** Generalize place value understanding for multi-digit whole numbers. | 4.NBT.A.1, 4.NBT.A.2, 4.NBT.A.3 |
| | **4.NBT.B** Use place value understanding and properties of operations to perform multi-digit arithmetic. | 4.NBT.B.4, 4.NBT.B.5, 4.NBT.B.6 |
| Grade 5 | **5.NBT.A** Understand the place value system. | 5.NBT.A.1, 5.NBT.A.2, 5.NBT.A.3, 5.NBT.A.4 |
| | **5.NBT.B** Perform operations with multi-digit whole numbers and with decimals to hundredths. | 5.NBT.B.5, 5.NBT.B.6, 5.NBT.B.7 |

using place value. As their understanding solidifies and skills develop, they will work with longer and more complex problems involving multi-digit numbers. To facilitate a deeper understanding of place value and operations, teachers can spend classroom time discussing these types of problems, allowing students to consider how other students might approach them and identifying similarities and differences between various approaches. In doing so, students will strengthen the skills they need to make sense of and persevere in solving problems—Mathematical Practice Standard 1.

As students illustrate and explain their calculations, using their understanding of strategies based on place value and the properties of operations to do so, they develop the capacity to "construct viable arguments" (Mathematical Practice Standard 3) and "communicate precisely to others" (a skill related to Mathematical Practice Standard 6). While constructing these explanations, students will also be selecting and using equations, arrays, or area models, evidencing Mathematical Practice Standard 5, "Use appropriate tools strategically."

Students will also "look for and make use of structure" (Mathematical Practice Standard 7) as they analyze both the base ten number system and the properties of operations and use both in the development of strategies to multiply and divide multi-digit numbers. Finally, as they begin to generalize these strategies and look for shortcuts, they will be using skills described by Mathematical Practice Standard 8, "Look for and express regularity in repeated reasoning."

## Conceptual Pathway Through the Grades

Figure 8.2 provides an overview of the concepts presented in grades K–2 that prepare students to master the standards within the Number and Operations in Base Ten domain for grades 3–5.

Reviewing this progression, it's clear that students in the primary grades work to develop a deep understanding of place value along with strategies for adding and subtracting multi-digit whole numbers. While this domain's focus on operations overlaps somewhat with that of the Operations and Algebraic Thinking domain (see Chapter 7), it is distinguished by an emphasis on multi-digit numbers and place value.

Let's move, now, to closer examination of the clusters and standards at each of the upper elementary grade levels.

## Grade 3

The content in the Number and Operations in Base Ten domain in 3rd grade is not identified as a critical area by the Common Core mathematics standards document (CCSSI, 2010g). However, multiplying single-digit whole numbers by multiples of 10 is supporting content for the critical areas of multiplication and division. PARCC has highlighted the addition, subtraction, multiplication, and division strategies found in this domain as

| Figure 8.2   **Number and Operations in Base Ten: Conceptual Pathway to Grades 3–5** | |
|---|---|
| **Grade Level** | **Concepts** |
| Kindergarten | • Compose and decompose numbers 11–19 to gain foundations for place value |
| Grade 1 | • Count to 120<br>• Read, write, and represent objects up to 120<br>• Understand place value up to the tens place<br>• Compare two two-digit numbers using the symbols >, <, and =<br>• Develop strategies based on place value, properties of operations, and the relationship between addition and subtraction to add within 100<br>• Use concrete models or drawings and strategies based on place value, properties of operations, and the relationship between addition and subtraction to subtract multiples of 10 from other multiples of 10 (both numbers in the range from 10 to 90) |
| Grade 2 | • Understand place value to the hundreds place<br>• Skip count by 5s, 10s, and 100s<br>• Fluently add and subtract within 100 using strategies based on place value, properties of operations, and the relationship between addition and subtraction<br>• Use concrete models or drawings and strategies based on place value, properties of operations, and the relationship between addition and subtraction to add and subtract within 1000<br>• Explain why addition and subtraction strategies work, using place value and the properties of operations |

recommended starting points for the transition to the Common Core standards, placing them among other "particularly rich areas of mathematical content" (2011, p. 68). Remember, these critical areas and PARCC's starting points are identified to help educators focus their instructional efforts and prioritize the most important content.

At the 3rd grade level, the Number and Operations in Base Ten domain has three standards in a single cluster.

## Use place value understanding and properties of operations to perform multi-digit arithmetic

Let's take a look at the standards associated with the Number and Operations in Base Ten domain for 3rd grade (see Figure 8.3).

Students' understanding of the place value system begins in 1st grade, when they are introduced to the idea of two-digit numbers having a "tens place" and a "ones place" (1.NBT.A.2). In 2nd grade, students begin to work with three-digit numbers, which have a "hundreds place" (2.NBT.A.1), and they begin to add and subtract numbers using both special and generalized strategies based on place value, properties of operations, and the relationship between addition and subtraction (2.NBT.B). Here, in 3rd grade, students further their understanding of place value within 1000, developing fluency (speed, accuracy, and comfort) with algorithms and strategies to add and subtract numbers (3.NBT.A.2).

Here, as elsewhere in the Common Core mathematics standards, there is a differentiation between algorithms and strategies. Algorithms, as defined by the Common Core Writing Team in *Progressions for the Common Core State Standards in Mathematics,* are a memorized set of steps that rely on students decomposing numbers and then performing operations with one-digit numbers. For example, the algorithm for multi-digit addition asks

**3.NBT.A**

Figure 8.3  |  **Use Place Value Understanding and Properties of Operations to Perform Multi-digit Arithmetic**

1. Use place value understanding to round whole numbers to the nearest 10 or 100.

2. Fluently add and subtract within 1000 using strategies and algorithms based on place value, properties of operations, and/or the relationship between addition and subtraction.

3. Multiply one-digit whole numbers by multiples of 10 in the range 10–90 (e.g., 9 × 80, 5 × 60) using strategies based on place value and properties of operations.

*Note:* A range of algorithms may be used.

students to add the ones column first to get a one-digit number, "carrying over" the one in the tens place if necessary. Next, students add the digits in the tens place, along with the carried-over 10s. They repeat the same process as long as necessary: for the hundreds place, for the thousands place, and so on. In contrast, mathematical strategies are about applying understanding, not process. A strategy for adding multi-digit numbers depends on students' understanding of both the base ten system and the properties of operations. For example, the ability to "make 10" and use the associative property when adding numbers such as 246 + 124 will allow students to change the problem to read (246 + 4) + 20 + 100, which may be an easier problem to solve. For additional examples of mathematical strategies, please see the *Progressions* document (Common Core Standards Writing Team, 2011).

Student-developed strategies may be specific to the problem being solved, or they may be generalized methods that will work on any problem of that type. Throughout the Common Core mathematics standards, students are asked to use strategies (in the case of 3.NBT.A.2, strategies for addition and subtraction) and become fluent with those strategies across multiple grades *before* they are introduced to the standard algorithms. So, for example, in the 3rd grade, students are asked to add and subtract within 1000, which lays the foundation for 4th grade, when they will be expected to fluently add and subtract all multi-digit whole numbers using the standard algorithm. Students' understanding of the place value system and of operations with multi-digit whole numbers will be further extended in 5th grade, as they begin to work with decimals and become fluent with standard algorithms for addition and subtraction of all multi-digit whole numbers.

In addition to noting the content connections across grade levels, we can also point to connections among the 3rd grade domains. As 3rd grade students begin to solve two-step word problems using the four operations, they are asked to assess the reasonableness of their answers using estimation strategies, including rounding (3.OA.D.8). In this domain, Standard 1 (3.NBT.A.1) asks students to develop those rounding skills using their understanding of place value. Standard 3 (3.NBT.A.3) provides another connection between domains, as it extends 3rd graders' ability to use strategies based on place value and properties of operations from just addition and subtraction to include multiplication—a concept that is also addressed in standards in the Operations and Algebraic Thinking domain (3.OA.A–C). Students' understanding of the place value system and of operations with multi-digit whole numbers will be further extended in 5th grade, as they begin to work with decimals and become fluent with standard algorithms for addition and subtraction of all multi-digit whole numbers.

# Grade 4

The Common Core mathematics standards document identifies the understanding of place value to 1,000,000; the use of generalizable methods to compute products and quotients of multi-digit whole numbers; and the use of estimation (including rounding) as critical content for the 4th grade. In addition, the use of strategies for addition, subtraction, multiplication, and division is highlighted by both the PARCC and the SBAC draft documents (PARCC, 2011; Schoenfeld et al., 2012).

The Number and Operations in Base Ten domain for 4th grade has six standards, grouped into two clusters.

## Generalize place value understanding for multi-digit whole numbers

The standards in Cluster A (see Figure 8.4) ask students to extend the knowledge of place value they developed in grades K–3 and generalize that understanding for whole numbers up to 1,000,000.

Students who understand the concept of multiplicative comparison as described in the Operations and Algebraic Thinking domain (4.OA.A.1–2) are well positioned to master Standard 1 (4.NBT.A.1), which focuses on understanding place value as a multiplicative comparison—that is, that a digit in one place represents 10 times what it represents in the place to its right. Students who developed a generalized understanding of place value in the early elementary grades will find it easier to read, write, compare,

Figure 8.4  |  **Generalize Place Value Understanding for Multi-digit Whole Numbers**

1.  Recognize that in a multi-digit whole number, a digit in one place represents ten times what it represents in the place to its right. For example, recognize that $700 \div 70 = 10$ by applying concepts of place value and division.

2.  Read and write multi-digit whole numbers using base-ten numerals, number names, and expanded form. Compare two multi-digit numbers based on meanings of the digits in each place, using >, =, and < symbols to record the results of comparisons.

3.  Use place value understanding to round multi-digit whole numbers to any place.

and round whole numbers, as described in Standard 2 (4.NBT.A.2) and Standard 3 (4.NBT.A.3). The understanding of place value for whole numbers as a multiplicative comparison will assist students in 5th grade, as they learn about decimals (see 5.NBT.A.3–4, p. 119).

## Use place value understanding and properties of operations to perform multi-digit arithmetic

Next, let's look at the second cluster in the 4th grade Number and Operations in Base Ten domain (see Figure 8.5).

As the mathematics standards document notes in its description of this domain at the 3rd grade level, students have been building the capacity to use the place value system to develop strategies for the addition, subtraction, and multiplication of whole numbers since 1st grade. In 4th grade, students are asked to become fluent with addition and subtraction algorithms (Standard 4—4.NBT.B.4), continue to use and develop additional multiplication strategies (Standard 5—4.NBT.B.5), and begin to use strategies for division (Standard 6—4.NBT.B.6). When applying these algorithms and strategies to perform any operation, students must explain what they are doing in terms of place value and the properties of operations.

One example of using strategies and place value to solve multiplication problems is breaking down the number 123 into its place value

**4.NBT.B**

Figure 8.5 | **Use Place Value Understanding and Properties of Operations to Perform Multi-digit Arithmetic**

4. Fluently add and subtract multi-digit whole numbers using the standard algorithm.

5. Multiply a whole number of up to four digits by a one-digit whole number, and multiply two two-digit numbers, using strategies based on place value and the properties of operations. Illustrate and explain the calculation by using equations, rectangular arrays, and/or area models.

6. Find whole-number quotients and remainders with up to four-digit dividends and one-digit divisors, using strategies based on place value, the properties of operations, and/or the relationship between multiplication and division. Illustrate and explain the calculation by using equations, rectangular arrays, and/or area models.

representations ($[1 \times 100] + [2 \times 10] + 3$) and then using the distributive property to ease the multiplication of the multi-digit number by another number (for example, $123 \times 4 = [(1 \times 100) + (2 \times 10) + 3] \times 4 = [100 \times 4] + [2 \times 10 \times 4] + [3 \times 4]$). The *Progressions* document contains a number of other examples (Common Core Standards Writing Team, 2011).

A deep understanding of strategies and algorithms for whole numbers will be helpful to students as they begin to perform operations on decimals in 5th grade.

## Grade 5

The Common Core mathematics standards document identifies understanding why division procedures work and fluency with multi-digit operations as critical content for 5th grade. This content is also highlighted by both the PARCC and SBAC documents (PARCC, 2011; Schoenfeld et al., 2012), so teachers are advised to consider the grade 5 standards within the Number and Operations in Base Ten domain as an important focus of instruction. There are seven standards, grouped in two clusters.

## Understand the place value system

The four standards in Cluster A (see Figure 8.6) add the concept of fractions to the foundational understanding of place value for whole numbers that students developed in grades K–4.

Students who understand the concept of multiplicative comparison as described in the 4th grade Operations and Algebraic Thinking domain (4.OA.A.1–2) and who understand the multiplication of fractions (5.NF.B.4) will find it easier to understand place value for decimals, the focus of Standard 1 (5.NBT.A.1).

The idea of patterns is first introduced in the mathematical concept standards in 4th grade and further developed in 5th grade (5.OA.B.3). Students' work over the prior two years explaining patterns will help them master Standard 2 (5.NBT.A.2), which introduces whole-number exponents. As is typical of the Common Core standards' emphasis on deeper understanding, recognition of patterns alone is not sufficient; students are asked

---

Figure 8.6  |  **Understand the Place Value System**

5.NBT.A

1. Recognize that in a multi-digit number, a digit in one place represents 10 times as much as it represents in the place to its right and 1/10 of what it represents in the place to its left.

2. Explain patterns in the number of zeros of the product when multiplying a number by powers of 10, and explain patterns in the placement of the decimal point when a decimal is multiplied or divided by a power of 10. Use whole-number exponents to denote powers of 10.

3. Read, write, and compare decimals to thousandths.
   a. Read and write decimals to thousandths using base-ten numerals, number names, and expanded form, e.g., $347.392 = 3 \times 100 + 4 \times 10 + 7 \times 1 + 3 \times (1/10) + 9 \times (1/100) + 2 \times (1/1000)$.
   b. Compare two decimals to thousandths based on meanings of the digits in each place, using >, =, and < symbols to record the results of comparisons.

4. Use place value understanding to round decimals to any place.

to explain *why* those patterns exist. To explain these patterns, students need to apply their understanding of the nature of the place value system— that is, that every digit is worth 10 times as much as it represents on the right or 1/10 of what it represents on the left, so that multiplying a number by a power of 10 results in that number shifting that many places. Developing this understanding opens students' eyes to connections in mathematics and keeps them from viewing multiplication and division as separate topics from place value.

The final two standards in this cluster, Standard 3 (5.NBT.A.3) and Standard 4 (5.NBT.A.4), extend students' abilities to read, write, compare, and round whole numbers to include decimals.

## Perform operations with multi-digit whole numbers and with decimals to hundredths

Cluster B of the 5th grade Number and Operations in Base Ten domain focuses on furthering students' abilities to work with whole numbers and decimals (see Figure 8.7).

**5.NBT.B**

Figure 8.7 ⏐ **Perform Operations with Multi-digit Whole Numbers and with Decimals to Hundredths**

5. Fluently multiply multi-digit whole numbers using the standard algorithm.

6. Find whole-number quotients of whole numbers with up to four-digit dividends and two-digit divisors, using strategies based on place value, the properties of operations, and/or the relationship between multiplication and division. Illustrate and explain the calculation by using equations, rectangular arrays, and/or area models.

7. Add, subtract, multiply, and divide decimals to hundredths, using concrete models or drawings and strategies based on place value, properties of operations, and/or the relationship between addition and subtraction; relate the strategy to a written method and explain the reasoning used.

Students begin performing operations on whole numbers in 1st grade, but it's not until 3rd grade that they are introduced to the concept of multiplication (3.OA.A–C) and begin to use strategies based on place value and properties of operations to multiply single-digit numbers by powers of 10 (3.NBT.A.3). They expand their use of these strategies in 4th grade, multiplying and dividing multi-digit whole numbers (4.NBT.B.5). This work prepares students for the requirements of Standard 5 (5.NBT.B.5), which asks them to become fluent with the multiplication algorithm. Similarly, the division strategies described in Standard 6 (5.NBT.B.6) and Standard 7 (5.NBT.B.7) will position students to master 6th grade standards focused on fluent use of the division algorithm (6.NS.B.2–3).

For an example of a 5th grade lesson addressing 5.NBT.A.1, 5.NBT.B.4, 5.NBT.B.6, and 5.NBT.B7 please see **Sample Lesson 6.**

As students describe and use these strategies and algorithms, they are learning the structure of the base ten number system. This point is underscored by the structure of the Common Core standards: the Number and Operations in Base Ten domain culminates in 5th grade and is succeeded by the Number System domain, which begins in 6th grade.

CHAPTER 9

# Number and Operations—Fractions

The Number and Operations—Fractions (NF) domain is found only in grades 3–5, and the content it covers is identified in the introduction to all three grade levels in the Common Core mathematics standards document (CCSSI, 2010g) as critical areas in those grades. As the overview in Figure 9.1 shows, students are introduced first to the concept of fractions and what fractions represent, then to the concept of equivalent fractions, and, finally, to how to perform operations on fractions.

Our examination of this domain begins with a look at the associated Standards for Mathematical Practice and goes on to consider how the content within each cluster builds and connects throughout the upper elementary grades.

## Connections to the Standards for Mathematical Practice

The Number and Operations—Fractions domain focuses on foundational understanding of fractions. Students learn what fractions are, how they're symbolized, and how to use them to solve problems.

Figure 9.1  |  **The Number and Operations—Fractions Domain: Grades 3–5 Overview**

| Grade Level | Clusters | Standards |
|---|---|---|
| Grade 3 | **3.NF.A** Develop understanding of fractions as numbers. | 3.NF.A.1, 3.NF.A.2, 3.NF.A.3 |
| Grade 4 | **4.NF.A** Extend understanding of fraction equivalence and ordering. | 4.NF.A.1, 4.NF.A.2 |
| | **4.NF.B** Build fractions from unit fractions by applying and extending previous understandings of operations on whole numbers. | 4.NF.B.3, 4.NF.B.4 |
| | **4.NF.C** Understand decimal notation for fractions, and compare decimal fractions. | 4.NF.C.5, 4.NF.C.6, 4.NF.C.7 |
| Grade 5 | **5.NF.A** Use equivalent fractions as a strategy to add and subtract fractions. | 5.NF.A.1, 5.NF.A.2 |
| | **5.NF.B** Apply and extend previous understandings of multiplication and division to multiply and divide fractions. | 5.NF.B.3, 5.NF.B.4, 5.NF.B.5, 5.NF.B.6, 5.NF.B.7 |

As students begin to make sense of fractions, they will be asked to use them to solve both mathematical and real-world problems. The foundation for this work is a solid grasp of ratios and proportions. To facilitate this understanding, teachers should assign complex tasks that help students build a deep, genuine understanding of the targeted concepts and allow for multiple solution methods. For example, a teacher might give groups of students a number of objects (e.g., tortillas) to divide equally among themselves (e.g., three tortillas to divide equally among five students). As the students share their solutions with one another, the teacher can pose questions designed to promote student reflection on how they solved the problem (e.g., "Why did you decide this way was the best way to divide the tortillas?"). Follow-up questions might address how the shape of the object factored into the way it was divided (e.g., "If the tortilla was a rectangle rather than a circle, how would you change your approach to the problem?"). In addition, teachers can encourage students to discuss how other students approached the problem, identifying how what they did is similar to or different from the approaches their classmates took. All these strategies are ways to promote the development of skills students need in order to persevere in solving problems, the focus of Mathematical Practice Standard 1.

As students solve problems involving operations with fractions in a context (whether it's a real-world context or a mathematical one), they need to be able to decontextualize the problem—that is, first restate the problem symbolically with equations involving fractions and then know how to manipulate those symbols in this new mathematical context. Students also strengthen their ability to make sense of and think through problems if they are able to contextualize—that is, see numbers as having a meaning in the context of the problem. The ability to reason both abstractly (to contextualize) and quantitatively (to decontextualize) is described in Mathematical Practice Standard 2.

The ability to apply the concepts of fractions to problems arising in everyday life, society, and the workplace is related to Mathematical Practice Standard 4, "Model with mathematics." These real-world problems may be posed by the teacher, or students might be asked to formulate problems that they find interesting. In grades 3–5, students who can express such a real-world problem in equation form are meeting the expectations of this standard.

As students explain why fractions are equivalent, or why performing a given operation on a fraction produces a certain result (such as why multiplying a given number by a fraction greater than 1 results in a product greater than the given number), they're developing their capacity to "construct viable arguments" (Mathematical Practice Standard 3). As they explain their reasoning and interpret relationships using terms associated with fractions, they are demonstrating the ability to communicate with precision, a skill related to Mathematical Practice Standard 6.

# Conceptual Pathway Through the Grades

Although the Number and Operations—Fractions domain is not introduced until 3rd grade, the foundational ideas necessary for understanding these relationships are laid in previous grades through concepts presented in different domains. Figure 9.2 summarizes and traces these ideas through 1st and 2nd grades.

Figure 9.2  |  **Number and Operations—Fractions: Conceptual Pathway to Grades 3–5**

| Grade Level | Concepts |
|---|---|
| Grade 1 | • Partitioning shapes into equal shares<br>• Fractional terms (halves, fourths, quarters) |
| Grade 2 | • Representing numbers on a number line<br>• Equal shares of identical wholes do not have to be the same shape<br>• Fractional terms (halves, thirds, half of, a third of)<br>• One whole equals two halves, three thirds, and four fourths |

As we explore the development of topics within each grade, we will refer to skills identified in this figure. Teachers may wish to consult it as they evaluate student readiness and plan their differentiation efforts.

With this overview of the domain complete, let's explore the clusters found within each grade level and take a closer look at the standards they contain.

# Grade 3

The Common Core identifies developing an understanding of fractions as a critical area for 3rd grade. In addition, PARCC and SBAC highlight this content in their draft documents (PARCC, 2011; Schoenfeld et al., 2012). As noted, critical areas provide educators with a place to focus their efforts, minimizing the risk that they will take on too much and struggle to implement the substantive changes that the Common Core standards may require.

In 3rd grade, there are three standards in the Number and Operations—Fractions domain, organized in a single cluster.

## Develop understanding of fractions as numbers

Students begin developing an informal understanding of fractions in 1st and 2nd grades as they learn about equal shares of shapes and learn some fractional language (1.G.A.3, 2.G.A.3). Third grade marks the start of students' formal study of fractions, which begins with a look at unit fractions and visual fractional models (see Figure 9.3).

The deep conceptual understanding students acquire through this foundational work will support them as they begin adding and subtracting whole numbers in grade 4 and multiplying and dividing fractions in grade 5.

The first two standards in this cluster focus on understanding fractions in two similar but distinct ways. Because both Standard 1 (3.NF.A.1) and Standard 2 (3.NF.A.2) have somewhat difficult wording, a close look, complete with illustration, is in order. We'll begin with Standard 1:

> 1. Understand a fraction $1/b$ as the quantity formed by 1 part when a whole is partitioned into $b$ equal parts; understand a fraction $a/b$ as the quantity formed by $a$ parts of size $1/b$.

The first part of the standard (before the semicolon) asks that students regard a unit fraction as a part of a whole. So, for example, if we say that the number of equal parts is 4 (i.e., $b = 4$), then each part is ¼, as shown in the diagram below:

| ¼ | ¼ | ¼ | ¼ |
|---|---|---|---|

The second part of Standard 1 (the text after the semicolon) develops the idea of a fraction as being composed of several unit fractions.

3.NF.A

Figure 9.3 | **Develop Understanding of Fractions as Numbers**

1. Understand a fraction $\frac{1}{b}$ as the quantity formed by 1 part when a whole is partitioned into $b$ equal parts; understand a fraction $\frac{a}{b}$ as the quantity formed by $a$ parts of size $\frac{1}{b}$.

2. Understand a fraction as a number on the number line; represent fractions on a number line diagram.
   a. Represent a fraction $\frac{1}{b}$ on a number line diagram by defining the interval from 0 to 1 as the whole and partitioning it into $b$ equal parts. Recognize that each part has size $\frac{1}{b}$ and that the endpoint of the part based at 0 locates the number $\frac{1}{b}$ on the number line.
   b. Represent a fraction $\frac{a}{b}$ on a number line diagram by marking off $a$ lengths $\frac{1}{b}$ from 0. Recognize that the resulting interval has size $\frac{a}{b}$ and that its endpoint locates the number $\frac{a}{b}$ on the number line.

3. Explain equivalence of fractions in special cases, and compare fractions by reasoning about their size.
   a. Understand two fractions as equivalent (equal) if they are the same size, or the same point on a number line.
   b. Recognize and generate simple equivalent fractions, (e.g., ½ = ²⁄₄, ⁴⁄₆ = ²⁄₃). Explain why the fractions are equivalent, e.g., by using a visual fraction model.
   c. Express whole numbers as fractions, and recognize fractions that are equivalent to whole numbers. *Examples: Express 3 in the form 3 = ³⁄₁; recognize that ⁶⁄₁ = 6; locate ⁴⁄₄ and 1 at the same point of a number line diagram.*
   d. Compare two fractions with the same numerator or the same denominator by reasoning about their size. Recognize that comparisons are valid only when the two fractions refer to the same whole. Record the results of comparisons with the symbols >, =, or <, and justify the conclusions, e.g., by using a visual fraction model.

*Note:* Grade 3 expectations in this domain are limited to fractions with denominators of 2, 3, 4, 6, and 8.

For example, the fraction ¾ is the quantity formed by three of the equal-sized boxes. This can be illustrated as follows:

| ¾ | ¼ |
|---|---|

Standard 2 develops the idea that fractions are numbers on a number line:

2. Understand a fraction as a number on the number line; represent fractions on a number line diagram.

a. Represent a fraction $1/b$ on a number line diagram by defining the interval from 0 to 1 as the whole and partitioning it into $b$ equal parts. Recognize that each part has size $1/b$ and that the endpoint of the part based at 0 locates the number $1/b$ on the number line.

Using the same example of ¼, we can see that partitioning a number line into four equal parts results in the following:

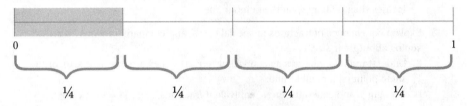

The shaded portion of this diagram illustrates the endpoint of the part based at 0, showing that the endpoint in this example locates the number ¼ ($1/b$) on the number line.

b. Represent a fraction $a/b$ on a number line diagram by marking off $a$ lengths $1/b$ from 0. Recognize that the resulting interval has size $a/b$ and that its endpoint locates the number $a/b$ on the number line.

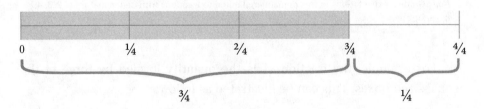

As the preceding diagram suggests, Standard 2 does not ask students to reduce the fractions. We're reminded in the *Progressions for the Common*

*Core State Standards in Mathematics* (Common Core Standards Writing Team, 2011) that there is nothing intrinsically better about a reduced fraction. The best format for a fraction is dependent on the situation, and while students are learning the concept of fractions, asking them to reduce the fraction before they truly understand what the fraction is representing may be confusing. (How to reduce fractions is introduced in 4th grade.)

Once 3rd graders have developed a solid understanding of fractions as part of a whole and as a number on a number line, they are ready to take on Standard 3 (3.NF.A.3) and begin to explain equivalence of simple fractions (e.g., $\frac{1}{2}$ = $\frac{2}{4}$, $\frac{4}{6}$ = $\frac{2}{3}$) and compare fractions based on their size using the models described in Standards 1 and 2. As students explore fractional comparisons, they will come to realize that comparisons are

For an example of a 3rd grade lesson addressing 3.NF.A.3, please see **Sample Lesson 4.**

only valid if the two fractions refer to the same whole—that is, that $\frac{1}{2}$ of a 12-inch ruler is not equivalent to $\frac{1}{2}$ of one inch. These concepts will be further developed at the 4th grade level, as students learn to generate equivalent fractions and to compare two fractions with different denominators.

# Grade 4

The Common Core mathematics standards document identifies understanding fractional equivalence and operations with fractions as a critical area in 4th grade. This same content was identified by both PARCC (2011) and SBAC (Schoenfeld et al., 2012) as an area of focus. As previously noted, critical areas identify priority content to help inform teachers' curricular decisions.

At the 4th grade level, the Number and Operations—Fractions domain contains seven standards, divided into three clusters.

## Extend understanding of fraction equivalence and ordering

The standards in Cluster A (see Figure 9.4) ask students to expand and articulate their understanding of why two fractions are equivalent, generate equivalent fractions, and, ultimately, compare two fractions with different numerators and denominators without using a picture or number line.

Figure 9.4  |  **Extend Understanding of Fraction Equivalence and Ordering**

1. Explain why a fraction $a/b$ is equivalent to a fraction $(n \times a)/(n \times b)$ by using visual fraction models, with attention to how the number and size of the parts differ even though the two fractions themselves are the same size. Use this principle to recognize and generate equivalent fractions.

2. Compare two fractions with different numerators and different denominators, e.g., by creating common denominators or numerators, or by comparing to a benchmark fraction such as ½. Recognize that comparisons are valid only when the two fractions refer to the same whole. Record the results of comparisons with symbols >, =, or <, and justify the conclusions, e.g., by using a visual fraction model.

To master Standard 1 (4.NF.A.1), students need to apply not only the understanding of fractions as numbers that they developed in 3rd grade but also what they know about multiplication and division. Students were first introduced to area models in 3rd grade, meaning that 4th graders should be prepared to use an area model as a visual fractional model to explain why a fraction $a/b$ (such as ½) is equivalent to $(n \times a) / (n \times b)$—for example, ½ = $(3 \times 1) / (3 \times 2)$. An example of this problem, shown as a visual fractional model, is provided here:

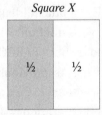

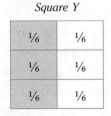

Square *X* is divided into two parts, but it can also be divided into three times as many parts ($3 \times 2$ parts = 6 parts). In Square *X,* one of the two parts is shaded. After we divide it by three times as many parts, we will shade three times as many parts of the square. When we do this, we can see that *shading* three times as many parts of the resulting new Square *Y* ($3 \times 1$ parts = 3 parts) produces the same amount of shading as was in the original square—that is, half of Square *Y* is shaded, as depicted above.

Another way of looking at this problem is to incorporate the concept of area, applying understandings developed in 3rd grade (3.MD.C.7, 3.G.A.2). Square *Y* above represents the whole; that square's area, as well as the area of its two halves (and its three thirds), can be measured.

The area of the shaded rectangle within Square *Y*, representing one-half, can be measured as $A = \frac{1}{2} \times 1 = \frac{1}{2}$. The whole area of the left rectangle within the square is equal to the whole area of the right rectangle within the square. The area of the two shaded portions is equivalent, so we can see that $(\frac{1}{6} + \frac{1}{6} + \frac{1}{6}) = \frac{1}{2}$; therefore (adding the unit fractions together), $\frac{3}{6} = \frac{1}{2}$. For more examples of fractional models, please see *Progressions for the Common Core State Standards in Mathematics* (Common Core Standards Writing Team, 2011).

Students' ability to develop an explanation like the one we have just provided will rely heavily on the understandings of unit fractions, area models, and multiplication that they developed in 3rd grade. Note that many of the concepts addressed here in Cluster A are also found in the next cluster, which focuses on building fractions from unit fractions.

Standard 2 (4.NF.A.2) extends students' ability to generate equivalent fractions and their understanding of the meaning of fractions. As is typical in the Common Core standards, the treatment of this content is more specific than what you would find in traditional state standards documents. Standard 2 asks that students be able not only to compare fractions with different numerators and denominators (common in older state standards documents) but also to generate equivalent fractions or compare a fraction to a benchmark fraction, recognize that the comparisons are valid only when referring to the same whole (e.g., $\frac{1}{4}$ of a dollar is not the same as $\frac{2}{8}$ of a cent), and justify their conclusions. Here in grade 4, the mathematical content standards look at unlike denominators in terms of comparison only, meaning teachers can devote time to ensuring students develop a deep understanding of the meaning of the fractions. Adding and subtracting fractions with unlike denominators will be addressed in 5th grade (5.NF.A.1).

## Build fractions from unit fractions by applying and extending previous understandings of operations on whole numbers

Students' firm grasp of what a fraction is and of the properties of operations—knowledge they've acquired in earlier grades—supports them as they learn to add and subtract fractions and mixed numbers and learn to multiply fractions by whole numbers. These concepts are addressed in Cluster B of the 4th grade Number and Operations—Fractions domain (see Figure 9.5). The sequencing of this domain—that is, how 4th graders are asked first to develop an understanding of the ordering of fractions with different numerators and denominators (in Standard 2—4.NF.A.2) and then to develop an understanding of how to perform operations on fractions, the focus of Standard 3 (4.NF.B.3) and Standard 4 (4.NF.B.4)—may be of particular interest to curriculum developers.

The idea that addition is "putting together" and subtraction is "taking from" has been instilled in students since kindergarten (K.OA.A); the two standards in this cluster require students to apply that understanding as they decompose fractions in a variety of ways, add and subtract mixed numbers with like denominators, and solve word problems involving addition and subtraction of fractions with like denominators. Decomposition, addition and subtraction, and solving word problems are all skills that have been developed throughout the early grades with whole numbers. Multiplication, on the other hand, is a relatively new skill, introduced in 3rd grade. Third graders learn to understand multiplication in terms of equal groups (3.OA.A.1) and to relate area to multiplication and addition (3.MD.C.7). Teachers may want to review all these concepts as part of instruction on how to multiply a fraction by a whole number.

## Understand decimal notation for fractions, and compare decimal fractions

The final cluster in this domain for 4th grade (see Figure 9.6) introduces the concept of decimals.

---

Figure 9.5 | **Build Fractions from Unit Fractions by Applying and Extending Previous Understandings of Operations on Whole Numbers**

4.NF.B

3. Understand a fraction $a/b$ with $a > 1$ as a sum of fractions $1/b$.
   a. Understand addition and subtraction of fractions as joining and separating parts referring to the same whole.
   b. Decompose a fraction into a sum of fractions with the same denominator in more than one way, recording each decomposition by an equation. Justify decompositions, e.g., by using a visual fraction model. *Examples: ⅜ = ⅛ + ⅛ + ⅛; ⅜ = ⅛ + 2/8; 2⅛ = 1 + 1 + ⅛ = 8/8 + 8/8 + ⅛.*
   c. Add and subtract mixed numbers with like denominators, e.g., by replacing each mixed number with an equivalent fraction, and/or by using properties of operations and the relationship between addition and subtraction.
   d. Solve word problems involving addition and subtraction of fractions referring to the same whole and having like denominators, e.g., by using visual fraction models and equations to represent the problem.

4. Apply and extend previous understandings of multiplication to multiply a fraction by a whole number.
   a. Understand a fraction $a/b$ as a multiple of $1/b$. *For example, use a visual fraction model to represent 5/4 as the product 5 × (¼), recording the conclusion by the equation 5/4 = 5 × (¼).*
   b. Understand a multiple of $a/b$ as a multiple of $1/b$, and use this understanding to multiply a fraction by a whole number. *For example, use a visual fraction model to express 3 × (2/5) as 6 × (1/5), recognizing this product as 6/5. (In general, n × (a/b) = (n × a)/b.)*
   c. Solve word problems involving multiplication of a fraction by a whole number, e.g., by using visual fraction models and equations to represent the problem. *For example, if each person at a party will eat ⅜ of a pound of roast beef, and there will be 5 people at the party, how many pounds of roast beef will be needed? Between what two whole numbers does your answer lie?*

Decimals will receive a more thorough introduction in 5th grade, in the Number and Operations in Base Ten domain (5.NBT.A.3). Here, students learn about decimals as fractions. As is typical in the Common Core standards, students are asked not merely to convert decimals and fractions but to reason about decimals. Focusing on the fractions with denominators of

4.NF.C

Figure 9.6 | **Understand Decimal Notation for Fractions, and Compare Decimal Fractions**

5. Express a fraction with denominator 10 as an equivalent fraction with denominator 100, and use this technique to add two fractions with respective denominators 10 and 100. *For example, express $\frac{3}{10}$ as $\frac{30}{100}$, and add $\frac{3}{10} + \frac{4}{100} = \frac{34}{100}$. Note: Students who can generate equivalent fractions can develop strategies for adding fractions with unlike denominators in general. But addition and subtraction with unlike denominators is not a requirement at this grade.*

6. Use decimal notation for fractions with denominators 10 or 100. *For example, rewrite 0.62 as $\frac{62}{100}$; describe a length as 0.62 meters; locate 0.62 on a number line diagram.*

7. Compare two decimals to hundredths by reasoning about their size. Recognize that comparisons are valid only when the two decimals refer to the same whole. Record the results of comparisons with the symbols >, =, or <, and justify the conclusions, e.g., by using a visual model.

10 or 100, students learn first how to add fractions with those denominators and then to use decimal notation to express these fractions. The examples given in Standard 6 (4.NF.C.6) make clear that students are expected not only to simply rewrite a decimal number as a fraction but also to relate that decimal number to concepts such as length. Such connections will further students' understanding of what fractions and decimals are, and they will allow students to see the equivalence of fractions and decimals in non-numeric forms.

The final standard in this cluster, Standard 7 (4.NF.C.7), extends students' understanding of fractions as a part of a whole (see our discussion of 4.NF.A.2 on p. 131) to include decimals, further cementing students' grasp of fraction and decimal equivalence. This understanding develops as students compare two decimals and justify these comparisons. The justification can be done using visual models (such as number lines or number strips) or with kinesthetic models (such as number blocks).

Students' understanding of fractional equivalence, operations on unit fractions, and decimal notation for fractions will be extended further in 5th grade, the culminating grade for the Number and Operations—Fractions domain.

# Grade 5

The Common Core mathematics standards document identifies as critical areas the topics addressed at the 5th grade level of Number and Operations—Fractions: generating equivalent fractions in order to add and subtract fractions with unlike denominators and an understanding of how to multiply and divide fractions. This content was also highlighted in the draft documents created by PARCC (2011) and SBAC (Schoenfeld et al., 2012). As noted, critical areas point teachers toward high-priority content, supporting their efforts to manage the curriculum more effectively.

There are seven standards in the Number and Operations—Fractions domain at the 5th grade level, organized into two clusters.

## Use equivalent fractions as a strategy to add and subtract fractions

Cluster A of the domain focuses on fractional equivalence and ordering (see Figure 9.7).

A typical structure for addressing operations in the Common Core is to introduce the concept of the operation in one grade, ask students to develop strategies (specific and general) in the grade that follows, and then focus on developing operational fluency and an understanding of the operational algorithm. This pattern can be seen as students learn operations with whole numbers from 1st grade to 5th grade, and it's also apparent in this domain, as students learn operations with fractions.

Students are introduced to the concept of fractions and fractional equivalence in 3rd grade. In 4th grade, they begin to perform operations on fractions, using fractional models as a strategy. Now, in 5th grade, students begin to use a generalized method of adding and subtracting with unlike denominators (Standard 1—5.NF.A.1), and they are expected to develop a degree of fluency with fractional concepts that will allow them not only to

---

Figure 9.7 | **Use Equivalent Fractions as a Strategy to Add and Subtract Fractions**

1. Add and subtract fractions with unlike denominators (including mixed numbers) by replacing given fractions with equivalent fractions in such a way as to produce an equivalent sum or difference of fractions with like denominators. *For example, $\frac{2}{3} + \frac{5}{4} = \frac{8}{12} + \frac{15}{12} = \frac{23}{12}$. (In general, $\frac{a}{b} + \frac{c}{d} = (ad + bc)/bd$.)*

2. Solve word problems involving addition and subtraction of fractions referring to the same whole, including cases of unlike denominators, e.g., by using visual fraction models or equations to represent the problem. Use benchmark fractions and number sense of fractions to estimate mentally and assess the reasonableness of answers. *For example, recognize an incorrect result $\frac{2}{5} + \frac{1}{2} = \frac{3}{7}$, by observing that $\frac{3}{7} < \frac{1}{2}$.*

---

solve word problems involving addition and subtraction of fractions but also to estimate the answers mentally to assess their reasonableness (Standard 2—5.NF.A.2).

## Apply and extend previous understandings of multiplication and division to multiply and divide fractions

The five standards in Cluster B (see Figure 9.7), most featuring numerous components, focus on fine-tuning students' understanding of the multiplication and division of fractions.

Students in 4th grade are introduced to the topic of multiplication of fractions with whole numbers, extending the concept of multiplication they developed in 3rd grade. Here in 5th grade, they are introduced to strategies and different ways to interpret the multiplication and division of fractions (as parts of a partition, as scaling, and in story contexts).

The introduction to the Common Core Standards for Mathematical Content explains that the standards are meant to show the structure inherent in mathematics. In this cluster, the writers highlight several connections between the multiplication and division of fractions and other

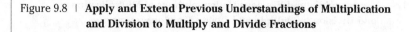

Figure 9.8 | **Apply and Extend Previous Understandings of Multiplication and Division to Multiply and Divide Fractions**

3. Interpret a fraction as division of the numerator by the denominator ($\frac{a}{b} = a \div b$). Solve word problems involving division of whole numbers leading to answers in the form of fractions or mixed numbers, e.g., by using visual fraction models or equations to represent the problem. *For example, interpret ¾ as the result of dividing 3 by 4, noting that ¾ multiplied by 4 equals 3, and that when 3 wholes are shared equally among 4 people, each person has a share of size ¾. If 9 people want to share a 50-pound sack of rice equally by weight, how many pounds of rice should each person get? Between what two whole numbers does your answer lie?*

4. Apply and extend previous understandings of multiplication to multiply a fraction or whole number by a fraction.

   a. Interpret the product ($\frac{a}{b}$) × $q$ as a part of a partition of $q$ into $b$ equal parts; equivalently, as the result of a sequence of operations $a \times q \div b$. *For example, use a visual fraction model to show (⅔) × 4 = ⁸⁄₃, and create a story context for this equation. Do the same with (⅔) × (⅘) = ⁸⁄₁₅. (In general, ($\frac{a}{b}$) × ($\frac{c}{d}$) = $\frac{ac}{bd}$.)*

   b. Find the area of a rectangle with fractional side lengths by tiling it with unit squares of the appropriate unit fraction side lengths, and show that the area is the same as would be found by multiplying the side lengths. Multiply fractional side lengths to find areas of rectangles, and represent fraction products as rectangular areas.

5. Interpret multiplication as scaling (resizing), by:

   a. Comparing the size of a product to the size of one factor on the basis of the size of the other factor, without performing the indicated multiplication.

   b. Explaining why multiplying a given number by a fraction greater than 1 results in a product greater than the given number (recognizing multiplication by whole numbers greater than 1 as a familiar case); explaining why multiplying a given number by a fraction less than 1 results in a product smaller than the given number; and relating the principle of fraction equivalence $\frac{a}{b}$ = $(n \times a)/(n \times b)$ to the effect of multiplying $\frac{a}{b}$ by 1.

*(continued)*

Figure 9.8 | **Apply and Extend Previous Understandings of Multiplication and Division to Multiply and Divide Fractions (*continued*)**

6. Solve real-world problems involving multiplication of fractions and mixed numbers, e.g., by using visual fraction models or equations to represent the problem.

7. Apply and extend previous understandings of division to divide unit fractions by whole numbers and whole numbers by unit fractions. *Note: Students able to multiply fractions in general can develop strategies to divide fractions in general, by reasoning about the relationship between multiplication and division. But division of a fraction by a fraction is not a requirement at this grade.*

   a. Interpret division of a unit fraction by a non-zero whole number, and compute such quotients. *For example, create a story context for ($\frac{1}{3}$) ÷ 4, and use a visual fraction model to show the quotient. Use the relationship between multiplication and division to explain that ($\frac{1}{3}$) ÷ 4 = $\frac{1}{12}$ because ($\frac{1}{12}$) × 4 = $\frac{1}{3}$.*

   b. Interpret division of a whole number by a unit fraction, and compute such quotients. *For example, create a story context for 4 ÷ ($\frac{1}{5}$), and use a visual fraction model to show the quotient. Use the relationship between multiplication and division to explain that 4 ÷ ($\frac{1}{5}$) = 20 because 20 × ($\frac{1}{5}$) = 4.*

   c. Solve real-world problems involving division of unit fractions by non-zero whole numbers and division of whole numbers by unit fractions, e.g., by using visual fraction models and equations to represent the problem. *For example, how much chocolate will each person get if 3 people share $\frac{1}{2}$ lb of chocolate equally? How many $\frac{1}{3}$-cup servings are in 2 cups of raisins?*

domains of mathematics, revealing some of that structure. As students learn how to multiply and divide fractions with whole numbers, they will also benefit from a deep understanding of the concepts addressed within the Measurement and Data domain (calculating area, the focus of 4.MD.3) and the Operations and Algebraic Thinking domain (interpretation of and understanding of multiplication and division, the focus of 3.OA.A.1–2 and 4.OA.A.1. Division of fractions in 5th grade is limited to dividing a unit fraction by a whole number and whole numbers by fractions, allowing teachers to spend a large amount of time on the meaning of division by a fraction before complicating the concept with the division of a fraction with another fraction. By giving students adequate time to truly develop a deep understanding, by the time they begin to divide fractions with other fractions in 6th grade (6.NS.A.1), they will be able to explain why the procedures for dividing fractions by fractions makes sense, rather than just memorizing that procedure.

# CHAPTER 10

# Measurement and Data

In grades K–5, the standards in the Measurement and Data domain focus on developing a conceptual understanding of data analysis and measurement, including area and volume. The writers of the Common Core have made several deliberate connections between the measurement and data standards and content addressed within other domains. Rather than isolating the concept of area, for example, the standards ask 3rd grade students to relate the concept of area to multiplication and 5th grade students to associate the concept of fractions with line plots.

This integration of mathematical content was not common in prior state standards documents. The *Progressions for Common Core State Standards in Mathematics* (Common Core Standards Writing Team, 2011) explains that by providing context related to other domains, the standards not only help students studying measurement and data analysis prepare for middle and high school mathematics but also reinforce students' understanding of the operations and fractions being studied in their current grades.

Figure 10.1 provides an overview of the Measurement and Data domain for grades 3–5.

In this chapter, we'll review each grade-level cluster individually and examine how its content connects and builds across the standards.

Figure 10.1  |  **The Measurement and Data Domain: Grades 3–5 Overview**

| Grade Level | Clusters | Standards |
|---|---|---|
| Grade 3 | **3.MD.A**  Solve problems involving measurement and estimation of intervals of time, liquid volumes, and masses of objects. | 3.MD.A.1, 3.MD.A.2 |
|  | **3.MD.B**  Represent and interpret data. | 3.MD.B.3, 3.MD.B.4 |
|  | **3.MD.C**  Geometric measurement: understand concepts of area and relate area to multiplication and to addition. | 3.MD.C.5, 3.MD.C.6, 3.MD.C.7 |
|  | **3.MD.D**  Geometric measurement: recognize perimeter as an attribute of plane figures and distinguish between linear and area measures. | 3.MD.D.8 |
| Grade 4 | **4.MD.A**  Solve problems involving measurement and conversion of measurements from a larger unit to a smaller unit. | 4.MD.A.1, 4.MD.A.2, 4.MD.A.3 |
|  | **4.MD.B**  Represent and interpret data. | 4.MD.B.4 |
|  | **4.MD.C**  Geometric measurement: understand concepts of angle and measure angles. | 4.MD.C.5, 4.MD.C.6, 4.MD.C.7 |
| Grade 5 | **5.MD.A**  Convert like measurement units within a given measurement system. | 5.MD.A.1 |
|  | **5.MD.B**  Represent and interpret data. | 5.MD.B.2 |
|  | **5.MD.C**  Geometric measurement: understand concepts of volume and relate volume to multiplication and to addition. | 5.MD.C.3, 5.MD.C.4, 5.MD.C.5 |

# Connections to the Standards for Mathematical Practice

The exploration of measurement and data concepts students do in upper elementary school will involve the use of several of the Standards for

Mathematical Practice. The Measurement and Data domain focuses on solving problems involving measurement and conversions of measurements (including geometric measurements) as well as on the representation and interpretation of data. As students begin to make sense of measurement systems, data representation, and geometric measurements, they will be asked to use these concepts and skills to solve multi-step, real-world problems. Teachers are advised to provide students with plenty of practice with such complex problems. For example, when addressing the first 3rd grade standard (3.MD.A.1), teachers may ask students to estimate what time a given event—a football game, a party, the school play—will end, given a starting time and time estimates for a component of the event—quarters, the cutting of the cake, the first act. (See the NCTM's *Principles and Standards for School Mathematics* [2000, pp. 183–184], for an example of a complex problem involving area and perimeter.) Teachers are further advised to spend classroom time discussing these problems, allowing students to consider their classmates' problem-solving approaches and prompting them to identify similarities and differences between their approaches and those of their peers. These strategies help students develop the skills necessary to make sense of and persevere in solving problems, as described in Mathematical Practice Standard 1.

As students solve multi-step measurement and data problems in a context (whether it's a real-world or a mathematical one), they need to be able to decontextualize the problem—that is, restate it symbolically with numbers or equations and know how to manipulate those symbols apart from the initial context. Students' ability to make sense of and think through problems is enhanced when they are also able to contextualize—that is, see numbers as having a meaning in the context of a problem. The ability to reason abstractly (contextualize) and quantitatively (decontextualize) is described in Mathematical Practice Standard 2.

Students' capability to apply the concepts of measurement to problems arising in everyday life, society, and the workplace is related to Mathematical Practice Standard 4, "Model with mathematics." As students learn about unit conversions, for example, they may be asked to apply the concept to real-world problems, taken from science or posed by the teacher, or to formulate problems that they find personally interesting.

Finally, the standards in the Measurement and Data domain offer upper elementary students multiple opportunities to "use appropriate tools strategically" (Mathematical Practice Standard 5) as they learn how to use graphs to illustrate data and as they measure area and volume.

## Conceptual Pathway Through the Grades

Figure 10.2 traces the concepts found in the Measurement and Data domain in grades K–2, illustrating how the concepts are developed over time.

Now that we've reviewed the domain and conceptual pathway through the grades as a whole, let's explore the clusters and standards within the different grades.

Figure 10.2  |  **Measurement and Data: Conceptual Pathway to Grades 3–5**

| Grade Level | Concepts |
|---|---|
| Kindergarten | • Measurable attributes<br>• Classification of objects into categories |
| Grade 1 | • Length measurement with non-standard units<br>• Time in hours and half hours<br>• Organization, representation, and interpretation of data with up to three categories<br>• Asking and answering simple questions about data and categories |
| Grade 2 | • Length measurement with standard units<br>• Addition and subtraction involving length<br>• Time to the nearest five minutes<br>• Money (dollar bills, quarters, dimes, nickels, and pennies)<br>• Line plots, picture graphs, and bar graphs with single-unit scale to represent a data set with up to four categories<br>• Solving simple problems using information presented in a bar graph<br>• Partitioning a rectangle into rows and columns of same-sized squares and counting them |

# Grade 3

Area—one of the concepts found within this domain—is marked as critical for 3rd grade and is also highlighted in both the PARCC and SBAC documents (PARCC, 2011; Schoenfeld et al., 2012). As noted, the Common Core's list of critical areas provides educators with a place to focus their efforts, minimizing the risk that they will take on too much and therefore be unable to implement the substantive changes the Common Core standards may require.

The 3rd grade Measurement and Data domain contains seven standards within four clusters.

## Solve problems involving measurement and estimation

The measurement and estimation problems students are asked to solve in Cluster A concern intervals of time, liquid volumes, and masses of objects (see Figure 10.3).

Standard 1 (3.MD.A.1) builds directly on students' work with time in 1st and 2nd grades. In 1st grade, students are asked to tell and write time in hours and half-hours (1.MD.B.3), and in 2nd grade, they are expected to tell and write time to the nearest five minutes (2.MD.C.7). Here in 3rd grade, students extend those abilities to include telling time to the nearest minute, and they are asked to solve word problems involving the addition and subtraction of minutes. The standards' focus on working with time culminates in 4th grade, when students must use the four operations to solve word problems involving measurements, including time.

The other standard in the cluster, Standard 2 (3.MD.A.2), introduces the concept of mass and liquid volume. Up to this point, the Common Core standards have limited measurement to length. Although weight is mentioned briefly in kindergarten as an example of a measurable attribute, neither weight nor mass is addressed again until the topics appear here, in 3rd grade. These basic measurement concepts will be revisited in 4th grade, when students are asked to apply them to solve real-world problems.

Figure 10.3  |  **Solve Problems Involving Measurement and Estimation of
Intervals of Time, Liquid Volumes, and Masses of Objects**

1. Tell and write time to the nearest minute and measure time intervals in minutes. Solve word problems involving addition and subtraction of time intervals in minutes, e.g., by representing the problem on a number line diagram.

2. Measure and estimate liquid volumes and masses of objects using standard units of grams (g), kilograms (kg), and liters (l). Add, subtract, multiply, or divide to solve one-step word problems involving masses or volumes that are given in the same units, e.g., by using drawings (such as a beaker with a measurement scale) to represent the problem. *Note: Excludes multiplicative comparison problems (problems involving notions of "times as much").*

## Represent and interpret data

Throughout elementary school, the Common Core standards present representing and interpreting data, the focus of Cluster B (see Figure 10.4), as a supporting area rather than a critical one. It's only when students enter middle school and begin to develop what the standards call "statistical thinking" that statistical standards gain the "critical area" designation. Nevertheless, the work students do here in 3rd grade helps form the foundation for this later study.

Standard 3 (3.MD.B.3), with its focus on solving "how many more" and "how many less" problems, not only helps prepare students for the

Figure 10.4  |  **Represent and Interpret Data**

3. Draw a scaled picture graph and a scaled bar graph to represent a data set with several categories. Solve one- and two-step "how many more" and "how many less" problems using information presented in scaled bar graphs. *For example, draw a bar graph in which each square in the bar graph might represent 5 pets.*

4. Generate measurement data by measuring lengths using rulers marked with halves and fourths of an inch. Show the data by making a line plot, where the horizontal scale is marked off in appropriate units—whole numbers, halves, or quarters.

statistical thinking they'll do in middle school but also reinforces addition and subtraction concepts covered in the Operations and Algebraic Thinking domain (2.MD.A.1). Furthermore, the use of scaled picture and bar graphs requires an understanding of multiplication, a concept that is first introduced here in 3rd grade and is considered a critical area (3.OA.A).

Working with data sets will not be new to 3rd graders (see Figure 10.2). In 1st grade, they learned how to work with up to three categories of data (1.MD.C.4), and in 2nd grade, they learned how to create bar graphs and line graphs with single-unit scales (2.MD.D.10). The development of multiple-unit scales here in 3rd grade is the major step forward for this skill.

Standard 4 (3.MD.B.4) builds on work in previous grades with measuring length and also reinforces the concept of fractions on a number line introduced at this grade level within the Number and Operations—Fractions domain (3.NF.A.2). Students first identify length as a measurable attribute in kindergarten. In 1st grade, they move on to measure length with non-standard units, and in 2nd grade, they begin to use standard units—measuring and estimating length using inches, feet, centimeters, and meters. In 3rd grade, the work students do with fractions, which is identified as a critical area, prepares them to use the fractional lengths of halves and quarters of an inch. Third graders are also expected to connect the idea of measurement with the concept of data generation while drawing a line plot. For example, each student measures the length of his or her pencil to the nearest quarter inch. The measurement data can then be collected, either for the whole class or for small student groups. After establishing an upper and lower boundary (the longest and shortest possible pencil lengths, respectively), students may then create a number line that demonstrates the quarter units, marking above the number line the number of times a given measurement was found, as illustrated here:

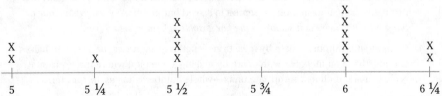

Teaching students to integrate measurement and graphing skills with their understanding of fractions increases their understanding of the interconnected structure of mathematics, which is a significant aim of the Common Core.

## Geometric measurement: understand concepts of area and relate area to multiplication and to addition

The next cluster in 3rd grade (see Figure 10.5) connects the geometric concept of area with measurement, multiplication, and addition.

---

**Figure 10.5  |  Geometric Measurement: Understand Concepts of Area and Relate Area to Multiplication and to Addition**

3.MD.C

---

5. Recognize area as an attribute of plane figures and understand concepts of area measurement.
   a. A square with side length 1 unit, called "a unit square," is said to have "one square unit" of area, and can be used to measure area.
   b. A plane figure which can be covered without gaps or overlaps by $n$ unit squares is said to have an area of $n$ square units.

6. Measure areas by counting unit squares (square cm, square m, square in, square ft, and improvised units).

7. Relate area to the operations of multiplication and addition.
   a. Find the area of a rectangle with whole-number side lengths by tiling it, and show that the area is the same as would be found by multiplying the side lengths.
   b. Multiply side lengths to find areas of rectangles with whole number side lengths in the context of solving real world and mathematical problems, and represent whole-number products as rectangular areas in mathematical reasoning.
   c. Use tiling to show in a concrete case that the area of a rectangle with whole-number side lengths $a$ and $b + c$ is the sum of $a \times b$ and $a \times c$. Use area models to represent the distributive property in mathematical reasoning.
   d. Recognize area as additive. Find areas of rectilinear figures by decomposing them into non-overlapping rectangles and adding the areas of the non-overlapping parts, applying this technique to solve real world problems.

In 2nd grade, students are asked to partition a rectangle into rows and columns of same-sized squares and count them (2.G.A.2). The first two standards in Cluster C—Standard 5 (3.MD.C.5) and Standard 6 (3.MD.C.6)—draw upon this foundation and formalize the concept of area. Students who understand area as a sum of the unit squares may find it easier to develop the notion of square units (e.g., square centimeters, square meters)—and understanding that will be useful when they are asked to contrast the concepts of perimeter and area in Cluster D of this domain and when they begin to use units to solve problems in grades to come. Grasping area as a sum of the unit squares also supports a better understanding of the properties of multiplication and addition, as described by the final standard in this cluster (Standard 7—3.MD.C.7). Typical state standards documents generally treat area and the properties of addition as separate concepts. Their deliberate connection here in the Common Core allows students to see mathematics as an integrated whole rather than a series of individual ideas. This sense of the structure of mathematics will assist students as they go on to consider new mathematical concepts and situations.

## Geometric measurement: Recognize perimeter

The final cluster in the 3rd grade Measurement and Data domain (see Figure 10.6) introduces the concept of perimeter as an attribute of plane figures and asks students to distinguish between linear and area measures.

The single standard constituting Cluster D combines the concepts regarding polygons found in the early elementary Geometry domains with

3.MD.D

Figure 10.6 | **Geometric Measurement: Recognize Perimeter as an Attribute of Plane Figures and Distinguish Between Linear and Area Measures**

8. Solve real world and mathematical problems involving perimeters of polygons, including finding the perimeter given the side lengths, finding an unknown side length, and exhibiting rectangles with the same perimeter and different areas or with the same area and different perimeters.

the measurement skills described in the Measurement and Data domain. Standard 8 (3.MD.D.8) draws on the measurement skills and mathematical problem-solving skills developed from kindergarten forward. In kindergarten, students are asked to compare two objects with a measurable attribute in common. In 1st grade, they learn to express the length of an object using nonstandard (comparison) units. By 2nd grade, students progress to using addition and subtraction within 100 to solve word problems involving lengths given in the same units. This preparation will be useful to students as they add the side lengths of rectangles to find the perimeter, and their work with area in Clusters A, B, and C of the 3rd grade Measurement and Data domain will allow them to readily compare the area and perimeter. This deep understanding of the two concepts gives students the foundation they'll need to work with the area and perimeter formulas in 4th grade.

# Grade 4

In 4th grade, students build on the concepts of measurement units, area, perimeter, and the representation of data they formed in previous grades and have their first exposure to the concept of angles. The Measurement and Data domain at this grade level contains seven standards in three clusters, and all the content covered is identified as supporting rather than critical.

## Solve problems involving measurement and conversion of measurements

The first cluster (see Figure 10.7) focuses on students' ability to use measurement concepts to solve problems that require converting a large unit into a smaller one.

Students have been working with standard units since the 2nd grade, when they measured the length of objects and learned to estimate lengths using units of inches, feet, centimeters, and meters (2.MD.A) and to tell time to the nearest five minutes (2.MD.C.7). In 3rd grade, students learned to measure and estimate liquid volumes and masses of objects, using the standard units of grams, kilograms, and liters (3.MD.A.2) and to tell time to

**4.MD.A**

Figure 10.7  |  **Solve Problems Involving Measurement and Conversion of Measurements from a Larger Unit to a Smaller Unit**

1. Know relative sizes of measurement units within one system of units including km, m, cm; kg, g; lb, oz; l, ml; hr, min, sec. Within a single system of measurement, express measurements in a larger unit in terms of a smaller unit. Record measurement equivalents in a two-column table. *For example, know that 1 ft is 12 times as long as 1 in. Express the length of a 4 ft snake as 48 in. Generate a conversion table for feet and inches listing the number pairs (1, 12), (2, 24), (3, 36), . . .*

2. Use the four operations to solve word problems involving distances, intervals of time, liquid volumes, masses of objects, and money, including problems involving simple fractions or decimals, and problems that require expressing measurements given in a larger unit in terms of a smaller unit. Represent measurement quantities using diagrams such as number line diagrams that feature a measurement scale.

3. Apply the area and perimeter formulas for rectangles in real world and mathematical problems. *For example, find the width of a rectangular room given the area of the flooring and the length, by viewing the area formula as a multiplication equation with an unknown factor.*

the nearest minute (3.MD.A.1). The three standards in this cluster teach students about conversion within all of the previously studied measurements—for length, liquid volume, mass, and time—allowing them to solve more complex problems involving different units of measurement, as articulated in Standard 1 (4.MD.A.1) and Standard 2 (4.MD.A.2). In addition to building on work in previous grades, Standard 2 also reinforces the concepts of fractions, decimals, and solving problems involving the four operations.

Standard 3 (4.MD.A.3) focuses on applying the formulas for area and perimeter. Students began informal work with area in the 2nd grade, when they were asked to partition a rectangle into rows and columns of same-sized squares and count them (2.G.A.2). In the 3rd grade, they began to formalize the concept of area, coming to understand area as a sum of the unit squares and contrasting that concept with perimeter in preparation for the application work they would be asked to do here in 4th grade. This progression is typical of the Common Core standards. Many mathematical concepts are informally introduced in a lower grade and gradually developed until the students can begin to use algorithms or formulas two to three years later.

## Represent and interpret data

The next cluster (see Figure 10.8) extends students' understanding of line plots.

Standard 4 (4.MD.B.4) builds on students' previous work representing data using a line plot and also reinforces the critical area of fractions. Students have been working with measurements since kindergarten. In 3rd grade, they learned how to use the fractional lengths of halves and quarters of an inch and tie that concept to generating data while drawing a line plot (see the example provided in the discussion of 3.MD.B.4, p. 146). Standard 4 is similar to 3.MD.B.4, simply adding the fraction ⅛ to the list of fractions of a unit and asking students to use the generated line plot to solve problems involving the addition and subtraction of fractions. It serves to reinforce the 3rd grade concepts and provide a context for problems involving the addition and subtraction of fractions, which is addressed in the Number and Operations—Fractions domain (4.NF.B.3).

The connection of line plots to the adding and subtracting of fractions is not typical in prior state standards documents, which often treat the two concepts separately. Again, deliberately connecting the two concepts allows students to see mathematics as an integrated whole rather than a series of individual ideas. This understanding of the structure of

Figure 10.8  |  **Represent and Interpret Data**

4.MD.B

4.  Make a line plot to display a data set of measurements in fractions of a unit (½, ¼, ⅛). Solve problems involving addition and subtraction of fractions by using information presented in line plots. *For example, from a line plot find and interpret the difference in length between the longest and shortest specimens in an insect collection.*

mathematics will help students to grasp new mathematical concepts and situations in the years to come.

## Geometric measurement: understand concepts of angles and measure angles

For an example of a 4th grade lesson addressing 4.MD.C.5 and 4.MD.C.6, see **Sample Lesson 5.**

Cluster C of the 4th grade Measurement and Data domain introduces the concept of angles and angle measurement (see Figure 10.9).

The concept of angles does not follow the typical Common Core pattern of introducing a topic in one grade, formally developing the topic in the next, and then expecting mastery in a third. Instead, angles are introduced and developed within a single grade; angle measurement is not found in the Common Core standards before it shows up here, in 4th grade. And while students

**4.MD.C**

---

Figure 10.9  |  **Geometric Measurement: Understand Concepts
of Angles and Measure Angles**

---

5. Recognize angles as geometric shapes that are formed wherever two rays share a common endpoint, and understand concepts of angle measurement:
   a. An angle is measured with reference to a circle with its center at the common endpoint of the rays, by considering the fraction of the circular arc between the points where the two rays intersect the circle. An angle that turns through $\frac{1}{360}$ of a circle is called a "one-degree angle" and can be used to measure angles.
   b. An angle that turns through $n$ one-degree angles is said to have an angle measure of $n$ degrees.

6. Measure angles in whole-number degrees using a protractor. Sketch angles of specified measure.

7. Recognize angle measure as additive. When an angle is decomposed into non-overlapping parts, the angle measure of the whole is the sum of the angle measures of the parts. Solve addition and subtraction problems to find unknown angles on a diagram in real world and mathematical problems, e.g., by using an equation with a symbol for the unknown angle measure.

will be familiar with the concept of a circle, introduced in kindergarten and developed over successive grade levels (K.G.A.1, 1.G.A.2, 2.G.A.3), rays are also first introduced here in grade 4, within the Geometry domain (4.G.A.1). What is typical of the treatment of angles found in Standard 5 (4.MD.C.5), Standard 6 (4.MD.C.6), and Standard 7 (4.MD.C.7) is the deep understanding students are asked to develop. While traditional standards may have focused on teaching students to measure angles with a protractor, this is not enough for the Common Core; students must also demonstrate that they understand the concept of an angle as $\frac{1}{360}$ of a circle and that they grasp the additive nature of angle measure. This may prove challenging for both students and teachers.

While not identified as a critical area, an understanding of angles will help to support students as they learn skills related to two-dimensional shapes—specifically, how to analyze, compare, and classify them (4.G.A.2, 5.G.B)—that *are* identified as a critical area in 4th grade.

# Grade 5

In 5th grade, students continue to work with measurement units and the representation and interpretation of data. Fifth grade marks students' formal introduction to the concept of volume as an attribute of solid figures, and they begin to solve problems involving volume. The Common Core mathematics standards document (CCSSI, 2010g) identifies student understanding of the concept of volume and the ability to measure the necessary attributes of shapes in order to determine volume as critical areas in 5th grade.

There are five standards for the Measurement and Data domain at the 5th grade level, grouped into three clusters.

## Convert like measurement units within a given measurement system

Figure 10.10 shows the single standard found in Cluster A of this domain.

Standard 1 (5.MD.A.1) is very similar to 4th grade Standard 2 (4.MD.A.2), which asks students to use the four operations to solve measurement

5.MD.A

**Figure 10.10  |  Convert Like Measurement Units Within a Given Measurement System**

1. Convert among different-sized standard measurement units within a given measurement system (e.g., convert 5 cm to 0.05 m), and use these conversions in solving multi-step, real world problems.

problems that require expressing measurements given in a larger unit in terms of a smaller unit (see p. 150). Fifth graders are asked to use measurement conversions to solve more complex problems; notably, this standard does not limit the conversion as being from larger to smaller, as 4.MD.A.2 does. In addition to building on work in previous grades, Standard 1 also reinforces the important concepts of decimals and the essential skill of solving multi-step, real-world problems.

## Represent and interpret data

Cluster B of the 5th grade Measurement and Data domain furthers students' understanding of line plots (see Figure 10.11).

This standard is very similar to the 4th grade Standard 4 (4.MD.B.4), which asks students to make a line plot to display a data set of measurement using the same fractions of a unit (see p. 151). The 4th grade standard asks students to add and subtract fractions with like denominators, and here in 5th grade, the requirement expands to the addition and subtraction

5.MD.B

**Figure 10.11  |  Represent and Interpret Data**

2. Make a line plot to display a data set of measurements in fractions of a unit (½, ¼, ⅛). Use operations on fractions for this grade to solve problems involving information presented in line plots. *For example, given different measurements of liquid in identical beakers, find the amount of liquid each beaker would contain if the total amount in all the beakers were redistributed equally.*

of fractions with different denominators. Like Standard 1 within Cluster A, Standard 2 builds on students' prior work representing data using a line plot and measurement while also reinforcing the critical area of fractions. (For an example of a simple line plot, see p. 145's discussion of the Represent and Interpret Data cluster at the 3rd grade level.)

The connection of line plots to the addition and subtraction of fractions is not typical in prior state standards documents, which often treat the two concepts separately. As discussed elsewhere in this chapter, deliberately connecting these concepts presents mathematics as an integrated whole rather than a series of individual ideas and enhances students' understanding of both concepts.

## Geometric measurement: Understand concepts of volume and relate volume to multiplication and to addition

The third cluster in the 5th grade Measurement and Data domain introduces the concept of geometric volume (see Figure 10.12).

In 3rd grade, students are introduced to the concepts of area and perimeter. The description of area as an attribute of plane figures is very similar to the description of volume as an attribute of solid figures that we see in Standard 3 (5.MD.C.3). Given the similarity in the development of the two concepts, students who understand area as a sum of the unit squares may find it easier to develop the notion of volume as the sum of unit cubes, which is addressed in Standard 4 (5.MD.C.4). In addition, grasping the idea of volume as a sum of the unit cubes will also allow students to use the concept of volume to better understand some of the properties of multiplication (e.g., the associative property), as described by the final standard in this cluster, Standard 5 (5.MD.C.5). The connection of volume to the properties of addition and subtraction is not typical in prior state standards documents, which often treat the two concepts separately. Once again, the deliberate connection of these two concepts underscores the integrated nature of mathematics, an understanding that will serve students well in middle school and beyond.

5.MD.C

Figure 10.12  |  **Geometric Measurement: Understand Concepts of Volume and Relate Volume to Multiplication and to Addition**

3. Recognize volume as an attribute of solid figures and understand concepts of volume measurement.

   a. A cube with side length 1 unit, called a "unit cube," is said to have "one cubic unit" of volume, and can be used to measure volume.

   b. A solid figure which can be packed without gaps or overlaps using $n$ unit cubes is said to have a volume of $n$ cubic units.

4. Measure volumes by counting unit cubes, using cubic cm, cubic in, cubic ft, and improvised units.

5. Relate volume to the operations of multiplication and addition and solve real world and mathematical problems involving volume.

   a. Find the volume of a right rectangular prism with whole-number side lengths by packing it with unit cubes, and show that the volume is the same as would be found by multiplying the edge lengths, equivalently by multiplying the height by the area of the base. Represent threefold whole-number products as volumes, e.g., to represent the associative property of multiplication.

   b. Apply the formulas $V = l \times w \times h$ and $V = b \times h$ for rectangular prisms to find volumes of right rectangular prisms with whole number edge lengths in the context of solving real world and mathematical problems.

   c. Recognize volume as additive. Find volumes of solid figures composed of two non-overlapping right rectangular prisms by adding the volumes of the non-overlapping parts, applying this technique to solve real world problems.

# CHAPTER 11

# Geometry

In this chapter, we'll examine Geometry (G), the last of the five mathematics domains for the upper elementary grades. After reviewing how the contents of this domain relate to the mathematical practice standards, we will look at how each cluster relates to the other mathematical content standards both within and across grades. This close analysis will clarify the meaning of each standard within the context of the entirety of the Common Core standards for mathematics and illuminate how standards that appear in the early elementary grades have prepared students to master the concepts.

Figure 11.1 provides an overview of the Geometry domain in grades 3–5.

Taken together, the Geometry domain at the upper elementary level focuses on reasoning with, drawing, and classifying geometric figures and on graphing points on the coordinate plane.

## Connections to the Standards for Mathematical Practice

Students in grades 3–5 will be using several mathematical practices as they build their knowledge of geometric concepts. As students become comfortable with graphing points on the coordinate plane, they're expected to begin to use these skills to solve real-world and mathematical problems

| Figure 11.1   |   **The Geometry Domain: Grades 3–5 Overview** | | |
|---|---|---|
| Grade Level | Clusters | Standards |
| Grade 3 | **3.G.A** Reason with shapes and their attributes. | 3.G.A.1, 3.G.A.2 |
| Grade 4 | **4.G.A** Draw and identify lines and angles, and classify shapes by properties of their lines and angles. | 4.G.A.1, 4.G.A.2, 4.G.A.3 |
| Grade 5 | **5.G.A** Graph points on the coordinate plane to solve real-world and mathematical problems. | 5.G.A.1, 5.G.A.2 |
| | **5.G.B** Classify two-dimensional figures into categories based on their properties. | 5.G.B.3, 5.G.B.4 |

involving the coordinate plane, activities that incorporate "making sense of problems," an important aspect of Mathematical Practice Standard 1. Representing these real-world problems using the coordinate plane also gives students the opportunity to use skills associated with "modeling with mathematics" (Mathematical Practice Standard 4).

As students learn how to classify two-dimensional figures into categories, they are also learning to use clear definitions with others and in their own reasoning, a skill related to Mathematical Practice Standard 6. In addition, because these content standards involve drawing and measuring geometrical figures using a wide variety of tools, students will have plenty of opportunity to "use appropriate tools strategically" (Mathematical Practice Standard 5).

Finally, as students look closely at shapes in order to classify them, they will be engaging in an important aspect of Mathematical Practice Standard 7 ("Look for and make use of structure").

## Conceptual Pathway Through the Grades

Geometry is a domain that extends through all grades, K–12. Several of the concepts introduced in the primary grades (e.g., shapes, modeling using geometry, geometric analysis) build and expand over the course of students' mathematics education.

Figure 11.2 highlights the concepts presented in grades K–2 that prepare students to master the standards within the Geometry domain for grades 3–5.

| Figure 11.2  |  **Geometry: Conceptual Pathway to Grades 3–5** | |
|---|---|
| **Grade Level** | **Concepts** |
| Kindergarten | • Basic two- and three-dimensional shapes <br> • Modeling objects in their environment <br> • Construction of more complex shapes |
| Grade 1 | • Composition and decomposition of plane or solid figures <br> • Perspective and orientation of combined shapes <br> • Geometric attributes <br> • How shapes are alike and different |
| Grade 2 | • Shape analysis (using sides and angles) <br> • Decomposition and combination of shapes |

With this overview complete, it's time to explore the domain's clusters and standards in greater detail.

# Grade 3

The Geometry domain in 3rd grade has just two standards, contained in one cluster.

## Reason with shapes and their attributes

The analysis and comparison of two-dimensional shapes, the content addressed in this cluster (see Figure 11.3), is identified by the Common Core mathematics standards document as critical content in 3rd grade (CCSSI, 2010g). As noted, critical areas are identified to help educators focus their instructional efforts and prioritize the most important content.

In kindergarten, students began looking at basic two- and three-dimensional shapes. In 1st and 2nd grades, they considered how shapes are alike

3.G.A

| Figure 11.3 | **Reason with Shapes and Their Attributes** |

1. Understand that shapes in different categories (e.g., rhombuses, rectangles, and others) may share attributes (e.g., having four sides), and that the shared attributes can define a larger category (e.g., quadrilaterals). Recognize rhombuses, rectangles, and squares as examples of quadrilaterals, and draw examples of quadrilaterals that do not belong to any of these subcategories.

2. Partition shapes into parts with equal areas. Express the area of each part as a unit fraction of the whole. *For example, partition a shape into 4 parts with equal area, and describe the area of each part as ¼ of the area of the shape.*

and different and were asked to recognize that shapes can have a given number of angles or faces. Now, in 3rd grade, Standard 1 (3.G.A.1) focuses students on more subtle differences and similarities between shapes, asking them to recognize that different shapes may belong to the same larger category of shapes (e.g., both rectangles and rhombuses are quadrilaterals).

Standard 2 (3.G.A.2) is also built on an understanding of shapes that students developed over several grades. In grades 1 and 2, they learned to partition circles and rectangles into equal shares (1.G.A.3, 2.G.A.3) and describe the whole using fractional language (halves, thirds, etc.); this work helped to develop students' sense of fractions as parts of a whole. Third graders are asked to partition shapes into equal areas and express the area of each part as a unit fraction. This partitioning not only strengthens their concept of unit fractions but also links unit fractions with the concept of area developed in the Measurement and Data domain (3.MD.C), helping prepare students to perform operations with fractions when they reach 4th grade (4.NF.B). Connecting the concepts of fractions, geometric figures, area measurement, and multiplication and addition provides a rich opportunity to demonstrate the interconnected nature of mathematics, which is one of the major goals of the Common Core. Students who can understand the connections that exist in mathematics rather than view mathematics as a series of unconnected topics will be better prepared to solve new and complex problems.

# Grade 4

In 4th grade, the introduction of new geometric concepts such as points, rays, and angles supports students' ability to begin formally classifying two-dimensional figures. Note that the classification and analysis of two-dimensional shapes and symmetry are identified as critical areas in 4th grade. Critical areas provide educators with a focus for their efforts, minimizing the chance that they will take on too much and be unable to implement the substantive changes the Common Core standards may require.

In this section, we'll take a closer look at the three standards in the 4th grade Geometry domain, which are grouped into a single cluster.

## Draw and identify lines and angles, and classify shapes by properties of their lines and angles

The standards in this cluster (see Figure 11.4) focus on concepts that will be new to 4th graders, including basic geometric concepts—points, lines, rays, and angles—and lines of symmetry. Angles and rays are also addressed in Cluster C of the 4th grade Measurement and Data domain (see p. 152), which focuses primarily on the concept of angles and angle measurement.

The first of the 4th grade geometry standards, Standard 1 (4.G.A.1), asks students to draw and identify all kinds of lines, rays, and angles. The

4.G.A

Figure 11.4  |  **Draw and Identify Lines and Angles, and Classify Shapes by Properties of Their Lines and Angles**

1. Draw points, lines, line segments, rays, angles (right, acute, obtuse), and perpendicular and parallel lines. Identify these in two-dimensional figures.

2. Classify two-dimensional figures based on the presence or absence of parallel or perpendicular lines, or the presence or absence of angles of a specified size. Recognize right triangles as a category, and identify right triangles.

3. Recognize a line of symmetry for a two-dimensional figure as a line across the figure such that the figure can be folded along the line into matching parts. Identify line-symmetric figures and draw lines of symmetry.

ability to classify two-dimensional figures, the aim of Standard 2 (4.G.A.2), proceeds directly from 3rd grade content (3.G.A.1), extending and formalizing the understanding that shapes in different categories may share attributes that define a larger category. Students in 4th grade are expected to integrate the new ideas about lines (parallel and perpendicular) and angles in order to classify shapes into categories and subcategories. They will continue this work in 5th grade, when they begin to classify two-dimensional figures in a hierarchy based on the figures' properties.

The final 4th grade standard for the Geometry domain, Standard 3 (4.G.A.3), introduces students to lines of symmetry—a concept that will not be formally addressed again until students reach high school, begin to study the symmetry of graphs, and learn to view symmetry from the perspective of geometric transformation.

# Grade 5

In 5th grade, students extend their ability to classify two-dimensional figures and are introduced to graphing points on the coordinate plane in order to solve problems. Note that the Common Core mathematics standards document identifies this material as supporting, not critical, content.

There are four standards for 5th grade, grouped into two clusters.

## Graph points on the coordinate plane to solve real-world and mathematical problems

Cluster A introduces the concept of the coordinate plane (see Figure 11.5).

Students who understand number lines, a concept first introduced in 2nd grade (2.MD.B.6) and explored further in 3rd and 4th grades, will be well prepared to grasp the concept of the coordinate plane. As is typical within the Common Core, Standard 1 (5.G.A.1) includes a detailed description of what students should know and do, including understanding points on the plane as distance from the axes. Although Standard 2 (5.G.A.2) requires students to represent and interpret problems by graphing points in the first quadrant of the coordinate plan, the 5th grade standards do not

Figure 11.5  |  **Graph Points on the Coordinate Plane to Solve Real-World and Mathematical Problems**

1. Use a pair of perpendicular number lines, called axes, to define a coordinate system, with the intersection of the lines (the origin) arranged to coincide with the 0 on each line and a given point in the plane located by using an ordered pair of numbers, called its coordinates. Understand that the first number indicates how far to travel from the origin in the direction of one axis, and the second number indicates how far to travel in the direction of the second axis, with the convention that the names of the two axes and the coordinates correspond (e.g., *x*-axis and *x*-coordinate, *y*-axis and *y*-coordinate).

2. Represent real world and mathematical problems by graphing points in the first quadrant of the coordinate plane, and interpret coordinate values of points in the context of the situation.

explicitly state that 5th graders' work with the coordinate plane should be *limited* to the first quadrant. Clarification comes in the text of a middle school standard within the Number System domain (6.NS.C.6), which states that students are not expected to extend their understanding of the coordinate system to include all four quadrants until 6th grade. Teachers may find this information useful when developing curriculum.

## Classify two-dimensional figures into categories based on their properties

As described in our look at the 3rd and 4th grade geometry standards, students have been developing their ability to classify two-dimensional objects since 1st grade's focus on how shapes are alike and different (1.G.A.1). Cluster B of the 5th grade Geometry domain builds on this foundation work and asks students to begin to use subcategories and classify figures in a hierarchy (see Figure 11.6).

The skills and understanding solidified in Standard 3 (5.G.B.3) and Standard 4 (5.G.B.4) will be extended further in 7th grade, when students begin to draw geometric shapes with given conditions (7.G.A.2) and describe

5.G.B

Figure 11.6  |  **Classify Two-Dimensional Figures into Categories Based on Their Properties**

3. Understand that attributes belonging to a category of two-dimensional figures also belong to all subcategories of that category. *For example, all rectangles have four right angles and squares are rectangles, so all squares have four right angles.*

4. Classify two-dimensional figures in a hierarchy based on properties.

the geometric shapes that result from slicing three-dimensional figures (7.G.A. 3). Ultimately, mastery of these concepts will support students' understanding of the more advanced geometric concepts they will encounter in high school.

# PART III

# Lesson Planning and Sample Lesson Plans

# CHAPTER 12

# Guidance for Instructional Planning

In this chapter, we provide a brief tutorial on designing lesson plans using the types of instructional strategies that appear in this guide's sample lessons. It includes a step-by-step outline for the development of lessons that make best use of proven instructional strategies and will help you ensure students master the new and challenging content represented by the Common Core standards.

## The Framework for Instructional Planning

To identify and use effective strategies to develop these lessons, we draw on the instructional planning framework developed for *Classroom Instruction That Works, 2nd edition* (Dean et al., 2012), presented in Figure 12.1.

The Framework organizes nine categories of research-based strategies for increasing student achievement into three components. These components focus on three key aspects of teaching and learning: creating an environment for learning, helping students develop understanding, and helping students extend and apply knowledge. Let's take a closer look at each.

Figure 12.1  |  **The Framework for Instructional Planning**

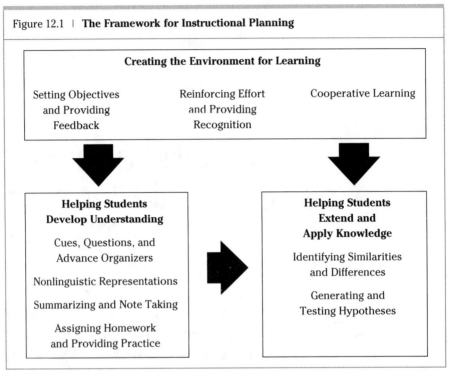

**Creating the Environment for Learning**

Setting Objectives and Providing Feedback

Reinforcing Effort and Providing Recognition

Cooperative Learning

**Helping Students Develop Understanding**

Cues, Questions, and Advance Organizers

Nonlinguistic Representations

Summarizing and Note Taking

Assigning Homework and Providing Practice

**Helping Students Extend and Apply Knowledge**

Identifying Similarities and Differences

Generating and Testing Hypotheses

*Source:* From *Classroom Instruction That Works, 2nd ed.* (p. xvi) by Ceri Dean, Elizabeth Hubbell, Howard Pitler, and Bj Stone, 2012, Alexandria, VA: ASCD; and Denver, CO: McREL. Copyright 2012 by McREL. Adapted with permission.

## Creating the environment for learning

Teachers create a positive environment for learning when they ensure that students are motivated and focused, know what's expected of them, and regularly receive feedback on their progress. When the environment is right, students are actively engaged in their learning and have multiple opportunities to share and discuss ideas with their peers.

A number of instructional strategies that help create a positive environment for learning may be incorporated into the lesson design itself. Other aspects, such as reinforcing effort and providing recognition, may not be a formal part of the lesson plan but are equally important. The following strategies are essential for creating a positive environment for learning:

- Setting objectives and providing feedback
- Reinforcing effort and providing recognition
- Cooperative learning

## Helping students develop understanding

This component of the Framework focuses on strategies that are designed to help students work with what they already know and help them integrate new content with their prior understanding. To ensure that students study effectively outside class, teachers also need strategies that support constructive approaches to assigning homework. The strategies that help students develop understanding include the following:

- Cues, questions, and advance organizers
- Nonlinguistic representations
- Summarizing and note taking
- Assigning homework and providing practice

## Helping students extend and apply knowledge

In this component of the Framework, teachers use strategies that prompt students to move beyond the "right answers," engage in more complex reasoning, and consider the real-world connections and applications of targeted content and skills, all of which help students gain flexibility when it comes to using what they have learned. The following strategies help students extend and apply knowledge:

- Identifying similarities and differences
- Generating and testing hypotheses

Figure 12.2 illustrates the three major components of teaching and learning described in *Classroom Instruction That Works,* along with the nine types, or categories, of strategies that further define the components and point you toward activities that will suit your learning objectives and support your students' success.

Figure 12.2 | **Framework Components and the Associated Categories of Instructional Strategies**

| Component | Category | Definition |
|---|---|---|
| Creating the Environment for Learning | Setting Objectives and Providing Feedback | Provide students with a direction for learning and with information about how well they are performing relative to a particular learning objective so they can improve their performance. |
| | Reinforcing Effort and Providing Recognition | Enhance students' understanding of the relationship between effort and achievement by addressing students' attitudes and beliefs about learning. Provide students with non-material tokens of recognition or praise for their accomplishments related to the attainment of a goal. |
| | Cooperative Learning | Provide students with opportunities to interact with one another in ways that enhance their learning. |
| Helping Students Develop Understanding | Cues, Questions, and Advance Organizers | Enhance students' ability to retrieve, use, and organize what they already know about a topic. |
| | Nonlinguistic Representations <br> • Graphic Organizers <br> • Pictures and Pictographs <br> • Mental Images <br> • Kinesthetic Movement <br> • Models/Manipulatives | Enhance students' ability to represent and elaborate on knowledge using mental images. |
| | Summarizing and Note Taking | Enhance students' ability to synthesize information and organize it in a way that captures the main ideas and supporting details. |
| | Providing Practice and Assigning Homework | Extend the learning opportunities for students to practice, review, and apply knowledge. Enhance students' ability to reach the expected level of proficiency for a skill or process. |

| Figure 12.2 | **Framework Components and the Associated Categories of Instructional Strategies (*continued*)** | |
|---|---|---|
| Component | Category | Definition |
| Helping Students Extend and Apply Knowledge | Identifying Similarities and Differences <br> • Comparing <br> • Classifying <br> • Creating/Using Metaphors <br> • Creating/Using Analogies | Enhance students' understanding of and ability to use knowledge by engaging them in mental processes that involve identifying ways in which items are alike and different. |
| | Generating and Testing Hypotheses | Enhance students' understanding of and ability to use knowledge by engaging them in mental processes that involve making and testing hypotheses. |

*Source:* From *Classroom Instruction That Works, 2nd ed.* (p. xviii) by Ceri Dean, Elizabeth Hubbell, Howard Pitler, and Bj Stone, 2012, Alexandria, VA: ASCD; and Denver, CO: McREL. Copyright 2012 by McREL. Adapted with permission.

# Lesson Development, Step by Step

To help you get started developing lessons that incorporate these strategies, we provide a step-by-step process to ensure that you've had an opportunity to consider where within a lesson the various strategies might be used most effectively. Those steps are as follows:

1. Identify the focus for the lesson.
2. Determine how learning will be assessed.
3. Determine the activities that will start the lesson.
4. Determine the activities that will engage students in learning the content.
5. Determine the activities that will close the lesson.

Let's look now at the details of each step and how you might incorporate the nine effective instructional strategies associated with each of the Framework's three components. We'll reference the sample lessons in this guide to illustrate particular aspects of this approach.

## Step 1: Identify the focus for the lesson

The critical first step in crafting a lesson is to identify what students should learn as a result of their engagement in the lesson activities. Setting objectives for students also means establishing the guidelines for your development of the lesson—namely, that you will select and develop only those activities that will help students meet the objectives set. A learning objective is built directly from a standard; the objectives found in this guide's sample lessons are constructed from Common Core standards and listed under the heading "Common Core State Standards—Knowledge and Skills to Be Addressed."

**Clarifying learning objectives.** To ensure that students are clear about what they will learn, you will want your lesson plans to include more specific statements of the objectives in clear, student-friendly language. Some teachers accomplish this by using stems such as "I can . . ." or "We will be able to . . ." or "Students will be able to . . ." and providing a paraphrased version of the standard, simplifying the language as necessary. In the sample lessons for this guide, such specifics may be found under the headings "Knowledge/Vocabulary Objectives" and "Skill/Process Objectives" and prefaced by either "Students will understand . . ." or "Students will be able to. . . ."

**Identifying essential questions and learning objectives.** Framing the lesson's objectives under a broader essential question provides students with alternate avenues to find personal relevance and can energize them to seek answers as they begin a unit or lesson. The essential question properly focuses on the broader purpose of learning, and it is most effective when it is open-ended and not a question that can be easily answered. Each of the sample lessons includes an essential question—the learning objectives reframed to clarify for students what value the lesson holds for them.

**Identifying foundational knowledge and possible misconceptions related to the learning objectives.** As you develop learning objectives for a lesson, consider the other skills students will need to use but that will not be the explicit focus of instruction or assessment. Our discussions of each standard in this guide identify the critical knowledge and skills that students are assumed to have mastered or practiced in lessons prior to learning the new content. In the sample lessons, you'll find these standards under the heading "Common Core State Standards—Prior Knowledge and Skills to Be Applied."

## Step 2: Determine how learning will be assessed

As important as identifying the learning objective for a lesson is identifying the criteria you will use to determine if students have met that objective. You will want to be clear about the rigor identified in the Common Core standards. As you develop scoring tools, such as checklists and rubrics that define the various levels of performance related to the objective's knowledge or skill, it is important to review the details of the objective's underlying standard to be sure you are looking for the appropriate level of mastery.

**Assessing prior knowledge.** Step 2 involves planning how to measure students' prior knowledge, especially the knowledge identified in Step 1 as prerequisite to mastery of the learning objective. For example, you might ask students to complete a short problem or share reflections on their prior experiences with similar tasks. This approach may also surface any lingering student misconceptions that you'll want to address before proceeding.

**Providing feedback.** This part of the planning process also includes deciding how you will provide students with feedback on their progress toward the outcome. Providing feedback is an important aspect of creating the environment for learning because understanding what good performance looks like, how to judge their own performance relative to a benchmark, and what they need to do to improve their performance helps students develop a sense of control over their learning. During lesson planning, you might also consider how peers can give their classmates feedback on progress toward the stated objective.

## Step 3: Determine the activities that will start the lesson

Step 3 of the planning process concerns the sequence of activities at the start of the lesson, which relate to the "Creating the Environment for Learning" component of the Framework for Instructional Planning. The beginning of each lesson should be orchestrated to capture students' interest, communicate the learning objectives, and encourage their commitment to effort.

**Communicating learning objectives.** You can share learning objectives by stating them orally, but be sure to post them in writing for reference throughout the lesson. Doing so not only reminds the class of the objectives' importance but also ensures that even students who weren't paying close attention or who came in late can identify what they are working to achieve.

**Identifying the essential question and providing a context.** Students engage in learning more readily when they can see how it connects to their own interests. The essential question you provide at the beginning of the lesson helps orient them to the purpose for learning. Students will also have a greater sense of involvement if you share with them what activities they'll be engaged in and how these activities will help build their understanding and skill. The sample lessons in this guide present this preview under the heading "Activity Description to Share with Students." It is something you might read aloud or post, along with the objectives and essential questions, as you create the environment for learning at the beginning of a lesson. To encourage greater involvement, you might also ask students to set personal goals based on the learning objectives in each activity. These personal goals may translate the learning objective to immediate goals that resonate for each student.

**Reinforcing effort.** As you develop the activities for the lesson, look for natural points where you might build in opportunities for students to receive the encouragement they need to continue their work. To reinforce student effort, we need to help students understand the direct connection between how hard they work and what they achieve. It's another way in which teachers can provide students with a greater sense of control over their own learning.

## Step 4: Determine the activities that will engage students in learning the content

At Step 4 we are at the crux of the lesson, deciding what students will do to acquire, extend, and apply knowledge or skills. This stage of planning includes identifying when formative assessment should take place, when you will provide students feedback from the assessment, and how you will ensure that students have a clear understanding of how they are doing. And, of course, you will need to decide which instructional activities will best serve the lesson's primary purposes, considering whether the activities need to focus on helping students acquire new knowledge and skill or help them extend and refine what they've already learned.

**Choosing activities and strategies that develop student understanding.** When your aim is to help students understand new information or a new process, then you will want to design activities that incorporate strategies associated with that component of the Framework for Instructional Planning. These are the strategies that help students access prior knowledge and organize new learning. Students come to every lesson with some prior knowledge, and the effective use of strategies such as using cues, questions, and advance organizers can enhance students' ability to retrieve and use what they already know about a topic in order to access something new. You can help students access and leverage their prior knowledge through simple discussion, by providing "KWL"-type advance organizers, by having students read or listen to short texts related to the targeted content, or any other number of ways. Activities incorporating the use of nonlinguistic representations (including visualization) in which students elaborate on knowledge, skills, and processes are other good ways to help students integrate new learning into existing knowledge. The strategies of note taking and summarizing also support students' efforts to synthesize information through the act of organizing it in a way that captures its main ideas and supporting details or highlights key aspects of new processes. Finally, homework can help students learn or review new content and practice skills so that they can more quickly reach the expected level of proficiency. However, you will want to think carefully about your homework practices, as the research on what makes homework effective shows mixed results. Dean and colleagues (2012) recommend that teachers design homework assignments that directly support learning objectives. Students need to understand how homework serves lesson objectives, and once homework is completed, it is important that teachers provide feedback on the assignment.

**Choosing activities and strategies that help students extend and apply knowledge.** When your aim is to help students extend or apply their knowledge or master skills and processes, they will need opportunities to practice independently. What are beneficial are activities that involve making comparisons, classifying, and creating or using metaphors and analogies. Research summarized in the second edition of *Classroom Instruction That Works* indicates that these strategies, associated with the "Helping Students Extend and Apply Knowledge" component of the Framework for Instructional Planning, are a worthwhile use of instructional time. They help raise students' levels of understanding and improve their ability to use what they learn. Because students need to understand the concepts or skills that they're comparing, you are more likely to insert these activities later in a lesson than at the outset.

Remember, too, that strategies that help students generate and test hypotheses are not meant just for science classrooms. They are a way to deepen students' knowledge by requiring them to use critical-thinking skills, such as analysis and evaluation.

**Grouping students for activities.** Cooperative learning can be tremendously beneficial, whether students are developing a new skill or understanding or applying or extending it. With every lesson you design, consider when it makes sense to use this strategy, what kind of student grouping will be most beneficial, and how these groups should be composed. Cooperative learning is a strong option, for example, when you want to differentiate an activity based on student readiness, interest, or learning style. Consider, too, that students' learning experiences will be different depending on whether you permit them to self-select into groups of their choosing or assign their group partners, whether the groups are larger (four or five students) or smaller (e.g., pair work), and whether these groups are homogeneous or heterogeneous.

Providing students with the opportunity to share and discuss their ideas with one another in varying cooperative learning arrangements lays a foundation for the world beyond school, which depends on people working interdependently to solve problems and to innovate. Interacting with one another also deepens students' knowledge of the concepts they are learning; in other words, talking about ideas and listening to others' ideas helps students understand a topic and retain what they've learned, and it may send their thinking in interesting new directions.

## Step 5: Determine the activities that will close the lesson

Bringing the lesson to a close provides an opportunity for you and students to look back on and sum up the learning experience.

During this part of the lesson, you want to return to the learning objectives and confirm that you have addressed each of them. This can be approached in one or more ways—through informal sharing, formative assessment, or even summative assessment. Students benefit from the opportunity to gauge their progress in learning. You might prompt them to reflect on the lesson in a journal entry, learning log, or response card, which can easily serve as an informal check for understanding. Note that asking students to share what they found most difficult as well as what worked well can provide you with insight you can apply during the next lesson and can use to refine the lesson just completed.

Depending upon the nature of the objective and whether the lesson appears late in the unit, you may elect to conduct a formal summative assessment. Alternatively, you may identify a homework assignment tied to the learning objective, making sure that students understand how the assignment will help them deepen their understanding or develop their skill.

\*\*\*

In the remaining pages of this guide, we offer sample lesson plans based on the Common Core standards for both English language arts/literacy and mathematics, the Framework for Instructional Planning, and the steps just outlined.

# Reading and Speaking for Understanding: Penguins on Display

**Course:** 3rd grade ELA
**Length of Lesson:** Two hours; two 60-minute class periods

## Introduction

The Common Core State Standards were developed to ensure that students complete their K–12 education experience prepared for a career or post-secondary education. A key characteristic of the K–5 ELA/literacy standards is the increased emphasis on reading informational text. As the Common Core standards state, students need many opportunities to "read widely and deeply from among a broad range of high-quality, increasingly challenging literary and informational texts" (CCSSI, 2010c, p. 10). This lesson, part of a social studies unit focused on animal habitats, is designed to give 3rd graders an opportunity to read award-winning nonfiction texts. The text complexity evident in the two books students will read requires the application of foundational and comprehension strategies.

The Common Core standards also encourage instruction that builds students' independence as learners and their critical-thinking skills. The literature circle, an instructional technique asking students to take on different roles or perspectives as they read, encourages students not only to share what they've learned, citing specific evidence, but also to assume responsibility for their learning. These are habits that are essential to success in college and in the workforce.

## Strategies from the Framework for Instructional Planning

- *Creating the Environment for Learning:* This lesson addresses two important aspects of this part of the Framework. First, at the beginning of each class session, the teacher highlights the essential question and gives students an opportunity to connect it to prior learning. Second, through partner reading and the use of literature circles, students can talk about their ideas with others while maintaining accountability for their own learning.
- *Helping Students Develop Understanding:* Several strategies are incorporated to help students understand the content presented in the two texts. During the lesson, students will read text aloud with their peers and will be prompted to access their prior knowledge about the topic. They will also practice summarizing texts during their partner reading experiences and during the literature circle.
- *Helping Students Extend and Apply Knowledge:* Students will extend and apply their knowledge and understanding by making connections between the two texts they read, to their prior knowledge, and to additional sources of information provided during the lesson.

## Common Core State Standards—Knowledge and Skills to Be Addressed

### Strand/Domain: Reading Informational Text

*Heading: Key Ideas and Details*

**RI.3.1** Ask and answer questions to demonstrate understanding of a text, referring explicitly to the text as the basis for the answers.

*Heading: Integration of Knowledge and Ideas*

**RI.3.9** Compare and contrast the most important points and key details presented in two texts on the same topic.

### Strand: Speaking and Listening

*Heading: Comprehension and Collaboration*

**SL.3.1** Engage effectively in a range of collaborative discussions (one-on-one, in groups, and teacher-led) with diverse partners on *grade 3 topics and texts*, building on others' ideas and expressing their own clearly.

d. Explain their own ideas and understanding in light of the discussion.

**SL.3.2** Determine the main ideas and supporting details of a text read aloud or information presented in diverse media and formats, including visually, quantitatively, and orally.

d. Explain their own ideas and understanding in light of the discussion.

## Common Core State Standards—Prior Knowledge and Skills to Be Applied

**Strand/Domain: Reading Informational Text**

*Heading: Key Ideas and Details*

**RI.3.2** Determine the main idea of a text; recount the key details and explain how they support the main idea.

*Heading: Craft and Structure*

**RI.3.6** Distinguish their own point of view from that of the author of a text.

**Strand: Speaking and Listening**

*Heading: Comprehension and Collaboration*

**SL.3.1** Engage effectively in a range of collaborative discussions (one-on-one, in groups, and teacher-led) with diverse partners on *grade 3 topics and texts*, building on others' ideas and expressing their own clearly.

b. Follow agreed-upon rules for discussions (e.g., gaining the floor in respectful ways, listening to others with care, speaking one at a time about the topics and texts under discussion).

## Teacher's Lesson Summary

In this lesson, students will demonstrate their ability to integrate information from two nonfiction texts: Sophie Webb's *My Season with Penguins: An Antarctic Journal*, a Sibert Award–winning book presenting the author's firsthand account of studying Adelie penguins, and Seymour Simon's *Penguins*, a nonfiction reference text. Students will partner-read excerpts from *My Season with Penguins* and summarize what they read with their partner. Using questioning strategies, students will identify information in that text to compare with the information about the Adelie penguin breed that is presented in *Penguins*. They will share their findings in a literature circle, following the rules for discussion. The literature circle gives students a structured format for talking about the text—one that encourages them to share their opinions and compare points of view.

**Essential Questions:** How does reading two different texts about the same topic help you understand the topic better? When you read the two texts, what kinds of questions do you have?
**Learning Objective:** To better understand the content of two texts by asking and answering questions with others.

### Knowledge/Vocabulary Objectives

At the conclusion of this lesson, students will understand

- The difference between an informational text (secondhand) and a journal or diary (firsthand).
- How reading different types of text about the same topic enriches knowledge.

### Skill/Process Objectives

At the conclusion of this lesson, students will be able to

- Compare and contrast two different texts on the same topic.
- Determine main ideas and key details.

### Resources/Preparation Needed

- Excerpts of the required texts, one per student; note that this lesson assumes students have had prior exposure, via a read-aloud, to the "December 1–December 16" journal entries in *My Season with Penguins: An Antarctic Journal*
- A handout on how to design text-based questions (see **Figure A: Designing Text-Based Questions,** p. 188)
- At the teacher's discretion, pair assignments for partner activities based on student readiness and behavioral expectations

## Activity Description to Share with Students

We have been learning a lot about animals and their habitats. Over the next two days, we will be taking a close look at one particular animal: Adelie penguins. We will do that by reading two different types of text. One is a firsthand account, which is a kind of writing that you might find in a journal or diary. The other is a reference book, which provides basic facts. You'll be doing your reading in pairs, and you and your partner will practice several reading strategies: using questions to help you understand what you read, summarizing what you've read, and using the text to support answers to your questions. You also will have the opportunity to discuss what you are learning about Adelie penguins in a literature circle with several of your classmates.

We can learn a lot about the world around us from reading—in school, obviously, but also out of school. When you read to learn information, you need to read a variety of texts. You also may find it helpful to talk to others (your classmates, family members, people in your community) to deepen your understanding of a topic. This lesson will teach you strategies for both finding information in texts and talking about what you've learned with others in order to understand topics better.

## Lesson Activity Sequence—Class #1

### *Start the Lesson*

1. Open the class by briefly reviewing the major events in the "December 1–December 16" journal entries from *My Season with Penguins.*
2. Post the essential questions. Ask students to share what the questions make them think about and what other reading strategies they have been learning with their partner.
3. Ask students to volunteer some things they know about penguins. Prompt them first to share some information they learned about Adelie penguins from the journal entries, and then open up the floor to information about penguins that they have learned from other sources: movies, stories, or other books about penguins or with penguins as main characters. Whenever a student offers information, prompt him or her to tell you the name of the "text" (movie, story, etc.) that was the source.

### *Engage Students in Learning the Content*

1. Tell students that they will continue reading from the firsthand account and their specific aim will be to gather more information about the Adelie penguins'

habitat and how they raise their babies. The reading assignment will be the entries for December 18 (which describes new penguin chicks hatching, how Adelies build their nests, and the local environment) and December 20 (which explains how the author and her colleague keep track of the penguins they are studying).

2. Ensure that each student has a reading partner and explain that they will read both of the journal entries and then work together to summarize the main ideas and details of the text. One student will read a page or paragraph out loud, while the other listens and then summarizes what was heard, focusing on the main ideas. At the end of a page or paragraph, they will switch roles.

3. To scaffold student learning, distribute copies of the **Designing Text-Based Questions** handout (see **Figure A,** p. 188). Explain to students that the handout will help them learn how to use questions to better understand the text that they are reading.

4. Explain to students that when they finish their reading and summarizing, they should work on their own to write two text-based questions related to the journal entries, referring to the guidelines in the handout. One must be a *Right There* question, and the other must be a *Think and Search* question. Explain the differences:

   • *Right There* questions ask students to respond at the text-based level. The words used to formulate the question and used to answer the question can be found "right there" in the text or title. Right There questions begin with words or statements such as "who is," "where is," "list," "what is," "when is," "how many," "when did," "name," or "what kind of." These questions usually elicit a one-word or short-phrase response and require one right answer.

   • *Think and Search* questions require students to "think" about how the information or ideas in the text relate to one another and to "search" through the entire passage they read to find information that applies. Think and Search questions may begin with words or statements such as "summarize," "what caused," "contrast," "retell," "how did," "explain," "find two examples," "for what reason," or "compare."

   Use the sample questions included in the Designing Text-Based Questions handout to demonstrate the formation of a Right There question and a Think and Search question.

5. Tell students that when they finish creating their questions, they should share each with their partner, getting feedback on its clarity and revising it as needed. When they are happy with their final questions, they should write the final versions on the handout. Observe students as they work, providing redirection and assistance as necessary.

## Close the Lesson

1. *Wrap up:* Review what the students accomplished during the class: read a text selection, summarized what they read, and created questions. Remind students that they worked with a classmate to help them deepen their knowledge.

2. *Assign homework:* Tell students that tomorrow, they will be asking and answering the questions they've written and discussing what they are learning about penguins in a literature circle. Briefly review this discussion format, including its various role responsibilities:

| Literature Circle Role | Description for Role Responsibilities |
| --- | --- |
| Discussion Director | Guide the discussion using the questions generated by your peers. Create a few additional questions based on what you thought about as you read the text selections. |
| Passage Master | Identify a few selections from both texts that you found interesting and would like to discuss with the group. |
| Vocabulary Enricher | Consider the following key vocabulary words: *stature, sly, curious, isolation,* and *unique.* Be prepared to lead a discussion of how the context helps or does not help to clarify the meaning of each word. |
| Connector | Think about and be prepared to share connections between what you've read and other experiences that you and your classmates have had (e.g., visiting penguins in the zoo, watching movies about penguins or with penguins as main characters). |
| Investigator | Select a topic related to the texts (e.g., Antarctica, sea ice, Emperor penguins). Find a few facts (e.g., 2 or 3) to share with the group. |
| Summarizer | Summarize what you consider to be the main ideas and key points of the texts that you read. |

*Source:* From *Literature Circles: Voice and Choice in the Student-Centered Classroom,* by Harvey Daniels, 1994, York, ME: Stenhouse. © 2002 by Stenhouse. Adapted with permission.

Give students role assignments, and explain that they should spend at least 15 minutes at home preparing for their assigned role in the literature circle: finding text selections, identifying connections, writing a summary, and so on.

## Lesson Activity Sequence—Class #2

### *Start the Lesson*

1. Open by reviewing the lesson's learning objectives and essential questions, asking students to share a few things they have learned about penguins and penguin habitats, and reviewing your behavioral expectations for group discussions.
2. Explain to students that today they will be reading a new text: a selection from the reference book *Penguins*. Once again, they will work with a partner to read and summarize the text, paragraph by paragraph. Then they will write a new set of Right There and Think and Search questions on their Designing Text-Based Questions handout. Finally, they will be discussing the questions they based on both today's text and yesterday's text in the literature circle format.

### *Engage Students in Learning Content*

1. Ensure that students have a reading partner. The partner can be the same or different from the previous class session. Ask them to partner-read pages 12–15 in *Penguins,* employing the same alternating read-and-summarize method they used the day before.
2. Remind students that after they finish their reading, they will need to generate new Right There and Think and Search questions, based on the reference book text.
3. Direct students who have finished writing their questions to turn to their partner and spend a few minutes comparing and contrasting the different information provided about penguins and their habitat found in the reference text's second-hand account and in the journal entries' firsthand account. Listen in on students' conversations, providing prompts as needed and focusing their attention on main ideas and details and the variations in the authors' point of view.
4. Organize the class into their assigned literature circles and quickly review the purpose of this discussion format: It gives them an opportunity to discuss text with their classmates and to assume responsibility for their own learning. They

have created the questions that will be asked and answered. They will guide the discussion. They will make their own connections—between the two texts and among the content in the texts and their prior knowledge and experiences.

5. Make sure every student has a copy of both texts to refer to during the discussion. Once the literature circles are underway, check in and offer guidance and support as needed.

### *Close the Lesson*

1. Ask students to write a brief learning journal entry explaining how reading the two types of text—firsthand and secondhand—enhanced their understanding of penguins and their habitat.

2. *Assign homework:* If the lesson will be extended another day, students should complete their preparation for the next literature circle, adding additional information based on the new text.

## Additional Resources for This Lesson

Information on Adelie penguins—for teacher reference or as an optional additional text for students—can be found at http://kids.nationalgeographic.com/kids/animals/creaturefeature/adelie-penguin and www.penguinscience.com/index.php

---

Figure A  |  **Handout: Designing Text-Based Questions**

---

Good readers routinely use questions to help them understand the text that they are reading. Two types of questions that readers often use are *Right There* questions and *Think and Search* questions.

***Right There* questions** are ones that you can find the answer to "right there" in the text, book, or story you are reading—and sometimes even in just the title. To write a Right There question, begin with words or statements such as "who is," "where is," "list," "what is," "when is," "how many," "when did," "name," or "what kind of." You usually can answer this type of question with one word or a short phrase, and there is one right answer.
*Examples: Where do penguins live? What is flat ice?*

***Think and Search* questions** are ones that you have to think about before you try to answer. This might mean thinking about how information or ideas in the text, book, or story you are reading relate to one another, and you may have to "search" through the entire passage that you read to find information that applies. To write a Think and Search question, begin with words or statements such as "summarize," "what caused," "contrast," "retell," "how did," "explain," "find two examples," "for what reason," or "compare."
*Examples: Find two examples that explain why penguins are considered birds but they do not fly. Explain the different stages that baby penguins go through as they mature.*

**Directions:** In the table below, write two Right There and two Think and Search questions related to each of this lesson's assigned readings. You'll fill in column one on the first day of the lesson and column two on the second day.

| Question Type | Text: *My Season with Penguins* | Text 2: *Penguins* |
|---|---|---|
| *Right There* | 1.<br><br><br>2. | 1.<br><br><br>2. |
| *Think and Search* | 1.<br><br><br>2. | 1.<br><br><br>2. |

# Using Text Structure to Understand Money

**Course:** 4th grade ELA/Social Studies
**Length of Lesson:** Two hours; two 60-minute class periods

## Introduction

The Common Core State Standards for English Language Arts and Literacy emphasize the need for students to interact with a variety of texts. The standards not only highlight the importance of informational text but also suggest that students review text and relevant information in formats such as graphs, tables, and timelines. These formats provide ways for students to observe the different types of text structures that authors rely on to convey information. Encouraging students to see the myriad ways in which text and visual representations of text are organized supports their reading experiences, enabling them to enter reading situations as detectives, looking for clues about the structure and using the structure to better understand the messages that authors convey.

This lesson is designed to give students the opportunity to interpret text in alternative formats and display these skills by developing a visual chart to represent text. It uses one of the informational texts highlighted in Appendix B to the Common Core ELA/literacy standards document (CCSSI, 2010e) and expands on the sample performance task suggested there.

## Strategies from the Framework for Instructional Planning

- *Creating the Environment for Learning:* It is important for students to understand what they are learning and how they can use their knowledge and skills to support future learning opportunities. In this lesson, students are prompted to reflect on and discuss essential questions and learning objectives.
- *Helping Students Develop Understanding:* Students will have multiple opportunities to practice interpreting different types of text structure. Both class sessions include time for students to collaborate by looking for examples similar to the structures presented and discussing what they find.
- *Helping Students Extend and Apply Knowledge:* Students will extend and apply their knowledge and understanding of text structure by analyzing a text and making decisions about how best to present that text's information in chart form so that the information will be accessible to other students.

## Common Core State Standards—Knowledge and Skills to Be Addressed

### Strand/Domain: Reading Informational Text

*Heading: Craft and Structure*

**RI.4.2** Determine the main idea of a text and explain how it is supported by key details; summarize the text.

**RI.4.5** Describe the overall structure (e.g., chronology, comparison, cause/effect, problem/solution) of events, ideas, concepts, or information in a text or part of a text.

*Heading: Integration of Knowledge and Ideas*

**RI.4.7** Interpret information presented visually, orally, or quantitatively (e.g., in charts, graphs, diagrams, time lines, animations, or interactive elements on Web pages) and explain how the information contributes to an understanding of the text in which it appears.

### Strand: Speaking and Listening

*Heading: Presentation of Knowledge and Ideas*

**SL.4.1** Engage effectively in a range of collaborative discussions (one-on-one, in groups, and teacher led) with diverse partners on *grade 4 topics and texts,* building on others' ideas and expressing their own clearly.

b. Follow agreed-upon rules for discussions and carry out assigned roles.

## Common Core State Standards—Prior Knowledge and Skills to Be Applied

**Strand: Speaking and Listening**

*Heading: Comprehension and Collaboration*

**SL.4.4** Report on a topic or text, tell a story, or recount an experience in an organized manner, using appropriate facts and relevant, descriptive details to support main ideas or themes; speak clearly at an understandable pace.

## Teacher's Lesson Summary

This lesson is part of a social studies unit designed to increase students' understanding of money management. Students will learn about different aspects of spending money by analyzing samples displayed in charts and comparing the charts with text that explains important ideas. The text analysis will focus on two types of expository text structure: Explanation/Process and Enumeration/Description. A third structure, Time Sequence, will be discussed for comparison.

The text for this lesson is an adaptation of the chapter on spending money in Steve Otfinoski's *The Kid's Guide to Money: Earning It, Saving It, Spending It, Growing It, Sharing It* (1996), which is one of the exemplar informational texts identified in Appendix B of the ELA/literacy standards document (CCSSI, 2010e). This lesson addresses two aspects of spending money: making a budget and understanding different types of advertising. Students will first analyze text and an accompanying chart that explain how to make a budget. By comparing the text and the chart, students will increase their understanding of the Explanation/Process text structure. Then they will apply the skills and knowledge they are developing to the analysis of additional pieces of text that exemplify the Enumeration/Description text structure.

**Essential Questions:** How does understanding how a text is structured help you understand the topic better? How does making your own chart help you explain a topic?

**Learning Objective:** To understand how text structure supports comprehension.

### Knowledge/Vocabulary Objectives

At the conclusion of this lesson, students will understand

- Three common expository text structures: Explanation/Process, Enumeration/Description, and Time Sequence.

### Skill/Process Objectives

At the conclusion of this lesson, students will be able to

- Interpret and summarize information read from a text.
- Incorporate summarized text information into a visual representation of the text structure.

### Resources/Preparation Needed

- Required text: Copies of a prepared adaptation of Chapter 2 of *The Kid's Guide to Money: Earning It, Saving It, Spending It, Growing It, Sharing It* by Steve Otfinoski (see **Figure A: "A Guide to Making a Budget"** and **Figure B: "Advertising—Let the Buyer Beware,"** pp. 197–200), one per student
- A prepared visual display that defines the common types of expository text structure addressed in this lesson (see Activity Description to Share with Students, beginning below)
- A collection of books, magazines, and printed online articles at various reading levels that feature the Explanation/Process text structure (e.g., pieces on how a bill becomes a law, how the three forms of government work, and how airplanes fly)
- Chart paper and markers

## Activity Description to Share with Students

In this lesson, you will learn about three different types of expository text structures: *Explanation/Process, Enumeration/Description,* and *Time Sequence.* Authors use these structures to present information about their chosen topics. They can use these structures in text, but they also can apply these structures to visual displays, such as charts and tables. Knowing the different types of structures that authors can use will help you understand the message that the author is trying to communicate. Understanding these structures can help you share what you have learned with others. We'll dig more deeply into what these structures mean, but you will find these definitions useful as a start:

**1. Explanation/Process:** This type of structure explains how something works or how something is done. It focuses on the steps in a process rather than the time.

**2. Enumeration/Description:** This type of structure describes and usually includes examples and definitions.

**3. Time Sequence:** This structure also describes, but it highlights time and includes signal words such as *first, then,* and *finally.*

For this lesson, you'll first read a selection from a book about money that explains how to make a budget, and then you will compare that explanation to the information the author presents in a chart. Next, you will read another selection of the text and create your own chart or table to capture the information that the text provides.

## Lesson Activity Sequence—Class #1

### *Start the Lesson*

1. Post the essential questions and explain the learning objective.
2. Ask students to tell you what they know about text structure. Prompting questions might include the following: *How are different texts organized? What are some different visual clues that authors use to help organize text? What do you notice about the order in which information is provided?*

3. Use the visual display you created (see p. 192) to explain Explanation/Process text structure.

4. Tell students that they will read a selection and view a chart about making a budget. Ask them to think about a time when they wanted to purchase something but did not have the money to do so. Tell students that making a budget can help them save money for something they might want to purchase or do.

### *Engage Students in Learning the Content*

1. Distribute copies of the student reading, **"A Guide to Making a Budget"** (see **Figure A,** pp. 197–198), adapted from "Chapter 2: Spending Your Money" of *The Kid's Guide to Money.* Ask students to read the steps for making a budget and the chart that depicts a budget.

2. Highlight the structures in the text, helping students distinguish between Time Sequence and Explanation/Process. Note that the text includes explicit steps but that the steps need not be undertaken in an explicit order. For example, it is important to know what needs you have every month, but you might create a list of needs before or after listing the items you want to save for.

3. Explain to students that the first step in making a budget can be to determine how much money you would like to save each week. Direct students' attention to the chart so that they can see how it reflects the different steps for making a budget.

4. Ask students to share how the chart helps them understand how to create a budget. Sample responses:
   • The headings are similar to the steps.
   • There are separate sections of the chart for most of the steps.
   • You don't have to read the table in order to understand how to create a budget.

### *Close the Lesson*

1. Divide students into small groups of three or four, with each group having a range of reading abilities.

2. Distribute sample texts (at least one per student) that include examples of the Explanation/Process text structure. Explain to students that the examples all use

the same text structure as the selection on budgeting. Ensure that your samples are accessible to the different reading levels in the class. Give students approximately 10 minutes to read and analyze their text, working on their own to find evidence that the text is an example of Explanation/Process.

3. Ask students to share with the other members in their group why their sample is an Explanation/Process and not a Time Sequence.
4. Back in a whole-class setting, invite students to explain how the Explanation/Process text structure helps them understand the process of creating a budget.
5. Tell students that they will review a different text structure during the next lesson.

## Lesson Activity Sequence—Class #2

### *Start the Lesson*
1. Review the lesson's essential questions and learning objective.
2. Ask students to share what they have learned about the Explanation/Process text structure, including what distinguishes it from the Time Sequence structure.
3. Explain to students that they will be reading another selection from *The Kid's Guide to Money* and will apply what they've learned about the Explanation/Process structure to create a chart explaining the content.

### *Engage Students in Learning the Content*
1. Distribute the student reading, **"Advertising—Let the Buyer Beware"** (see **Figure B,** p. 199), noting that it illustrates the Enumeration/Description text structure. Highlight the fact that the text includes a definition and includes an example to help the reader understand the different techniques that advertisers use.
2. Review the general skill of summarizing text.
3. Ask students to return to the groups they worked in during the previous day. Explain that each member of the group will work individually to present the text's information in a table format, but that they will first read the text and work together in their group to determine the table headings that everyone in the group will use. With the headings decided, the members of the group will fill in their individual tables, summarizing each method that advertisers use and

identifying an example to illustrate the method. Then they will come together and collaborate to turn the individual tables into a single group chart that conveys the information presented in the text.

4. Each student within every group will select one advertising strategy and example from the group's chart to share with the whole class.

### *Close the Lesson*

Ask students to explain how understanding the Enumeration/Description text structure helped them understand the text and create the table.

## Additional Resources for This Lesson

Information about text structure for teachers:

- *Creating Literacy Instruction for All Students* by Thomas G. Gunning
- *Nonfiction Matters: Reading, Writing, and Research in Grades 3–8* by Stephanie Harvey

Figure A │ **Student Reading: "A Guide to Making a Budget"**

One way to be sure you have enough money to pay for everything you need is to make a budget. A **budget** is a plan for managing your money on a regular basis. When you follow a budget, you have enough money to meet all your expenses.

**Five Steps to Making a Budget**

**Step 1:** Figure out your weekly income, the money you receive from all sources. Count only the money you get regularly—for example, a weekly allowance or money earned from a steady job such as delivering newspapers.

**Step 2:** Every week, make a list of the things you need to spend money on, such as bus fare, school supplies, and lunches.

**Step 3:** Make a list of the things you want but could get along without if you had to. These could include going to a movie or buying snacks or music.

**Step 4:** Now list any things that you need to save for.

**Step 5:** Subtract your needs (the total amount from Step 2) from your income. You can spend or save whatever's left. This is your weekly budget.

Here is a sample weekly budget:

| Total weekly income: $10.00 | | | |
|---|---|---|---|
| **Needs** | | **Wants** | |
| lunch/milk tickets | $2.00 | snacks at school | $3.00 |
| bus fare (to piano lesson) | $1.50 | movie | $3.50 |
| **Total needs:** | $3.50 | **Total wants:** | $6.50 |
| **Total weekly income:** | $10.00 | **Saving for new bike** | $2.00 |
| **Total weekly needs:** | $3.50 | **Giving donation** | $1.00 |
| **Money remaining:** | $6.50 | | |

**Budget notes:**
I need to rethink my "want" spending.
I really want to go to the movies this week, so if I bring my own snacks to school, I can cut that expense and still have money to save for the bike and make a donation to charity.

*(continued)*

Figure A  |  **Student Reading: "A Guide to Making a Budget"** (*continued*)

Even if you don't have much of a weekly income, it's still a good idea to create a budget. Managing your money is a habit that's best to develop early in life—starting right now!

Once you plan your budget, it's important to stick to it. Keep track of your spending and budget goals in a notebook. You might want to call it your **Money Management Book.** Add up each week's total spending. If you managed to keep within your budget that week, you should give yourself a great big pat on the back and 27 hip-hip-hoorays.

**Money Jars**

Here's one way to make sure you stick to your budget. Take four empty glass or plastic jars and write the following labels on them: NEEDS, OTHER SPENDING, SAVINGS, and GIVING. Put the jars on your dresser or desk in your room. Every week take your money and split it into the four jars, according to your budget. Take the money out of each jar as you need it.

---

Figure B | **Student Reading: "Advertising—Let the Buyer Beware"**

---

Every day we are bombarded by advertising—on television and radio, in magazines and newspapers, and now even on DVDs. Advertising can educate and inform consumers about products, but it can influence you to buy things you don't need or can't afford. Advertising can also be misleading and dishonest. Most manufacturers rely on advertising not just to tell people about their products but to persuade consumers to buy them. The more you are aware of the techniques of advertising, the more you will be able to look objectively at a product and make a sensible decision. Here are . . .

**Six Ways Advertisers Try to Grab You**

**1. The Bandwagon Technique**
This ad tells you that everyone else is buying the product and you'd better get on the bandwagon too, if you don't want to be left out. Don't be motivated by this attempt at peer pressure. Look for a better reason to buy a product.
*Example:* Every kid on the block is wearing Snappy Sneakers. Get your pair today and be part of the crowd!

**2. The Celebrity Endorsement**
A famous person you admire is endorsing this product. If this celebrity uses it, it must be great, right? Not necessarily. Celebrities advertise products because they get paid big bucks by the manufacturer.
*Example:* Basketball star Jamal Kamal says: "My Snappy Sneakers give me the winning edge on the court. They'll do it for you, too!"

**3. The Image-Is-Everything Technique**
The advertiser uses pleasing images, music, and fancy camera work to create a favorable impression. In truth, there may be no connection between the images and the product.
*Example:* In a TV commercial, a pretty girl runs down a country road on a sunny day wearing a pair of Snappy Sneakers. Soft, romantic music plays. As the image fades, a persuasive voice says: "Get back to nature—get a pair of Snappy Sneakers."

**4. The Emotional Appeal**
This ad also uses persuasive images to get a strong emotion from the viewer. The ad makes you happy, sympathetic, or excited—anything to get you to want to buy the product it's pitching.
*Example:* A boy is about to make a foul shot in the last seconds of a basketball game. He's the smallest player on either team, and his teammates are looking at him intently. He looks down at the Snappy Sneakers he's wearing and then up at the hoop. He throws the ball, and you watch in slow motion as it goes through the hoop, winning the game. The small guy's teammates give a cheer and lift him up on their shoulders. The picture dissolves into the words "Snappy Sneakers—Footwear for Winners."

*(continued)*

Figure B  |  **Student Reading: "Advertising—Let the Buyer Beware" (*continued*)**

### 5. Misleading Claims

This ad makes impossible claims, but does it in such a way that it never actually promises anything. You should be alert to this sneaky technique.

*Example:* An actor dressed like a doctor is sitting behind a desk with a pair of Snappy Sneakers in front of him. He says, "Wearing the right shoes can correct problem feet." (This may or may not be true, but who says Snappy Sneakers are the right shoe?)

### 6. The We're-the-Best Technique

This ad leads you to believe its product is better than other brands but doesn't offer any hard evidence.

*Example:* Four runners are lined up for a footrace. One runner is wearing Snappy Sneakers. The others wear competing brands. The runner in Snappy Sneakers crosses the finish line first. Announcer's voice: "Snappy Sneakers leave the competition in the dust every time!"

By now, you're probably convinced you need a pair of Snappy Sneakers. Go to a store and try some on. But if they don't fit—or you like another kind better or if your old sneakers are perfectly good—don't buy them.

### Becoming a Smart Consumer

Being a smart spender is a good way to get the most out of the money you have. It's important that you spend your money wisely and make smart choices when you buy.

### Shopping in Stores

We all shop at stores—department stores, boutiques, music stores, supermarkets. We want to get the most value for our money. To do that you need to think very cleverly. Let's suppose you go to the market to buy some cereal. There are about 200 different kinds of cereal on the supermarket shelves. Which one is the best value?

### *Comparison Shopping*

One way to find the best buy is to comparison shop. When you shop this way, you compare different brands of a product, whether cereal or laundry detergent. Here are a few things to look for when you comparison shop:

- **Price.** How much a product costs is important. A cheaper brand is often just as good as one that's more expensive. In supermarkets, for example, name brands often cost more than store brands, because name manufacturers spend more on promotion and advertising. Actually, the two brands may not be that different. Look for items on sale and discount too.
- **Size.** Don't be fooled by the size of the package. When you're buying food, look at the weight of the product, which should be listed on the box or container. A smaller box of cereal, for example, might contain the same amount or nearly the same as a larger box of a different brand that costs more.

# Reading and Writing Hurricane Katrina: Exploring Theme in Historical Fiction

**Course:** 5th grade ELA
**Length of Lesson:** Two hours; two 60-minute class periods

## Introduction

The Common Core standards make clear that students need multiple opportunities to interact with a wide range of texts, including different texts about the same topic. In addition, the expectation that students should write from resources is a significant shift from prior state standards. This means that rather than writing predominately from personal experiences, students need extended opportunities to write about information they encounter in both fiction and nonfiction texts and learn to cite the sources. One way to deepen students' understanding of information they encounter in such resources is to help them interpret personal experiences in light of material that they read.

During this lesson, students will identify themes in two pieces of historical fiction, citing supporting evidence, and then identify and recognize the prevalence of themes in their own lives.

## Strategies from the Framework for Instructional Planning

- *Creating the Environment for Learning:* The lesson starts with an opportunity for students to reflect on and discuss the essential questions ("Why is it important to identify themes in stories? How do themes help me as a reader?"). These questions are designed to pique students' interest in theme. Posing these questions also helps students to understand not just what they will be learning but also how it will contribute to their development as readers and writers.

- *Helping Students Develop Understanding:* This lesson includes several strategies to help students grasp its concepts. Students will connect themes they identify in stories with themes found in other texts and themes that they recognize in their own lives. Seeing the relationships among themes in multiple contexts (e.g., stories, personal experience) not only deepens students' understanding of the particular literary works they are reading but also gives them a better sense of theme as a way of making sense of literature and real life, providing a solid foundation for future learning.

- *Helping Students Extend and Apply Knowledge:* Students will extend and apply their knowledge and understanding by comparing themes in different texts and by analyzing actions and dialogue in the texts to support their observations.

## Common Core State Standards—Knowledge and Skills to Be Addressed

### Strand/Domain: Reading Literature

*Heading: Key Ideas and Details*

**RL.5.2** Determine a theme of a story, drama, or poem from details in the text, including how characters in a story or drama respond to challenges or how the speaker in a poem reflects upon a topic; summarize the text.

*Heading: Integration of Knowledge and Ideas*

**RL.5.9** Compare and contrast stories in the same genre (e.g., mysteries and adventure stories) on their approaches to similar themes and topics.

### Strand: Writing

*Heading: Text Types and Purposes*

**W.5.2** Write informative/explanatory texts to examine a topic and convey ideas and information clearly.

b. Develop the topic with facts, definitions, concrete details, quotations, or other information and examples related to the topic.

*Heading: Research to Build and Present Knowledge*

**W.5.8** Recall relevant information from experiences or gather relevant information from print and digital sources; summarize or paraphrase information in notes and finished work, and provide a list of resources.

## Common Core State Standards—Prior Knowledge and Skills to Be Applied

**Strand/Domain: Reading Literature**

*Heading: Key Ideas and Details*

**RL.5.1** Quote accurately from a text when explaining what the text says explicitly and when drawing inferences from the text.

**Strand/Domain: Reading Foundational Skills**

*Heading: Fluency*

**RF.5.4** Read with sufficient accuracy and fluency to support comprehension.

## Teacher's Lesson Summary

In this lesson, students will identify the themes in two fictional accounts of young people who survived Hurricane Katrina: *Ninth Ward* by Jewell Parker Rhodes and *I Survived Hurricane Katrina, 2005* by Lauren Tarshis. These novels clearly illustrate ways that the main characters encounter challenges as they attempt to survive precarious conditions. As a result of overcoming these challenges, the characters learn important information about themselves.

Themes evident in the texts include but are not limited to personal strength, fortitude, courage, and perseverance. Identifying themes in texts supports students in their reading because many themes repeat, and the repetitive nature of themes helps student readers construct meaning. For example, when students are familiar with the common theme of perseverance, they can make predictions about what will happen and then read to confirm or disconfirm the veracity of their predictions.

**Essential Questions:** Why is it important to identify themes in stories? How do themes help me as a reader?

**Learning Objective:** To use the themes identified in two fictional accounts of an historic event to write a text describing an experience that illustrates the same or a similar theme.

### Knowledge/Vocabulary Objectives

At the conclusion of this lesson, students will understand

- The use of thematic metaphors within a novel.
- How characters respond to challenges in a text.

### Skill/Process Objectives

At the conclusion of this lesson, students will be able to

- Identify similar themes in two different texts.
- Use concrete examples to illustrate a point.
- Write a short essay/piece of explanatory text.

### Resources/Preparation Needed

- Required texts: *Ninth Ward* by Jewell Parker Rhodes and *I Survived #3: I Survived Hurricane Katrina* by Lauren Tarshis, one copy per student; *note:* it is assumed that students will have read both novels prior to this lesson's activities
- A prepared note-taking template to support deep reading (see **Figure A: Examining Character Actions to Identify Theme,** pp. 209–210), one per student
- A prepared writing sample to share with students that illustrates the writing assignment in Class Session #2 (see p. 208)

## Activity Description to Share with Students

Stories often have themes that convey big ideas to readers. Being able to identify themes supports your development as a reader, because knowing a theme will help you understand the text. In addition, many themes repeat across different stories. You will start to recognize themes in the different kinds of stories you read and see them in your own life. This recognition can help you make better sense of texts and of the things that happen to you.

In this lesson, you will identify the themes in two stories: *Ninth Ward* and *I Survived Hurricane Katrina, 2005.* These stories are what's known as "historical fiction": made-up stories set among events that really happened. Both of these stories tell about how the main character battled challenges related to the real-life hurricane that devastated the city of New Orleans, Louisiana, in 2005. You will then make note of the themes you notice in the stories and identify an instance in which a similar theme occurred in your own life. Next, you will use what you have learned about theme in these two stories to write a nonfiction essay explaining the connection between the themes in the stories and themes from your personal experience.

## Lesson Activity Sequence—Class #1

### Start the Lesson

1. Post the essential questions and discuss the learning objective.
2. Ask students to turn to a sharing partner and explain what a theme is.
3. Ask various student volunteers to share their concept of theme, using this opportunity to clarify understanding and to correct misunderstandings.
4. Revisit the distinction between plot (what a story is about) and theme (the bigger ideas inferred from the story).
5. Ask student volunteers to share themes they have noticed in different texts. Be prepared to share several examples from familiar stories in case students need additional clarity.

### Engage Students in Learning the Content

1. Explain to students that one way to identify themes within a story is to look at what the characters do: *Character actions often demonstrate theme.* In many stories, it's possible to begin to figure out themes by paying attention to how characters respond to the personal challenges they face.
2. Distribute copies of the note-taking template **Examining Character Actions to Identify Theme** (see **Figure A**, pp. 209–210), which students will use to guide their reflection on the lesson's two texts. Highlight the need to find and cite specific information in the text rather than describe general impressions. Tell students that their goal is to find examples of actions and use these to infer themes. Remind them that each novel may have more than one theme.

Model the process of filling out the table, using an example from either text. For example, one of the challenges Lanesha faces in *Ninth Ward* is her fear of darkness. She responds to it by learning to trust TaShon and getting him to trust her. Here is the relevant text, which should be posted for students to see:

> "You should sleep, Lanesha. I'll stay awake in case Mama Ya-Ya needs anything. That's why you're awake, isn't it?"
>
> "Yes." But Mama Ya-Ya isn't the only reason. I don't want to tell TaShon about the rising water.
>
> "Try to sleep, Lanesha. I'll keep watch."
>
> "That's okay, TaShon."
>
> "No, please. I can look out for you and Mama Ya-Ya."
>
> TaShon's words feel like a cool breeze. No one has looked out for me and Mama Ya-Ya, except me and Mama Ya-Ya.
>
> "I'll sleep," I say. But I know I won't. Just in case. . . just in case. . . . Don't think it, I tell myself. But I think it anyway. Just in case the water keeps rising.
>
> "Good," says TaShon, and I can tell by his voice that he's feeling proud. "I'm on duty," he says. "Spot's second-in-command." Even though I can't see him, I know he's smiling. (Rhodes, 2010, pp. 174–175)

Lanesha's actions and words tell a reader that she feels safe with TaShon and that she experiences someone taking care of her in a way that hasn't happened before. Applicable themes are courage and perseverance.

One of Barry's challenges in *I Survived Hurricane Katrina, 2005* is that he's separated from his parents. He responds by relying on his knowledge of the neighborhood to find a safe place to wait out the storm:

> The house hit the tree with a smash and a groan and then got stuck there. The current started to drag Barry. He fought against it and somehow managed to swim to the house. He reached up and grabbed hold of a window frame, careful of the jagged glass around the edge. A piece of wood fell into the water right next to Barry. Its bright color glowed in the ghostly light: sky blue. Barry

stared at the house. Could it be? Yes. It was Abe's house. Abe Mackay's. And that wasn't all. The sound of ferocious barking rang out. Somewhere in that ripped-apart house was Cruz. The killer dog. (Tarshis, 2011, p. 57)

Here, Barry's actions and words tell the reader that he pays attention to his surroundings and uses what he knows to determine where he is and what dangers he may face. Themes include strength and trusting yourself. Ask students to skim back through both books, rereading passages in which the characters' actions might offer clues to the texts' themes, and then fill out their organizer.

### *Close the Lesson*

1. Ask students to share two examples of challenges and corresponding evidence from their handouts with a partner. Partners will listen to ensure that the identified challenges are supported with evidence from the text.
2. Ask students to share the themes they think are in the texts with their partners.
3. Ask students to share several examples with the whole group. Listen to ensure that the students identify challenges and conclusions that are supported by the text. Also listen to ensure that the themes are appropriate for the text. If they are not appropriate, ask probing questions about the books that will lead students to reexamine the evidence. Ask students to talk about how the authors of *Ninth Ward* and *I Survived Hurricane Katrina, 2005* present similar events and themes in different ways, prompting them to consult their handouts and provide text-based evidence for their conclusions.
4. *Assign homework:* Ask students to think about other books or stories they've read with events and themes that are similar to the ones they identified for each text. To prepare for the writing exercise they'll be doing the following day, they should also think about one or two instances from their own lives that illustrate the themes identified in the novels (perseverance, courage, strength, trusting yourself, trusting others). Mention that the circumstances in their own lives may not be as dramatic as those in the two novels but that they should look for experiences that are *thematically similar.* Be prepared to share an example from your own experience if students are confused about the assignment.

## Lesson Activity Sequence—Class #2

### *Start the Lesson*

1. Review the essential question.
2. Ask students to share their responses to the homework assignment with the rest of the class.
3. Share a writing sample that you created that demonstrates writing about theme.

### *Engage Students in Learning the Content*

1. Explain to students that they will now draft an essay—a piece of explanatory text—that first describes the themes evident in *Ninth Ward* and *I Survived Hurricane Katrina, 2005,* using specific evidence from the texts, and then compares the themes in the two novels with a similar theme in their own life.
2. As students work on their essays, interact with them, one on one. Ask them to describe the connection between the themes in the books and the personal experience they are writing about. Remind students that identifying themes can help us get a better understanding of not only what is happening in the texts we read but also what has happened or is happening in our own lives.

### *Close the Lesson*

1. Gather the students and ask several to share the personal example of overcoming a challenge they have decided to write about.
2. Create a visual display (e.g., wall poster, whiteboard presentation, pocket chart) that captures the variety of themes that students discuss. Post the display in the classroom and remind students that they should look for these themes as they read additional literature.
3. *Homework:* Ask students to complete their essays and be prepared to share their work during the next lesson.

## Additional Resources for This Lesson

Good information on theme can be found at www.readwritethink.org.

Figure A  |  **Handout: Examining Character Actions to Identify Theme**

| Personal Challenges Lanesha Faced *Describe and provide page #s* | Actions Lanesha Took in Response to These Challenges *Describe and provide page #s* | What Lanesha Said in Response to These Challenges *Quote and provide page #s* | What This Tells Me About Lanesha |
| --- | --- | --- | --- |
| | | | |

Themes I think are in *Ninth Ward:*

|  |
| --- |
| |

(*continued*)

Figure A  |  **Handout: Examining Character Actions to Identify Theme (*continued*)**

| Personal Challenges Barry Faced *Describe and provide page #s* | Actions Barry Took in Response to These Challenges *Describe and provide page #s* | What Barry Said in Response to These Challenges *Quote and provide page #s* | What This Tells Me About Barry |
|---|---|---|---|
| | | | |

Themes I think are in *I Survived Hurricane Katrina, 2005:*

# Understanding Equivalent Fractions

**Course:** 3rd grade Mathematics
**Length of Lesson:** Two hours; four 30-minute class periods

## Introduction

In 3rd grade, students begin to develop a deep understanding of fraction concepts. Up to this point in their education, students will have had minimal exposure to the fraction concepts included in the Common Core State Standards, and what exposure they have had will have come through geometric representation of halves, thirds, and fourths. Grade 3 marks the first time students are expected to understand fraction notation as well as equivalent fractions with denominators of 2, 3, 4, 6, and 8.

This lesson is designed to provide a foundation for building students' understanding of equivalent fractions. Additional problems, practice, exploration, and discussion will be needed to refine and cement this understanding.

Note that this 3rd grade lesson focuses on content that state mathematics standards typically address in later grade levels. The National Council of Teachers of Mathematics' *Principles and Standards for School Mathematics* (2000), for example, identifies equivalent fractions as a topic students should master by the end of grade 5. Due to the repositioning of this content within the progression of elementary mathematics, even seasoned 3rd grade teachers may find teaching this material to be an unfamiliar challenge.

## Strategies from the Instructional Planning Framework

- *Creating the Environment for Learning:* Both the essential question ("Why are equivalent fractions important to us?") and learning objective ("To understand the concept of a fraction, be able to recognize equivalent fractions, and compare fractions") will be visible in the classroom—posted and written in student-friendly language. Students will be asked to personalize the learning objectives by identifying how the objectives connect to their lives outside the classroom. The teacher will provide immediate corrective feedback in whole-group and individual contexts.

- *Helping Students Develop Understanding:* Students will be engaged in the mathematics content through real-world situations that interest them—in this case, technology and digital devices like mp3 players and tablets. They will have opportunities to engage in cooperative learning and independent practice throughout the lesson. Small-group instruction will also be incorporated, differentiated by student readiness. The use of nonlinguistic representation in the lesson will be critical, providing a visual reference for students learning about equivalent fractions. Teacher cues and questions will help to assess student understanding and facilitate mathematical dialogue in the classroom.

- *Helping Students Extend and Apply Knowledge:* During this lesson, students will apply mathematical content knowledge in a real-world situation—comparing and contrasting the storage space of electronic devices in a variety of formats.

## Common Core State Standards—Knowledge and Skills to Be Addressed

### Standards for Mathematical Practice

**MP3** Construct viable arguments and critique the reasoning of others.

**MP5** Use appropriate tools strategically.

**MP6** Attend to precision.

**MP7** Look for and make use of structure.

### Standards for Mathematical Content

**Domain: Number and Operations—Fractions**

*Cluster: Develop Understanding of Fractions as Numbers\**

**3.NF.A.3** Explain equivalence of fractions in special cases, and compare fractions by reasoning about their size.

---

\*Grade 3 expectations in this domain are limited to fractions with denominators of 2, 3, 4, 6, and 8.

a. Understand two fractions as equivalent (equal) if they are the same size or the same point on a number line.

b. Recognize and generate simple equivalent fractions (e.g., $\frac{1}{2}$ = $\frac{2}{4}$, $\frac{4}{6}$ = $\frac{2}{3}$). Explain why the fractions are equivalent, e.g., by using a visual fraction model.

c. Express whole numbers as fractions, and recognize fractions that are equivalent to whole numbers. *Examples: Express 3 in the form 3 = $\frac{3}{1}$; recognize that $\frac{6}{1}$ = 6; locate $\frac{4}{4}$ and 1 at the same point of a number line diagram.*

d. Compare two fractions with the same numerator or the same denominator by reasoning about their size. Recognize that comparisons are valid only when the two fractions refer to the same whole. Record the results of comparisons with the symbols >, =, or <, and justify the conclusions, e.g., by using a visual fraction model.

## Common Core State Standards—Prior Knowledge and Skills to Be Applied

**Domain: Geometry**

*Cluster: Reason with Shapes and Their Attributes*

**2.G.A.3** Partition circles and rectangles into two, three, and four equal shares, describe the shares using the words *halves, thirds, half of, a third of,* etc., and describe the whole as two halves, three thirds, four fourths. Recognize that equal shares of identical wholes need not have the same shape.

**Domain: Number and Operations—Fractions**

*Cluster: Develop Understanding of Fractions as Numbers*

**3.NF.A.1** Understand a fraction $\frac{1}{b}$ as the quantity formed by 1 part when a whole is partitioned into $b$ equal parts; understand a fraction $\frac{a}{b}$ as the quantity formed by $a$ parts of size $\frac{1}{b}$.

**3.NF.A.2** Understand a fraction as a number on the number line; represent fractions on a number line diagram.

## Teacher's Lesson Summary

This lesson is divided into four parts, which could be presented over the course of four days or combined and presented in fewer days, depending on the portion of the school day allotted for mathematics. In the lesson, students will explore fraction concepts by working with fraction strips and fraction circles. They will also use a number line to identify equivalent fractions and compare two fractions with the same numerator or same denominator. Once students understand equivalent fractions, they will be asked to generate two equivalent fractions, compare two fractions, and explain their reasoning.

In order to properly support student success, you will need to pre-assess students to determine their current understanding of fraction concepts; you may need to review fraction concepts, especially those presented in 2.G.A.3 and 3.NF.A.1–2, with students before teaching this lesson. It's also advisable to think through what you know about your students' background, extracurricular activities, hobbies, and interests; use this knowledge to provide contextual background for the learning objectives. Learning becomes more meaningful when students are able to connect classroom assignments to the world outside the classroom.

Throughout the lesson, be sure to ask students to explain their reasoning on a frequent and regular basis in order to gain formative assessment data on their developing comprehension and skills. Additional resources are provided at the end of the lesson to support integrating technology into the lesson or making connections to literature.

**Essential Question:** Why are equivalent fractions important to us?

**Learning Objective:** To understand the concept of a fraction, be able to recognize equivalent fractions, and compare fractions.

### Knowledge/Vocabulary Objectives

At the conclusion of this lesson, students will understand that

- Two fractions are equal if they are of equal size.
- Two fractions are equal if they are at the same location on the number line.
- Two fractions can only be compared when they are part of the same whole.

### Skill/Process Objectives

At the conclusion of this lesson, students will be able to

- Recognize and generate equivalent fractions.
- Explain why two fractions are equal (e.g., use a visual model).
- Recognize fractions that are equivalent to whole numbers (e.g., $\frac{1}{1} = 1$; $\frac{3}{1} = 3$; $\frac{4}{4} = 1$ are at the same point of a number line diagram).
- Compare two fractions with the same numerator or same denominator by reasoning about their size.

- Use the symbols >, =, and < to compare two fractions with the same numerator or same denominator and justify their conclusions.

### Resources/Preparation Needed

- Scissors, one pair per student
- Prepared sets of four 8" × 1" strips of construction paper, each strip a different color, plus three paperclips and one plastic storage bag, one set per student plus extras)
- A prepared practice activity handout focused on recognizing and generating equivalent fractions (see **Figure A: Recognizing and Generating Equivalent Fractions Practice Activity,** p. 228), one per student
- Prepared fraction circles (wholes, halves, thirds, fourths, sixths, and eighths), one set per student
- A blank sheet of unlined white paper, one per student
- Prepared 8" × 2" strips of construction paper, one per student
- A prepared practice activity handout focused on comparing fractions (see **Figure B: Comparing Fractions Practice Activity,** p. 229), one per student

## Activity Description to Share with Students

What is a fraction? When do we use fractions? What do the numerator and denominator in a fraction represent? We are about to start a lesson that will help you understand when two fractions represent the same amount of something (equivalent fractions). You will use hands-on tools and number lines to generate equivalent fractions and compare two fractions using >, =, and < symbols. We will also examine some real-world connections to the topic of equivalent fractions, including eating pizza and storing media files on digital devices like an iPod or an iPad.

## Lesson Activity Sequence—Class #1

### Start the Lesson

1. Ask students to share what they know about fractions.
2. Ask students where they see or use fractions in their lives, drawing their attention to connections between the real world and fraction concepts. Students may offer examples such as portioning food, sharing space, sports matches, money,

time, and so forth. Use a graphic organizer, such as the one below, to display student contributions:

| Where do you see/use fractions? | Types of fractions used . . . |
| --- | --- |
| Putting fuel in a car | ½ tank, ¼ tank, etc. |
| Cutting up a sandwich | ½ sandwich, ¼ sandwich, etc. |
| Basketball game | ½ game ("first half and second half"); ¼ game ("first quarter, second quarter," etc.) |

3. Post and explain the essential question and learning objectives for this class session:
   - To understand the concept of a fraction
   - To be able to recognize equivalent fractions
   - To be able to compare fractions
4. Ask students to write one sentence in their notebook about what they hope to learn relating to fractions.

### Engage Students in Learning the Content

1. Distribute sets of fraction strips: four different-colored strips of paper, each eight inches long. Once every student has a set, explain that they will be creating a model of different fractions that can be used to help them identify equivalent fractions. Using a different-colored strip for each fraction, guide students through the process of creating strips equivalent to one whole, halves, fourths, and eighths. Model for students how to cut their strips into the fractional parts and label each part as shown:

| 1 | | | | | | | |
| --- | --- | --- | --- | --- | --- | --- | --- |
| ½ | | | | ½ | | | |
| ¼ | | ¼ | | ¼ | | ¼ | |
| ⅛ | ⅛ | ⅛ | ⅛ | ⅛ | ⅛ | ⅛ | ⅛ |

2. Throughout the activity, present students with problems:
   - Hold up a piece you have cut and ask students: *If you were to represent this part as a fraction, what would it be? Why?*
   - Hold up the one-half piece you have cut and ask students: *If you were to use the half part to cover the strip labeled "1," how many parts would you need?* Then: *How can you write this as a fraction? (²⁄₂)* Repeat for the quarter piece.
   - Model the meaning of *numerator* and *denominator* for students: *This is one out of two pieces that cover the one whole.* (Write the fraction ½.) *This is one out of four pieces that cover the one whole.* (Write the fraction ¼.)
   - *What do you think the numerator and the denominator in a given fraction represent?*
   - Show the students two one-quarter pieces. Ask: *What fraction would you write to name these two parts of the whole? How would you know your answer is correct?*
   - *Predict how many one-eighth parts you will need to cover the one whole strip exactly, then test your prediction.*
   - *The number "1" can also be written as various fractions: ²⁄₂, ⁴⁄₄, and ⁸⁄₈. Write other fractions that would represent the number "1" and explain your reasoning.*
   - *The number "2" could also be written as various fractions: ²⁄₁, ⁴⁄₂, and ⁶⁄₃. Why is this true?*
   - *What other whole numbers could you write as a fraction?* (Students may need to use additional whole strips to model this concept visually.)
   - *How many one-quarter parts are needed to cover the one-half part exactly? How do you know? Why would we need to use a 2 for the numerator in the fraction ²⁄₄? Does this mean that ½ and ²⁄₄ are equivalent fractions?* Repeat for other fractions.
3. Have students work in pairs to write as many equivalent fractions as they can in five minutes. If necessary, students should use their fraction strips as a visual model to help them to write the fractions on paper or a whiteboard and explain their equivalencies to their partner. As students work, be sure to check for understanding and clarify any misconceptions with the entire class. Ask students to paperclip the like fractions together and store all the strips in a plastic storage bag in their desk for future use.

### Close the Lesson

1. Display a set of sample mp3 player or tablet capacity bars, as illustrated here:

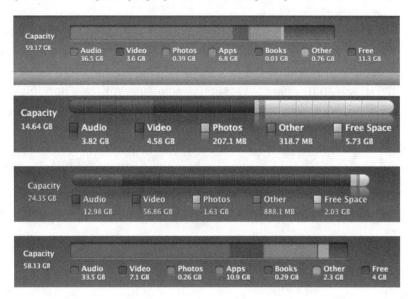

2. Discuss with students what the bar represents and what *memory* and *capacity* mean. If you can print and talk about the capacity bar of one of your own devices, students will be more engaged ("As you can see, I use one-half of my storage for audio files—music and audio books—and only one-fourth of my storage for video."). Ask students questions ("Approximately how much memory is being used by audio files? Video files? Apps?"), requesting that they frame their answers using fractions.

3. Explain to students that if they or someone in their family owns an mp3 player or tablet, you would like them to take a screenshot of that device's capacity bar and e-mail it to you tonight. With an iPod, students can find the capacity bar when they plug their device into their computer, open iTunes, and choose the device. The easiest way to take a screenshot is to use the Print Screen key and then paste the image into e-mail; model this for students. If you like, prepare and distribute a small sheet of instructions on how to take a screenshot or post these

instructions on your class website. Explain that you will be using the screen-shots in class the next day.

4. Close by reviewing the learning objectives with students and asking them to give you a thumbs-up or thumbs-down to represent their individual understanding of each objective; make note of where the areas of uncertainty seem to be and of the students who express greater or lesser degrees of understanding. This kind of informal formative assessment, along with observations and student explanations, is recommended as a way to monitor student understanding throughout the lesson.

## Lesson Activity Sequence—Class #2

### *Start the Lesson*

1. Display various capacity bars from the screenshots students e-mailed to you the night before. Assign a number to each capacity bar, and have students determine the fraction that would represent various types of files for each capacity bar. (*Note:* If students do not have access to this technology, another option is to use the Fraction Bar virtual manipulative at http://nlvm.usu.edu/en/nav/frames_asid_203_g_2_t_1.html?from=grade_g_2.html.)

2. Explain to students that in today's class, you will continue to review equivalent fractions but will also include fractions of denominators 3 and 6. Explain, too, that during Class Session #1, they used fraction strips as their physical models; today they will learn to use fraction circles to model equivalent fractions.

3. Review the essential question and learning objectives with students:
   • To understand the concept of a fraction
   • To be able to recognize equivalent fractions
   • To be able to compare fractions

### *Engage Students in Learning the Content*

1. Divide the students into two or three homogeneous groups based on the readiness data you gathered at the close of the previous class session (e.g., a "struggling" group, an "on-target" group, and an "advanced" group). Distribute to every

student a set of fraction circles: the whole circle and the parts that represent halves, thirds, fourths, sixths, and eighths. Use the small groups to provide differentiated guided instruction in order to lead students to an understanding of equivalent fractions. Facilitate a discussion around the following points:

- *Find the "whole" fraction circle. Choose any of the five other colors to cover the whole. What fraction names one of the pieces you chose?*
- *Find the part that represents ⅓. Look for another color you could use to cover that part exactly and write a fraction sentence to represent the situation. [⅓ = ⅖]*
- *Find all equivalent fractions to ½. Write a fraction sentence for each.*

2. Have students work independently for five minutes to write as many equivalent fraction sentences as possible, using their fraction circles to support their work. Explain that they must write at least one fraction with the following denominators: 2, 3, 4, 6, and 8.

3. Distribute the **Recognizing and Generating Equivalent Fractions Practice Activity** handout (see **Figure A**, p. 228). Provide corrective feedback to students as they complete the worksheet.

### *Close the Lesson*

1. Call the class back together and take a few minutes to clarify any common misconceptions you observed during students' independent practice time.

2. Review the learning objectives, and ask students to compare their understanding today to their understanding after the prior class. Are they making progress?

3. Have students write a one-sentence summary of their learning for the day to be turned in and used as a formative assessment to guide the instruction in the next lesson.

## Lesson Activity Sequence—Class #3

### *Start the Lesson*

1. Use a fraction circle to review the work from the previous class session and the lesson's objective: understanding and generating equivalent fractions with denominators of 2, 3, 4, 6, and 8.

2. Mention to students that fraction circles call to mind charts that display the memory capacity of computers and flash drives. On the "Properties" screen of some computers, the memory displayed is a circle showing space that is used and space that is available (demonstrate this via computer projection or with prepared examples as seen here). Display various memory circle graphs and have students approximate in a fraction the amount of memory used and the amount of memory still available.

3. As preparation for the session's focus on number lines, activate students' prior knowledge by dividing the class into pairs and asking the pairs to draw a number line and generate, in writing, a statement of what a number line is and what a number line's purpose is. After a few minutes, ask various pairs of students to share their responses in order to generate a class definition. Ask students to predict how a number line would incorporate fractions and what a number line including fractions might look like. Capture these responses.

4. Explain to students that they will now start expanding their knowledge of equivalent fractions to the number line. They will continue to use their fraction strip and fraction circle models to aid in their understanding as they work toward the following learning objectives:

   • Understand that two fractions are equal if they are at the same location on the number line.

   • Recognize and generate equivalent fractions.

### Engage Students in Learning the Content

1. Distribute to every student an 8" × 1" strip of construction paper and a blank, unlined sheet of white paper. Guide students through the process of creating a number line on the white paper. Students will begin by using the strip of construction paper to draw an 8" line on the white paper. Next, they will place a point at each end of the line, labeling one end "0" and the other "1." Model for students how to fold their strip in half, align the strip with their number line, and place a point at the fold mark. Discuss with students why this point should be labeled ½. Continue this process of modeling until students have created a number line like the one illustrated, including all fractions of denominators 2, 3, 4, 6, and 8. (*Note:* This exercise could be confusing for some students; it may be necessary to scaffold student learning by having students create separate number lines for each different denominator and go back later to create one number line that integrates all fractions of denominators 2, 3, 4, 6, and 8.)

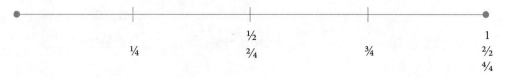

2. Throughout the process, ask students questions such as the following:
   - *Look at the ½ mark, now also labeled ²⁄₄. Why is it OK to do this? Does this mean that they are equivalent?*
   - *What are some ways we could be more accurate when it comes to placing the marks for thirds and sixths?* (One idea might be to use a ruler to help mark the thirds, and then the sixths would be halfway between the thirds marks. If you decide to use a ruler, it may be helpful to use a 9" strip of paper rather than the 8" strip suggested. Be sure to walk students through the reasoning for this strategy.)
3. Have students work with a partner to use the number line to help them write as many equivalent fraction sentences as possible in five minutes. As they work, be sure to check for understanding, provide corrective feedback, and clarify any misconceptions with the whole class.

4. Tell students that ½ is equivalent to ⁴⁄₈. Then ask students to respond to the following prompt, working independently: *Write in words how you can use a number line to prove that the statement "½ = ⁴⁄₈" is true.*

### Close the Lesson

1. Review the class session's learning objectives.
2. Ask students to pull out a scrap of paper, write their name on it, and then write either a star (meaning they understand or have mastered these objectives) or a question mark (meaning they do not yet understand or haven't yet mastered the objectives). Collect these exit slips and review them to guide your differentiation efforts.

## Lesson Activity Sequence—Class #4

### Start the Lesson

1. Remind students that over the past few days they have been studying equivalent fractions; now, they will be looking at fractions that may not be equivalent. Their challenge will be to determine which fraction is larger. To do this, they will continue to use the comparison tools they have used so far: fraction strips, fraction circles, and the number line.
2. Review the class session's learning objectives:
   - Compare two fractions with the same numerator or same denominator by reasoning about their size.
   - Use symbols >, =, and < to compare two fractions with the same numerator or same denominator.
   - Understand two fractions can only be compared when they are part of the same whole.
3. Take a minute to review with students the symbols >, =, and < and how to use them in a number sentence.
4. Give each student an 8" × 2" strip of construction paper. Have students compare the new strip to the 8" × 1" strip they have been using. Ask students: *If you were to cut the 8" × 2" strip in half, would it be equivalent to the 8" × 1" half we cut a*

*few days ago? Why, or why not?* Guide students to the realization that in order to compare fractions, they must be comparing the same whole.

### Engage Students in Learning the Content

1. Guide students to use their visual models of fraction strips and fraction circles to compare a variety of given examples of two fractions of either the same numerator or same denominator.
2. Have students write a fraction sentence comparing two given fractions.
3. Read the following situation to the students:

   *Several students attend a birthday party that has a large pepperoni pizza and a small cheese pizza for lunch. One of the boys at the party, Ian, says he is going to eat half of the cheese pizza. Another boy, Devin, claims he is starving and he is going to eat half of the pepperoni pizza.*

   Remind students that they know $\frac{1}{2} = \frac{1}{2}$. Ask students: *Does $\frac{1}{2} = \frac{1}{2}$ in this story? Are Ian and Devin going to eat the same amount of pizza?* Have students explain their reasoning.
4. Read the following situation aloud:

   *Tasha saved $20 to spend while shopping. Finley saved $8 to spend. They both spent $\frac{1}{4}$ of their money.*

   Remind students that they know $\frac{1}{4} = \frac{1}{4}$. Ask students: *Does $\frac{1}{4} = \frac{1}{4}$ in this story? Did Tasha and Finley spend the same amount of money?* Have students explain their reasoning.
5. Facilitate a discussion to guide students to the following understanding: *In order to compare fractions, the fractions must both be a part of the same whole.*
6. Have students use a number line to compare a variety of given examples of two fractions of either the same numerator or same denominator. Facilitate a discussion to guide students to the following understanding: *The farther a number is to the right on a number line, the larger it is in size.*
7. Have students compare the following fractions using any tool they choose. Ask them to explain in writing why they chose the tool they did and how they used the tool to make each comparison.

   (a) $\frac{4}{4}$ and $\frac{3}{4}$           (b) $\frac{2}{6}$ and $\frac{5}{6}$           (c) $\frac{1}{4}$ and $\frac{1}{8}$

8. Allow students to self-select into pairs to complete the **Comparing Fractions Practice Activity** handout (see **Figure B,** p. 229). As the pairs work collaboratively on the task, observe their work and discussion to check for understanding, provide corrective feedback, and clarify any misconceptions with the whole class. Offer more comprehensive support to those students who are still struggling with comparing fractions.

### *Close the Lesson*

1. Display two mp3 player or tablet capacity bars (e.g., "Sophie's Device" and "Hunter's Device"), and ask students to approximate how much space is being used on video or on audio, is free, and so on. Then have students compare the two graphs and write a number sentence to represent the capacity of each device. For example:

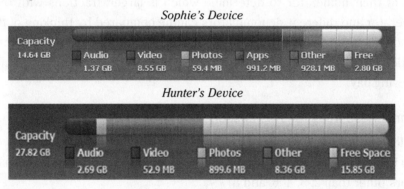

- *Sophie's device has approximately ¾ of the space used. Hunter's device has approximately ½ of the space used. Sophie's ¾ > Hunter's ½.*
- *Sophie's device has approximately ½ of the space used by video. Hunter's device has zero space used by video. Hunter's 0 < Sophie's ½.*

Point out to students that Sophie's device (14.64 GB) has a total capacity of about ½ of the total capacity of Hunter's device (27.82 GB). Sophie's device has used ¾ of the capacity and Hunter's device has used ½ of the capacity. Yes, ¾ is greater than ½, but has Sophie's device actually used more storage space than Hunter's device has? How could we figure this out? Have students model this concept with their fraction strips or with a diagram. Have students justify their reasoning to an elbow partner and critique one another's reasoning.

2. Repeat Step 1 with two computer device memory circles. This is also a good time to talk about the same fraction representing different amounts, such as when comparing devices with different storage capacities. For example, an iPod with 8 GB of storage that has ¼ of memory used by audio and an iPod with 16 GB of storage that has ¼ of memory used by audio have different amounts of audio on file because different wholes are being compared.

3. Review the learning objectives with students, making connections between the visual fraction models and the number line.

4. *Homework:* Ask students to explore any patterns that might exist when comparing fractions of the same numerator or fractions of the same denominator. For example, fractions with the same denominator can be compared by looking only at their numerator to determine which is larger; fractions with the same numerator and different denominators can be compared by thinking of the fraction divided into fewer pieces, so the smaller denominator is in fact the larger fraction. Explain that they will be sharing their discoveries with the class the following day.

## Additional Resources for This Lesson

The following can support mastery of this lesson's learning objectives:

- Ratio Blaster at www.arcademicskillbuilders.com (includes fractions with denominators other than 2, 3, 4, 6, and 8)
- Dirt Bike Comparing Fractions at www.arcademicskillbuilders.com (includes fractions with denominators other than 2, 3, 4, 6, and 8)
- Balloon Pop Fractions at www.sheppardsoftware.com/mathgames/fractions/Balloons_fractions1.htm (students pop fraction balloons in order from least to greatest—has the fraction notation as well as a visual model; includes fractions with denominators other than 2, 3, 4, 6, and 8)
- Thirteen Ways of Looking at a Half at http://pbskids.org/cyberchase/math-games/thirteen-ways-looking-half/ (students use a visual model to find ways ½ could be represented in the model)

- Equivalent Fractions at http://illuminations.nctm.org/ActivityDetail.aspx?ID=80 (students see the fraction, a visual model—either square or circle, as well as the number line to facilitate the connection among the three; includes fractions with denominators other than 2, 3, 4, 6, and 8)
- Fun with Fractions lesson at http://illuminations.nctm.org
- Science Network—*What Is One-Half?* K2 Math Education Video with Ted Tunes at http://youtube.com/QXekR9HLSC4 (a good introduction to the Equivalent Fractions unit)
- Cover Up and Uncover Game at www.ehow.com/way_5299621_fraction-games-second-grade.html

*Literature Connections:* Literature is an excellent way to provide a real-world connection for students as well as to make content connections across disciplines. The following texts support the mathematical content of the lesson and could be introduced in concurrent ELA class sessions to reinforce the mathematics learning:
- *The Doorbell Rang* by Pat Hutchins
- *Gator Pie* by Louise Mathews
- *The Hershey's Milk Chocolate Bar Fractions Book* by Jerry Pallotta and Rob Bolster
- *Apple Fractions* by Jerry Pallotta and Rob Bolster
- *Give Me Half* by Stuart J. Murphy and G. Brian Karas
- *Jump, Kangaroo, Jump!* by Stuart J. Murphy and Kevin O'Malley

Figure A  |  **Handout: Recognizing and Generating Equivalent Fractions Practice Activity**

**Shade the fraction strips and the fraction circles to represent the equivalent fraction sentence.**

1. ⅓ = ⅖                                    2. ¾ = ⁶⁄₈

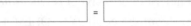

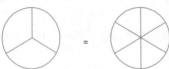    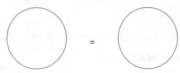

**Complete the following fraction sentences and draw a picture to represent each sentence.**

3. (a)  ½ = ?⁄₈                    (b) Draw a picture for this fraction sentence.

4. (a)  ⁴⁄₆ = ?⁄₃                   (b) Draw a picture for this fraction sentence.

5. (a)  ?⁄₄ = 1                     (b) Draw a picture for this fraction sentence.

6. The fraction ⅖₈ is equivalent to ¼. Explain in words why this is true; draw a picture to help you.

Figure B  |  **Handout: Comparing Fractions Practice Activity**

**Complete the fraction strips or circles, then complete each statement with a symbol: >, =, or <.**

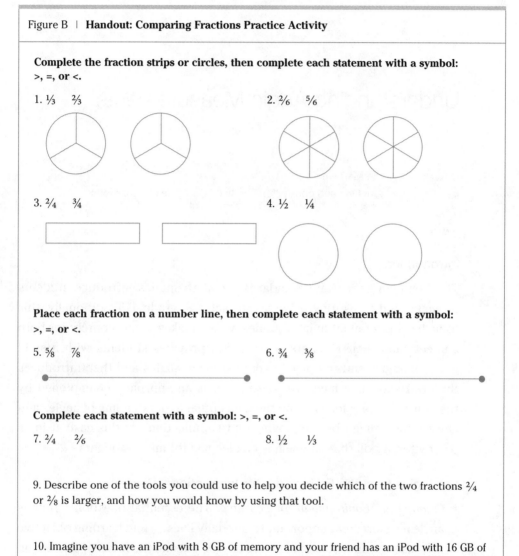

1. ⅓   ⅔

2. 2/6   5/6

3. 2/4   ¾

4. ½   ¼

**Place each fraction on a number line, then complete each statement with a symbol: >, =, or <.**

5. 5/8   7/8

6. ¾   3/8

**Complete each statement with a symbol: >, =, or <.**

7. 2/4   2/6

8. ½   ⅓

9. Describe one of the tools you could use to help you decide which of the two fractions 2/4 or 2/8 is larger, and how you would know by using that tool.

10. Imagine you have an iPod with 8 GB of memory and your friend has an iPod with 16 GB of memory. You each look at your capacity bar and see that ¾ of your memory has been used by audio files. Does this mean that you each have the same amount of space available for additional files? Why, or why not?

# Understanding Angle Measurements

**Course:** 4th grade Mathematics
**Length of Lesson:** One and one-half hours; two 45-minute class periods

## Introduction

The Common Core State Standards for Mathematics introduce students to angles and measuring using a protractor in grade 4. Traditionally, this topic has been taught in later grades, which makes it new content for both students and their teachers. This lesson provides students with a solid grasp of angles and the process of measuring angles and then introduces the protractor as a measurement tool. It is an approach championed by the Common Core: focusing on the conceptual understanding of angles and angle measurement before moving on to application—in this case, using a protractor, a skill that, in itself, is challenging for many students.

## Strategies from the Framework for Instructional Planning

- *Creating the Environment for Learning:* The essential question ("How is angle measurement important to our daily lives?") and learning objective ("To use various tools to measure angles") define the focus of this lesson and will be posted in the classroom and referred to during both class sessions. The teacher will provide feedback throughout the lesson, and students will give feedback to one another. Cooperative learning will take place with informal partnering, and all students will have the opportunity to contribute to discussions and learn from one another. Real-world examples will be incorporated to help students understand how the concepts of this lesson are reflected in situations beyond the mathematics class.

• *Helping Students Develop Understanding:* Guided practice incorporating teacher-prepared notes will help support student learning by providing an organized format in which they can record their own notes related to vocabulary instruction and conceptual understanding. Direct vocabulary instruction will incorporate nonlinguistic representation, which students will use to summarize their learning.

• *Helping Students Extend and Apply Knowledge:* Students will collect and compare measurement data using non-standard units (e.g., student-created wedges as a unit of angle measure) and a conventional protractor. This will provide an opportunity for students to identify similarities and differences between non-standard and standard measuring units and extend their understanding of why standard units are necessary for measurement.

## Common Core State Standards—Knowledge and Skills to Be Addressed

### *Standards for Mathematical Practice*

**MP3** Construct viable arguments and critique the reasoning of others.

**MP5** Use appropriate tools strategically.

### *Standards for Mathematical Content*

### **Domain: Measurement and Data**

*Cluster: Geometric Measurement: Understand Concepts of Angles and Measure Angles*

**4.MD.C.5** Recognize angles as geometric shapes that are formed wherever two rays share a common endpoint, and understand concepts of angle measurement.

a. An angle is measured with reference to a circle with its center at the common endpoint of the rays, by considering the fraction of the circular arc between the points where the two rays intersect the circle. An angle that turns through $\frac{1}{360}$ of a circle is called a "one-degree angle" and can be used to measure angles.

b. An angle that turns through *n* one-degree angles is said to have an angle measure of *n* degrees.

**4.MD.C.6** Measure angles in whole-number degrees using a protractor. Sketch angles of specified measure.

## Common Core State Standards—Prior Knowledge and Skills to Be Applied

### Domain: Geometry

*Cluster: Draw and Identify Lines and Angles, and Classify Shapes by Properties of Their Lines and Angles.*

**4.G.A.1** Draw points, lines, line segments, rays, angles (right, acute, obtuse), and perpendicular and parallel lines. Identify these in two-dimensional figures.

## Teacher's Lesson Summary

Because students should understand what an angle is and the process of measuring an angle before they are introduced to the protractor, the lesson is divided into two parts. In Class Session #1, your focus will be communicating a conceptual understanding of angles via direct vocabulary instruction and by guiding student through the process of measuring angles with non-standard units and non-standard measuring tools. In Class Session #2, you will focus on helping students connect what they have learned about measuring angles with non-standard units and tools to measuring angles with the standard unit and tool—the degree and the protractor (a fairly complex tool). Throughout the lesson, hands-on use of measuring tools and frequent discussion will give you plenty of opportunity to focus students on two Common Core Standards for Mathematical Practice: "Use appropriate tools strategically" (Mathematical Practice Standard 5) and "Construct viable arguments and critique the reasoning of others" (Mathematical Practice Standard 3).

**Essential Question:** How is angle measurement important to our daily lives?

**Lesson Objective:** Students will use various tools to measure angles.

### Knowledge/Vocabulary Objectives

At the conclusion of this lesson, students will understand

- The concept of an angle with reference to a circle.
- The concept of a degree as a unit of measure ($\frac{1}{360}$ of a circle), its relationship to a circle, and why the degree unit is necessary.
- How degree relates to previously introduced mathematical measurement terms such as *angle, ray, acute, obtuse,* and *right.*

### Skill/Process Objectives

At the conclusion of the lesson, students will be able to

- Use non-standard units to measure angles.
- Use a protractor to measure angles.
- Use benchmarks to determine if angle measures are reasonable.

### Resources/Preparation Needed

- A prepared note-taking template focused on background vocabulary, foundational understanding for measuring angles, and measuring angles with non-standard units (see **Figure A: Note-Taking Template for Class Session #1,** p. 240), one per student
- A prepared practice activity handout focused on measuring angles (see **Figure B: Measuring Angles Practice Activity,** p. 241), one per student
- A prepared note-taking template focused on the key vocabulary term *degree* and on measuring with a protractor (see **Figure C: Note-Taking Template for Class Session #2,** p. 242), one per student
- Modeling clay and various materials students can use to create non-standard units (e.g., toothpicks, craft sticks, or Anglegs™—different-sized legs that snap together to create angles)
- Coffee filters, tracing paper, wax paper, or other material students can use to create a measuring tool
- Protractors, one per student (or per pair of students)
- Online video projection and access to the Internet

## Activity Description to Share with Students

The world we live in is full of angles. Just sitting in this classroom, there are angles all around you. Many of these are right angles: the trim around the door and windows and the walls themselves. Angles are important in many professions, including art, interior design, engineering, and architecture. It is important that we have methods and tools to measure not only lengths, areas, and volumes but also angles. This lesson will help you understand angles and develop your skill at measuring angles. You will also learn how you can apply the concept of angles and angle measurement when you are drawing, designing, and building things.

## Lesson Activity Sequence—Class Session #1

### *Start the Lesson*

1. Lead a whole-class discussion to focus students on their prior knowledge of angles. Begin by asking students to draw and label an angle on a piece of unlined paper. Next, have students display their angles in the classroom. Ask students to examine all the angles on display and discuss how they could be grouped according to similar properties. Lead students to group the angles by those greater than, less than, or equal to 90 degrees.

2. Reorganize the angles on display according to the agreed-upon groups. Use the grouped angles to discuss *acute*, *right,* and *obtuse* angles.

3. Distribute the **Note-Taking Template for Class Session #1** (see **Figure A,** p. 240), and ask students to complete the background knowledge section focused on vocabulary, either with a self-selected partner or working independently.

4. Next, share and explain the lesson's learning objectives—that students will be working to understand the concept of an angle with reference to a circle and use non-standard units to measure angles. Encourage students to keep the essential question ("How is angle measurement important to our daily lives?") in mind throughout the lesson.

### *Engage Students in Learning the Content*

1. Explain to students that they will now create their own unit of measurement to measure various angles. Here are two suggestions for how students could complete this task:

   - They might use two toothpicks, popsicle sticks, or Anglegs to create an acute angle the size of their choosing (a small amount of modeling clay can ensure the vertex of the angle remains intact).
   - They might draw an acute angle on a piece of paper or cardstock and cut the wedge out.

   Provide the necessary supplies and guidance.

2. Once students have created their own non-standard units, model the process of measuring an angle by aligning one edge of the non-standard unit to an edge of the angle. Make a mark and move the unit edge to align with the new mark; continue until you can estimate the measure. For example, if the non-standard

unit fits completely in the measured angle twice and fits halfway the third time, the measure would be 2½ non-standard units.

3. After demonstrating this skill for students, have them work with a partner to measure the angles on the **Measuring Angles Practice Activity** handout (see **Figure B,** p. 241) and then answer the discussion point questions. (Decide if students should self-select a partner or if they would benefit from working in assigned heterogeneous pairs, based on past formative assessment information.) Stress that each student within the pair should use the measuring unit that he or she created. Monitor students as they work, providing immediate, corrective feedback and additional instruction as necessary.

4. Reconvene as a whole class, and ask pairs to share their explanations from their discussions. Be sure that students understand the idea that if we all measure the same angle using different units of measurement, we won't have a common language to discuss the size of angles.

5. Explain that now everyone will create a common measuring device for measuring angles—one that represents a circle divided into 16 equal wedges. Walk students through the process of creating this tool, using supplies you have available. Here are two options:

   • *Use a coffee filter.* Fold in half four times, each time matching the folded sides together. (*Note:* If using this method, it works best to iron the coffee filters to produce a smooth surface.)

   • *Use tracing paper or wax paper.* Begin with a square of paper (it does not need to be a perfect square). Fold the paper in half twice. Now fold twice at an angle, matching the two folded sides together and keeping the endpoint intact. Once you've done this, you can cut off the ragged edges. When the wax paper is opened, you will have a circle that looks something like this:

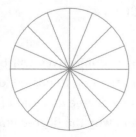

6. Hold up the measurement device you have created, and explain to students that one wedge is equivalent to one unit. Ask students to share a method they might use to measure an angle with this tool. Lead students to the conclusion that (a) the center of the circle needs to lie on the endpoint of the angle and (b) one fold should align with one side of the angle. The paper circle will be slightly transparent, allowing students to see the angle beneath to allow students to measure.

7. Explain that an angle is often referred to as "a turn" around a circle (e.g., a 90 degree angle is a quarter turn). Model "turning" using Anglegs, craft sticks, or another material. Ask students questions like these: *If you were to make a ¼ turn around the circle, what would the angle measure?* [4 wedges] *If you had an angle that measured 8 wedges, what type of turn would that be?* [½]

8. Have students return to the **Measuring Angles Practice Activity** (see Figure B) and, with their partners, measure all five angles again, using the now common non-standard unit. Clarify any misconceptions or confusion for students as they work.

### *Close the Lesson*

1. Give student pairs a minute or so to compare their new measurements to another pair's measurements.

2. Ask the class if their compared measurements were the same the second time around. There may be slight differences in measurements due to variety in students' estimation skills; however, overall, the new measurements should be the same.

3. Direct students to independently complete questions in the section "New Understanding: Angle Measurement with Non-Standard Units" on their note-taking template (see Figure A).

## Lesson Activity Sequence—Class #2

### *Start the Lesson*

1. Explain to students that today's objectives will build on the objectives in the previous lesson. Direct their attention to posted learning objectives:
   - Understand the concept of a degree as a unit of measure ($\frac{1}{360}$ of a circle), its relationship to a circle, and why the degree unit is necessary.

- Use a protractor to measure angles.
- Use reference angles to determine if angle measures are reasonable.

2. Show the approximately two-minute video from PBS CyberChase titled *What's a 360?* This look at a young snowboarder's attempts to do a trick called "a 360" introduces the concept of measuring angles in reference to a circle, which consists of 360 equal slices, or degrees. The video is streaming online at www.teachersdomain.org/resource/vtl07.math.geometry.pla.whatis360/.

3. Distribute the **Note-Taking Template for Class Session #2** (see **Figure C,** p. 242), and give students a minute or two to record what they learned from the video.

4. Ask students to share the key information they recorded with the rest of the class. Referring back to the video, ask students: *What type of turn would a snowboarder make if the turn measured 90 degrees? If the snowboarder turns in a half circle, what is the degree measure?*

### *Engage Students in Learning the Content*

1. Guide students to the realization that a degree is a unit used to measure angles. Facilitate a discussion around the number of degrees in a complete circle, making connections to the video they watched. Lead students to the following key points:

- A degree is a very small unit used to measure angles.
- There are 360 degrees in a complete circle.
- One degree is $\frac{1}{360}$ of a circle.
- There are 90 degrees in a right angle (a right angle is $\frac{1}{4}$ of a circle).
- An acute angle is smaller than a right angle, therefore less than 90 degrees.
- An obtuse angle is larger than a right angle, therefore greater than 90 degrees.
- A right angle is used as a reference angle (benchmark) to determine if angle measures appear reasonable.

Throughout the lesson, pause to prompt students to record information in their note-taking template.

2. Ask students to take out the common measuring tool they created in the previous class (the paper circle). Discuss the characteristics of this tool (e.g., circular, 16 wedges of equal size), and ask them how it reflects what they now know about degrees (e.g., one degree is a slice of a circle; there are 360 equal-size wedges in a circle, and each wedge measures one degree).

3. Have students fold their tools in half to create a semicircle. Then ask students to work with an elbow partner to discuss and answer the following questions:
   - *How many wedges are contained in the semicircle?*
   - *How many degrees are contained in the semicircle? How do you know?*
   - *There is a tool similar to the one we created that measures in degrees. What is it called?* [Students may be familiar with the term *protractor,* but most will not know how to use it.]
   - *How are degrees labeled?*
   - *Do you think it would be possible to have an angle that measured greater than 360 degrees? Explain your reasoning.*

   As student pairs finish answering these questions, direct them to discuss their answers with other pairs.

4. Explain to students that now they will learn how to use a protractor to measure angles. Ask them to think of the protractor as half of a circle, pointing out where the "center" of this circle is. When measuring an angle, they should place the center on the endpoint of the angle and align the line on the protractor going through zero degrees with one side of the angle. Then they need to read the protractor at the point that the other side of the angle intersects. Be prepared to address student challenges, misconceptions, and measurement errors. For example,
   - Make sure students are aligning the angles properly, which will require you to pay close attention to all students as they begin to practice the skill.
   - If the protractors that students will be using have the degrees marked from both ends, be sure to explain to students how to read the correct measurement.
   - If the sides of the angle are not long enough to read accurately on the protractor, students should use a straightedge to extend one or both sides.

5. Ask students how they might use the reference angle of 90 degrees to help them determine if their angle measurement is reasonable. Be sure students understand that if the angle is acute, their measurement should be less than 90 degrees and if the angle is obtuse, their measurement should be greater than 90 degrees.

6. Practice measuring angles as a whole class using the online activity at Math Playground (www.mathplayground.com/measuringangles.html).

### *Close the Lesson*

1. Discuss with students critical misconceptions and key points to measuring angles with a protractor. Remind students of the learning objectives and ask students to share what they have learned about the essential question, "How is angle measurement important to our daily lives?"

2. Ask students to retrieve the notes they took during Class Session #1 (see Figure A) and make corrections and additions.

3. Conclude the lesson by giving students time to practice using a protractor to measure angles. They might go back and use a protractor and the degree unit to measure the five angles on the Measuring Angles handout (see Figure B). Circulate as they work, providing corrective feedback.

## Additional Resources for This Lesson

Students will need many opportunities over time to practice using a protractor to accurately measure angles. Early on, students need supervised guided practice with corrective feedback. Once they have a very firm understanding of the process of measuring angles, they can be given more independent practice opportunities, such as those available through www.mathplayground.com and other technology websites and virtual manipulatives.

*Other Online Resources:*
• Khan Academy (www.khanacademy.org)
• Wolfram MathWorld (http://mathworld.wolfram.com)
• PBS Kids Cyberchase video: *Now That's What I Call an Angle!* (http://pbskids.org/cyberchase/videos/now-thats-what-i-call-an-angle/)
• Math Is Fun on degrees (www.mathsisfun.com/geometry/degrees.html)

*Extension or Cross-Content Connection to Social Studies/History:*
As either a social studies activity or an extension activity for those who are interested, students might do online research on the origin of the degree measure. You might direct them to http://kids.britannica.com, and ask them to gather information regarding the unit's origin.

Figure A  |  **Note-Taking Template for Class Session #1**

### 1. BACKGROUND KNOWLEDGE: ANGLES

| Key Vocabulary | Definition/Description | Drawing/Description to Help You Remember What This Is |
|---|---|---|
| Angle | | |
| Right Angle | | |
| Acute Angle | | |
| Obtuse Angle | | |

### 2. NEW UNDERSTANDING: ANGLE MEASURMENT WITH NON-STANDARD UNITS

Explain in your own words why it is important to measure angles using a common unit.

How is measuring angles similar to measuring length or area? How does measuring angles differ from measuring length or area?

Figure B  |  **Handout: Measuring Angles Practice Activity**

**Directions:** Measure each angle using your non-standard unit. Write your measurement next to each angle.

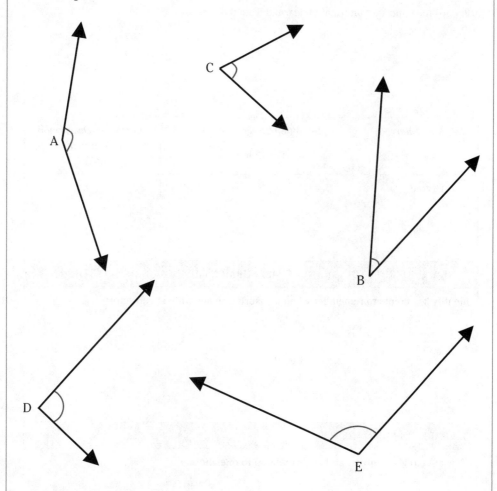

**Discussion Points:**

Compare your measurements to your partner's. Are they the same? Why, or why not? If the measurements are not the same, do you think this could be a problem? Explain your reasoning on the back of this page.

Figure C | **Note-Taking Template for Class Session #2**

### 1. NEW UNDERSTANDING: *WHAT'S A 360?*

Record the important information learned from the video.

| Key Vocabulary | Definition/Description | Drawing or Description to Help You Remember What This Is |
|---|---|---|
| Degree | | |

### 2. NEW UNDERSTANDING: ANGLE MEASURMENT USING A PROTRACTOR

Identify key points to remember when measuring angles with a protractor:

- 
- 
- 
- 

### 3. LEARNING SUMMARY

How are circles, degrees, and angles related to one another?

# Division of Decimals Through Concrete Models

**Course:** 5th grade Mathematics
**Length of Lesson:** One hour; one 60-minute class period

## Introduction

Throughout the Common Core State Standards for Mathematics, students are expected to develop deep conceptual understandings. That priority is reflected in the 5th grade Number and Operations in Base Ten content standard—5.NBT.C.7—that is the focus of this lesson. Whereas in the past, state standards for elementary mathematics often placed greater emphasis on the division algorithm than on conceptual understanding of decimal division, the Common Core aims to balance conceptual understanding and procedural fluency to ensure that 5th grade students develop not only skills in computation with decimals but also a conceptual understanding of operations on decimals. This shift, along with the increased focus on concrete models, will prove a challenge for many 5th graders. This lesson provides ways to increase students' conceptual understandings by helping them progress from a concrete and representational understanding of division to a more abstract comprehension.

## Strategies from the Framework for Instructional Planning

- *Creating the Environment for Learning:* Together, the essential question and learning objectives define the focus of this lesson and will be posted in the room and referred to throughout the lesson. The teacher will provide feedback throughout the lesson, and students will give feedback to one another. Cooperative learning will take place both formally and informally through the use of paired learning.

- *Helping Students Develop Understanding:* This lesson incorporates several strategies to help students develop a conceptual understanding of decimal division. The teacher will use an advance organizer to help engage students and illustrate the connections between the concept of division of whole numbers and the new concept of division of decimals. The teacher will question students throughout the lesson to encourage higher-order thinking and check for understanding. Based on formative data collected, follow-up support will be provided to students who need it. Non-linguistic representation—the use of drawings and concrete models—will be critical to this lesson. Students will take notes throughout the guided instruction and summarize their understanding during the lesson closure. These strategies will work in tandem to build student understanding.

- *Helping Students Extend and Apply Knowledge:* During this lesson, students will be prompted to reflect on what they know about the division of whole numbers and about how to work with models and leverage this understanding to solidify what they are learning about the new concept, division of decimals.

## Common Core State Standards—Knowledge and Skills to Be Addressed

### Standards for Mathematical Practice

**MP1** Make sense of problems and persevere in solving them.

**MP3** Construct viable arguments and critique the reasoning of others.

**MP4** Model with mathematics.

**MP5** Use appropriate tools strategically.

### Standards for Mathematical Content

#### Domain: Number and Operations in Base Ten

*Cluster: Perform Operations with Multi-digit Whole Numbers and with Decimals to Hundredths*

**5.NBT.C.7** Add, subtract, multiply, and divide decimals to hundredths, using concrete models or drawings and strategies based on place value, properties of operations, and/or the relationship between addition and subtraction; relate the strategy to a written method and explain the reasoning used.

## Common Core State Standards—Prior Knowledge and Skills to Be Applied

**Domain: Number and Operations in Base Ten**

*Cluster: Understand the Place Value System*

**5.NBT.A.1** Recognize that in a multi-digit number, a digit in one place represents 10 times as much as it represents in the place to its right and $\frac{1}{10}$ of what it represents in the place to its left.

**5.NBT.A.4** Use place value understanding to round decimals to any place.

*Cluster: Perform Operations with Multi-digit Whole Numbers and with Decimals to Hundredths*

**5.NBT.B.6** Find whole-number quotients of whole numbers with up to four-digit dividends and two-digit divisors, using strategies based on place value, the properties of operations, and/or the relationships between multiplication and division. Illustrate and explain the calculation by using equations, rectangular arrays, and/or area models.

*Cluster: Use Place Value Understanding and Properties of Operations to Perform Multi-digit Arithmetic*

**4.NBT.B.6** Find whole number quotients and remainders with up to four-digit dividends and one-digit divisors, using strategies based on place value, the properties of operations, and/or the relationship between multiplication and division. Illustrate and explain the calculation by using equations, rectangular arrays, and/or area models.

## Teacher's Lesson Summary

The concept of decimal division can be a difficult one for students to grasp. By the time they reach 5th grade, they are familiar with dividing whole numbers, so it makes sense to them for the quotient to be a number smaller than the dividend. The idea that the quotient could be larger than the dividend can be confusing. To help your students gain a deep understanding of decimal division, you must address concrete concepts that will serve as the foundation for more representational and abstract understanding to come. This lesson focuses on ways to help students understand the basic concepts of decimal division. Future lessons could extend the learning to written methods used for division of decimals.

**Essential Question:** How can models help us understand real-world decimal division problems?

**Learning Objective:** To understand the concept of dividing decimals through the use of drawings or concrete models.

### Knowledge/Vocabulary Objectives

At the conclusion of this lesson, students will understand that when the divisor is less than one, the quotient will be larger than the dividend.

### Skill/Process Objectives

At the conclusion of the lesson, students will be able to

- Use concrete models and drawings to divide decimals to the hundredths.
- Estimate the quotient when dividing decimals in order to assess the reasonableness of a solution.

### Resources/Preparation Needed

- A prepared handout focused on decimal division that provides guided, partner, and individual practice (see **Figure A: Decimal Division Practice Activities,** pp. 253–254), one per student
- A sheet of hundreds grids (see **Figure B: Hundreds Grids,** p. 255), ideally laminated and reusable, one per student
- Dry- or wet-erase markers (to use with laminated grids), one per student
- Student mathematics notebooks/journals
- Online video projection and access to the Internet

## Activity Description to Share with Students

We encounter decimals on a regular basis when dealing with money, finding unit rates at the grocery store, or putting fuel into our cars. Decimals are simply another way to write a fraction. In this lesson, we'll look at how using models will help you understand the meaning of a decimal and easily see its connection to fractions. You'll also learn how to use estimation to approximate the solution to various decimal division problems and arrive at a quick answer, and then use a model to help find the exact answer. You will practice applying your knowledge about decimal division to solve real-world problems.

## Lesson Activity Sequence

### *Start the Lesson*

1. Show the two-minute streaming video clip *Ma and Pa Kettle Math* (www.teacher tube.com/viewVideo.php?video_id=45749&title=Ma_and_Pa_Kettle_Math) to hook student interest and help them make the first connections between division of whole numbers and the new concept of division of decimals. Before the video begins, tell students what they are about to see: an argument that 25 divided by 5 is equal to 14. Write the equation on the board, and ask students to tell you what the answer should be.

2. Give students five minutes to work with an elbow partner to answer the following questions:
   - How would you use a model or diagram to prove to Ma and Pa Kettle that 25 divided by 5 really does equal 5?
   - What do Ma and Pa Kettle not understand about numbers? How could you teach them the concepts they do not understand?

   As students work, take time to visit each pair to listen to their mathematical dialogue and correct any misconceptions you overhear. Make note of the demonstration strategies different pairs are suggesting.

3. Select two or three groups who used different strategies to share their arguments with the class. Have the students provide input on whether or not they think each argument is effective and explain their reasoning.

4. Explain to students that today they will begin to understand the concept of dividing decimals. Post and describe to students the objectives for the lesson, and make sure the objectives remain in a visible location for reference throughout the lesson:

- Understand that when the divisor is less than one, the quotient will be larger than the dividend.
- Use concrete models and drawings to divide decimals to the hundredths.
- Estimate the quotient when dividing decimals.

### Engage Students in Learning the Content

1. Begin with guided practice using real-life problems related to money. Most 5th grade students will be familiar with the concept of money and understand some basic decimal concepts that will be useful for instruction (e.g., there are four quarters [0.25] in one dollar [1.00]). Distribute copies of the **Decimal Division Practice Activities** handout (**Figure A,** pp. 253–254). As you and the students work through the problems in Part A (Guided Practice) together, ask them to record their work in their math journal—a notebook in which they record the critical concepts they learn.

   Here's an example of how you might approach the first problem:

   *1. You have decided you will save your money to purchase an iPod that costs $200. Your grandma says she will match every dollar you save toward the purchase. If you are able to save $7.50 of your allowance each week, how many weeks will you need to save until you can make the purchase?*

   Ask students: *How much money will you need to save if Grandma is matching your funds? Estimate how many weeks you will need to save before you can make the purchase, and then explain your reasoning.* Encourage students to think about reference decimals, such as 0.25, 0.50, and 0.10, when they estimate, and be sure to model this kind of thinking (e.g., "I know that 100 divided by 10 is 10. Since 7.5 is less than 10, it can go into 100 more times, so I think my answer will be greater than 10.").

3. Next, show students how they might use a concrete model or drawing to represent the problem and use a think-aloud technique to describe each step in your thought process as you reason through the problem. Here is an example:

*We know: A $100 bill can be broken apart into twenty $5 bills.*

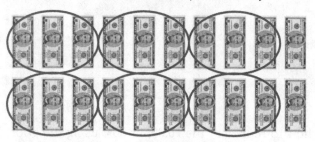

*Each group of 3 $5 bills is equal to 2 weeks of $7.50 savings, or $15.*
*Each circle represents 2 weeks; there are 6 circles, which would equal 12 weeks.*
*Will we have saved enough money after 12 weeks? How do you know?*
*How many weeks do we need to save?*
*How can we use our estimate to check our answer?*

4. Model another decimal division problem, this time using a hundreds grid as a concrete model. Distribute copies of the **Hundreds Grids** handout (see **Figure B, p. 255**), along with erasable markers if the sheet is laminated, so that students can work along with you.

> *2. You have $2.70 left on your school lunch account. The end of the year is approaching, and you don't want to add any money to your account. If one carton of milk costs $0.30, how many days can you buy a milk before your lunch account balance is zero (assuming that you don't buy anything else)?*

Ask students to estimate the number of days they could buy milk. Have students turn to their elbow partner and explain their reasoning.

5. Model how to use hundreds grids to represent money, and discuss the importance of representing the quantity using the same units (e.g. $0.30 is the same as 30¢, and $2.70 is the same as 270¢). In the example provided, each grid

represents $1.00 and each individual square represents 1¢. Have students shade their grids, as depicted, to represent $2.70, or 270¢:

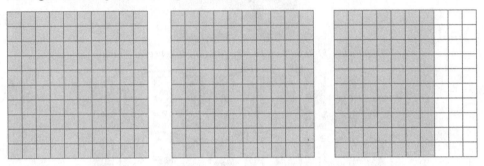

6. Ask students how to represent the $0.30, or 30¢, using the grids. Students may need guidance to understand that the shaded area would be partitioned into groups that represent $0.30:

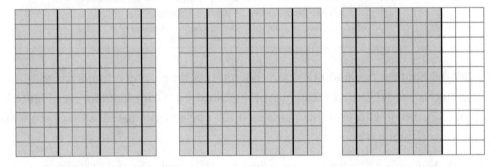

Be sure students understand that each partitioned area represents one carton of milk. Ask students questions such as the following:

• How many days can you buy milk?
• Will the ending balance of your lunch account be exactly zero? How do you know?
• Compare your solution to your estimate. Is your solution reasonable?
• Why is the quotient greater than the dividend?

7. Check for student understanding by referring to the objectives posted in the classroom and asking students to raise their hands and show five fingers if they

completely understand the learning objectives to this point, three fingers if they feel that they have a good start but a couple of questions, and one finger if they are very confused. Be sure to make note of those students who self-assess as being very confused or having some questions.

8.  Tell students that the problems you have been working on together are division problems, and have students write the division equation that corresponds with the previous example (i.e., $2.70 ÷ $0.30). Ask one student to write the equation on the board for the class. Tell the students to show a thumbs-up if they agree or a thumbs-down if they disagree with the student's equation, then discuss if necessary.

9.  Guide students through the next two guided practice problems on the Decimal Division Practice sheet, checking for understanding and providing corrective feedback as needed.

10. Have students work in assigned, heterogeneous pairs to collaborate on the problems in Part B of the Decimal Division Practice sheet (see Figure A). While they do so, offer further small-group or individualized support to students who exhibited or expressed confusion during the guided instruction. Continue to observe all pairs of students to identify any who are struggling and to correct misconceptions.

11. Explain to students that once they have finished their partner problems, they should move on to Part C: Independent Practice. If it appears that students are still struggling, complete another problem using guided practice or have students continue to work with partners while you provide additional assistance. *Note:* Practice on this skill should occur during class with teacher/peer feedback until students reach a reasonable level of proficiency. Practicing a problem incorrectly could instill incorrect habits of thinking and be difficult to correct. If students do not have time to complete the Independent Practice problems in Part C of the handout, or if they are not proficient enough to work independently, use the problems in Part C to open an additional class session the following day. You might have students use scissors to cut out the Independent Practice problems to attach in their notes or math journals next to the models they have created.

### Close the Lesson

1. Remind students of the learning objective and the essential question for the lesson. Ask students to share what they have learned and how they would answer the essential question.
2. Post two exit ticket questions (shown), and instruct students to copy them down and then think about what they learned during the lesson before responding in writing.

---

**EXIT TICKET**                                          **NAME:**

How can estimation help us solve problems involving division of decimals?


How does division by a number less than one affect the quotient?

---

Collect these responses, and use them to develop a clearer picture of students' current level of mastery and gain a better idea of which conceptual understandings should be reinforced through additional practice activities or clarified through additional instructional attention.

## Additional Resources for This Lesson

The following resources can be used to support the mathematical concepts being taught in this lesson. The literature could be read to introduce the topic of decimal division, while the technology component could be used to provide additional, engaging practice of the mathematical concepts addressed in the lesson and in Standard 5.NBT.C.7.

*Reinforcing with Technology:* Quotient Café: http://illuminations.nctm.org/Activity-Detail.aspx?ID=224

*Literature Connections: A Remainder of One* by Elinor J. Pinczes

---

| Figure A   &#124;   **Handout: Decimal Division Practice Activities** |
|---|

NAME_____ DATE _____

## A. Guided Practice

Complete the problems with your teacher's help. Use a drawing or concrete model to represent each problem in your Math Journal.

| | |
|---|---|
| **1.** You have decided you will save your money to purchase an iPod that costs $200. Your grandma says she will match every dollar you save toward the purchase. If you are able to save $7.50 of your allowance each week, how many weeks will you need to save until you can make the purchase? | **2.** You have $2.70 left on your school lunch account. The end of the year is approaching, and you don't want to add any money to your account. If one carton of milk costs $0.30, how many days can you buy a milk before your lunch account balance is zero (assuming that you don't buy anything else)? |
| **3.** You are part of an ice hockey league. You attend practice three nights per week. Often the Zamboni is working on the ice when you arrive. Your friend tells you the Zamboni can resurface a stripe of ice that is 9.5 feet wide. You decide to watch the operator to see how many stripes he makes to resurface the 85-feet-wide ice rink. How many stripes should the operator make? | **4.** Your school is remodeling the auditorium. You class has been assigned the task of determining how many seats need to be ordered. Each seat is 0.4 meters wide. If the fourth row is 15.2 meters long, how many seats can fit in the row if there is no space left between each seat? |

Answers: **1.** 14 weeks  **2.** 9 days  **3.** 9 stripes  **4.** 38 seats

*(continued)*

Figure A  |  **Handout: Decimal Division Practice Activities (*continued*)**

**B. Partner Practice**

Work with your partner to complete the problems. Use a drawing or concrete model to represent each problem in your Math Journal.

| | |
|---|---|
| **5.** You bought a bag of chips at the store for your mom. The bag cost $4.50, and you noticed on the store tag that the price per ounce was $0.15. How many ounces were in the bag of chips? | **6.** Your school is hosting a cross-country meet, and you are helping to map out the course. The length of the course is 3.6 miles. You need to place a marker for the runners at every 0.3 mile. How many markers will you need to mark the entire 3.6 mile course? |
| **7.** Your dad owns a lawn care business and asks if you would like to help him on Saturday. He will be working at the local high school to care for the football field. He needs you to mow the field. The tractor he is using can mow a stripe that is 8.25 feet wide. The field is 165 feet wide. What is the minimum number of stripes up and down the field you will need to make with the lawn mower to complete the job? | **8.** Each week you earn up to $12.50 in allowance for completing your chores. You have been saving your money each week to buy a mountain bike. So far you have saved $62.50. How many weeks have you been saving? (Assume you haven't spent any money since you began to save your allowance.) |

**C. Independent Practice**

Complete the problems independently. Use a drawing or concrete model to represent each problem in your Math Journal.

| | |
|---|---|
| **9.** You are going to summer sport camp and need to bring money to buy snacks from the vending machines. Your parents say they will give you $12.00 in quarters. If snacks are 75¢ each, how many snacks will you be able to buy? Will you have any money left over? | **10.** You are making cupcakes for a bake sale for the school choir. Each cupcake requires 0.25 cup of frosting. You make 15 cups of frosting. How many cupcakes will you be able to frost for the bake sale? |

Answers: **5.** 30 ounces **6.** 12 markers (also accept 13 markers) **7.** 20 stripes  **8.** 5 weeks **9.** 16 snacks; no money left  **10.** 60 cupcakes

Figure B  |  **Handout: Hundreds Grids**

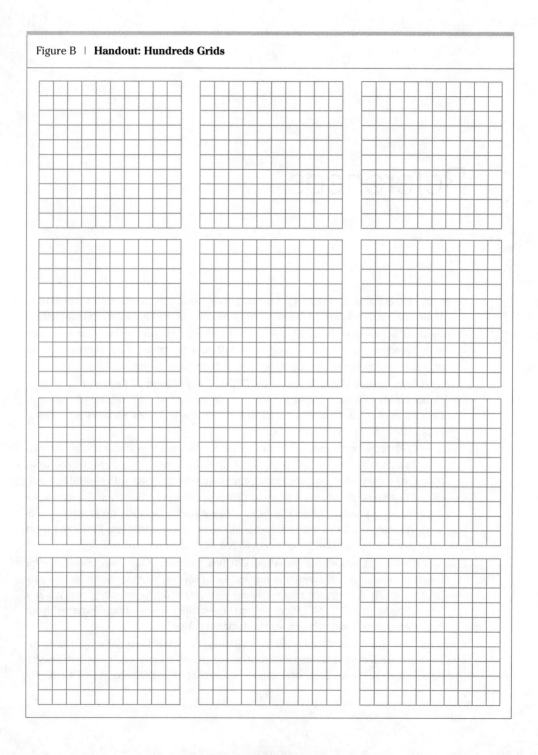

# References

Clements, D., & Sarama, J. (2004). Learning trajectories in mathematics education. *Mathematical Thinking and Learning, 6*(2), 81–89. doi: 10.1207/s15327833mtl0602

Coleman, D., & Pimentel, S. (2012, April 12). *Publisher's criteria for the Common Core State Standards in English language arts and literacy, grades 3–12*. Retrieved from http://www.corestandards.org/assets/Publishers_Criteria_for_3-12.pdf

Common Core State Standards Initiative. (2010a). *Application of Common Core State Standards for English language learners*. Washington, DC: CCSSO & National Governors Association. Retrieved from http://www.corestandards.org/assets/application-for-english-learners.pdf

Common Core State Standards Initiative. (2010b). *Application to students with disabilities*. Washington, DC: CCSSO & National Governors Association. Retrieved from http://www.corestandards.org/assets/application-to-students-with-disabilities.pdf

Common Core State Standards Initiative. (2010c). *Common Core State Standards for English language arts & literacy in history/social studies, science, and technical subjects*. Washington, DC: CCSSO & National Governors Association. Retrieved from http://www.corestandards.org/assets/CCSSI_ELA%20Standards.pdf

Common Core State Standards Initiative. (2010d). *Common Core State Standards for English language arts & literacy in history/social studies, science, and technical subjects. Appendix A: Research supporting key elements of the standards, glossary of key terms*. Washington, DC: CCSSO & National Governors Association. Retrieved from http://www.corestandards.org/assets/Appendix_A.pdf

Common Core State Standards Initiative. (2010e). *Common Core State Standards for English language arts & literacy in history/social studies, science, and technical subjects. Appendix B: Text exemplars and sample performance tasks*. Washington, DC: CCSSO

& National Governors Association. Retrieved from http://www.corestandards. org/assets/Appendix_B.pdf

Common Core State Standards Initiative. (2010f). *Common Core State Standards for English language arts & literacy in history/social studies, science, and technical subjects. Appendix C: Samples of student writing.* Washington, DC: CCSSO & National Governors Association. Retrieved from http://www.corestandards.org/assets/ Appendix_C.pdf

Common Core Standards Writing Team. (2011, April 17). *Progressions for the Common Core State Standards in mathematics* [draft]. Available: commoncoretools.word press.com

Common Core State Standards Initiative. (2010g). *Common Core State Standards for mathematics.* Washington, DC: CCSSO & National Governors Association. Retrieved from http://www.corestandards.org/assets/CCSSI_Math%20Standards.pdf

Daniels, H. (1994). *Literature circles: Voice and choice in the student-centered classroom.* Portland, ME: Stenhouse.

Dean, C. B., Hubbell, E. R., Pitler, H., & Stone, B. (2012). *Classroom instruction that works: Research-based strategies for increasing student achievement* (2nd ed.). Alexandria, VA: ASCD.

Hess, K. (2011). *Learning progressions frameworks designed for use with the Common Core State Standards in English language arts & literacy K–12.* Retrieved from http:// www.nciea.org/publication_PDFs/ELA_LPF_12%202011_final.pdf

Hess, K. (2012, January 6). *Content specifications with content mapping for the summative assessment of the Common Core State Standards for English language arts and literacy in history/social studies, science, and technical subjects* [draft]. Retrieved from http://www.smarterbalanced.org/smarter-balanced-assessments/

Hess, K., & Hervey, S. (2011). *Tools for examining text complexity.* Retrieved from http:// www.nciea.org/publication_PDFs/Updated%20toolkit-text%20complexity_KH12. pdf

Kansas State Department of Education. (2011). *Text complexity resources.* Retrieved from http://www.ksde.org/Default.aspx?tabid=4778#TextRes

Kendall, J. S. (2011). *Understanding Common Core State Standards.* Alexandria, VA: ASCD.

Kosanovich, M., & Verhagen, C. (2012). *Building the foundation: A suggested progression of sub-skills to achieve the reading standards: Foundational skills in the Common Core State Standards.* Portsmouth, NH: RMC Research Corporation, Center on Instruction.

Measured Progress & ETS Collaborative. (2012, April). Smarter Balanced Assessment Consortium: English language arts item and task specifications. Retrieved from http://www.smarterbalanced.org/smarter-balanced-assessments/#item

National Assessment Governing Board. (2010a). *Reading framework for the 2011 National Assessment of Educational Progress.* Washington, DC: U.S. Government

Printing Office Superintendent of Documents. Retrieved from http://www.nagb.org/publications/frameworks/reading-2011-framework.pdf

National Assessment Governing Board. (2010b). *Writing framework for the 2011 National Assessment of Educational Progress.* Washington, DC: U.S. Government Printing Office Superintendent of Documents. Retrieved from http://www.eric.ed.gov/PDFS/ED512552.pdf

National Council of Teachers of Mathematics. (2000). *Principles and standards for school mathematics.* Reston, VA: Author.

National Reading Panel. (2000). *Teaching children to read: An evidence-based assessment of the scientific research literature on reading and its implications for reading instruction.* Author. Retrieved from http://www.nationalreadingpanel.org

National Research Council. (2001). *Adding it up: Helping children learn mathematics.* Washington, DC: National Academies Press.

National Research Council, Committee on a Conceptual Framework for New K–12 Science Education Standards. (2012). *A framework for K–12 science education: Practices, crosscutting concepts, and core ideas.* Washington, DC: National Academies Press. Retrieved from http://www.nap.edu/openbook.php?record_id=13165&page=1

National Research Council, Committee on How People Learn: A Targeted Report for Teachers. (2005). *How students learn: Mathematics in the classroom.* Washington, DC: National Academies Press.

Nelson, J., Perfetti, C., Liben, D., & Liben, M. (2012). *Measures of text difficulty: Testing their predictive value for grade levels and student performance.* Retrieved from http://www.ccsso.org/Documents/2012/Measures%20ofText%20Difficulty_final.2012.pdf

Otfinoski, S. (1996). *The kids' guide to money: Earning it, saving it, spending it, growing it, sharing it.* New York: Scholastic.

Partnership for Assessment of Readiness for College and Careers. (2010, June). *Application for the Race to the Top comprehension assessment systems competition.* Retrieved from http://www.parcconline.org/sites/parcc/files/PARCC%20Application%20-%20FINAL.pdf

Partnership for Assessment of Readiness for College and Careers. (2011, October). *PARCC model content frameworks: Mathematics grades 3–8 only.* Retrieved from http://www.parcconline.org/sites/parcc/files/PARCCMCFfor3-8MathematicsFall2011Release.pdf

Partnership for Assessment of Readiness for College and Careers. (2012, August). *PARCC model content frameworks: English language arts/literacy, grades 3–11.* Retrieved from http://www.parcconline.org/sites/parcc/files/PARCC%20MCF%20for%20ELA%20Literacy_Fall%202011%20Release%20%28rev%29.pdf

Rhodes, J. P. (2010). *Ninth ward.* New York: Little, Brown.

Schmidt, W. (2012). *Common Core State Standards math: The relationship between high standards, systemic implementation and student achievement.* Lansing, MI: Michigan State University.

Schoenfeld, A., Burkhardt, H., Abedi, J., Hess, K., & Thurlow, M. (2012, March). *Content specifications for the summative assessment of the Common Core State Standards for mathematics* [draft]. Olympia, WA: Smarter Balanced Assessment Consortium. Available: http://www.smarterbalanced.org/wordpress/wp-content/uploads/2011/12/Math-Content-Specifications.pdf

Tarshis, L. (2011). *I survived Hurricane Katrina, 2005* (I Survived #3). New York: Scholastic Paperbacks.

# About the Authors

**Amber Evenson** is a lead consultant at Mid-continent Research for Education and Learning (McREL), providing services, strategies, and materials to support improvement in mathematics education, curriculum development, instructional coaching, and instructional technology. She also works with schools and districts to assist them as they align, plan, and implement the Common Core State Standards while building the internal capacity of the school or district. Ms. Evenson holds an MA in Teaching and Learning from Nova Southeastern University and a BA in Mathematics from Beloit College. Prior to coming to McREL, she served as a K–12 mathematics coach and has many years of experience as a secondary mathematics educator.

**Monette McIver** is a principal consultant at McREL and has worked on several design and development projects related to school leadership and systemic improvement efforts. A former assistant professor in the School of Education at the University of Colorado at Boulder, she taught a writing methods course for elementary teacher candidates and conducted research about writing instruction that focused on the interaction between teachers and students in the writing conference. Ms. McIver is an experienced elementary classroom teacher who has taught kindergarten through 4th grade. Her elementary classroom experiences include working with English language learners, adapting instruction to meet the diverse needs of learners, and mentoring preservice teachers. She is the coauthor of *Teaching Writing in the Content Areas*.

**Susan Ryan** is a senior consultant at McREL. She has reviewed, revised, and developed language arts standards documents for many districts, state agencies, and education organizations. Ms. Ryan has conducted alignment reviews on assessment items, instructional materials, and curriculum materials. Her work with the Common Core State Standards includes the production of gap analyses, crosswalks, transition documents, alignment reviews, and research support for state departments of education. Ms. Ryan has also facilitated teacher leaders in curriculum development and implementation of the Common Core. She was a consulting state content expert for English language arts during the development of the Common Core and a state consultant to the Partnership for Assessment of Readiness for College and Careers (PARCC) consortium. A former high school language arts teacher, she holds a BA in English from the University of Colorado and a secondary teaching license through Metropolitan State University of Denver.

**Amitra Schwols** serves as a consultant at McREL. She has reviewed, revised, and developed standards documents for many districts, state agencies, and organizations. She has also reviewed instructional materials, created lesson plans, and conducted research on a wide variety of education topics. Ms. Schwols's work with the Common Core State Standards includes developing gap analysis, crosswalk, and transition documents, as well as facilitating implementation with groups of teacher leaders. She was a consulting state content expert for mathematics during the development of the Common Core standards and a state consultant to the Partnership for Assessment of Readiness for College and Careers (PARCC) consortium. A former classroom teacher at the secondary grades and a Navy veteran, Ms. Schwols holds a BS in science with an emphasis in physics and mathematics and a minor in English from Colorado State University.

**John Kendall** (Series Editor) is Senior Director in Research at McREL in Denver. Having joined McREL in 1988, Mr. Kendall conducts research and development activities related to academic standards. He directs a technical assistance unit that provides standards-related services to schools, districts, states, and national and international organizations. He is the author of *Understanding Common Core State Standards,* the senior author of *Content Knowledge: A Compendium of Standards and Benchmarks for K–12 Education,* and the author or coauthor of numerous reports and guides related to standards-based systems. These works include *High School Standards and Expectations for College and the Workplace; Essential Knowledge: The Debate over What American Students Should Know;* and *Finding the Time to Learn: A Guide.* He holds an MA in Classics and a BA in English Language and Literature from the University of Colorado at Boulder.

**About McREL**

Mid-continent Research for Education and Learning (McREL) is a nationally recognized nonprofit education research and development organization headquartered in Denver, Colorado, with offices in Honolulu, Hawaii, and Omaha, Nebraska. Since 1966, McREL has helped translate research and professional wisdom about what works in education into practical guidance for educators. Our more than 120 staff members and affiliates include respected researchers, experienced consultants, and published writers who provide educators with research-based guidance, consultation, and professional development for improving student outcomes.

## ASCD and Common Core State Standards Resources

ASCD believes that for the Common Core State Standards to have maximum effect, they need to be part of a well-rounded whole child approach to education that ensures students are healthy, safe, engaged, supported, and challenged.

For a complete and updated overview of ASCD's resources related to the Common Core standards, including other *Quick-Start Guides* in the Understanding the Common Core Standards Series, professional development institutes, online courses links to webinars and to ASCD's free EduCore™ digital tool, and lots more, please visit us at www.ascd.org/commoncore.